Rail and the City

Urban and Industrial Environments

Series editor: Robert Gottlieb, Henry R. Luce Professor of Urban and Environmental Policy, Occidental College

For a complete list of books published in this series, please see the back of the book.

Rail and the City

Shrinking Our Carbon Footprint While Reimagining
Urban Space

Roxanne Warren

The MIT Press
Cambridge, Massachusetts
London, England

MIT Press books may be purchased at special quantity discounts for business or sales promotional use. For information, please email special_sales@mitpress.mit.

This book was set in Sabon LT Std 10/14 pt by Toppan Best-set Premedia Limited. Printed and bound in the United States of America.

Library of Congress Cataloging-in-Publication Data
Warren, Roxanne.
Rail and the city : shrinking our carbon footprint while reimagining urban space / Roxanne Warren.
    pages cm.—(Urban and industrial environments)
Includes bibliographical references and index.
ISBN 978-0-262-02780-9 (hardcover : alk. paper)
1. Urban transportation—United States. 2. Land use—United States. 3. Housing—United States. 4. Sustainable development—United States. 5. Urban transportation—Europe. 6. Land use—Europe. 7. Housing—Europe. 8. Sustainable development—Europe. I. Title.
HE308.W37 2014
388.40973—dc23
2014003868

10 9 8 7 6 5 4 3 2 1

Contents

Preface

This book is written with the purpose of stirring public awareness about the possibilities for reversing currently damaging trends in transportation and land use. It aims to achieve this through a synthesis of the thinking of the most qualified and insightful experts in related fields.

The book sets our recent and ongoing history of energy and land use within the context of the formidable reality of climate change, and points toward more rational and potentially hopeful scenarios. A central theme is the critical importance of cities to humanity and the planet, and our need to enable their more humane, environmentally compatible, and fluid functioning through the most appropriate means of transportation.

Chapter 1 traces the history of urban sprawl in the United States, its foundations and its negative repercussions for the climate and for society, and notes our currently shifting paradigm of re-urbanization. Chapter 2 analyzes the challenges, and some solutions, to providing affordable, truly transit-oriented development for a society that is so dominated by the private automobile and by the zoning codes that have helped to reinforce this dominance.

Chapter 3 is the heart of the book. It describes the key attributes of common, as well as less common public transit options, and focuses on the unique features of rail modes that qualify them as city-reinforcing infrastructure. Chapter 4, in considering our existing spread-out development, hones in on issues of access to rail stations, and the need to reduce the physical scale, environmental impact, and costs of our access modes—emphasizing the potential that can be realized by improving conditions for walking and cycling. Progress on this front in the nations of northern Europe, Japan, and North America is reviewed.

Chapter 5 very briefly addresses the issue of high motor vehicle speeds, their legitimate and inappropriate contexts, and some solutions for residential neighborhoods that have already been achieved, and whose application is spreading. Urban design qualities for pedestrian-oriented- and transit-oriented cities and suburbs are then discussed in chapter 6. The different approaches in Europe and the United States are compared, and experiences with traffic calming, pedestrianization, and coordinating pedestrian zones with transit are described.

Chapter 7 brings the discussion back to the hard realities and urgencies of climate change, which is tremendously aggravated by the massive use of fossil fuels for transportation. It outlines the promise and potential of completely clean, renewable energy, and reviews some steps that we as a society can take to radically shrink our ecological footprint. This final chapter observes that many of our youth are already gravitating in this direction.

The United States has by now evolved into a nation of some twenty densely populated mega-regions. In the late nineteenth century, it was explicitly argued by US geographer–social scientist Henry Gannet that it was only the highly developed parts of the nation that should be considered in determining the infrastructural needs of those areas. That is, while the country's *overall average* population density is roughly only half that of Europe, this average includes vast areas that are only sparsely populated, and *should not be conflated with the densities of the heavily populated areas in determining infrastructural needs.* But such conflation has been pervasive in the twentieth and twenty-first centuries. Combined with an over-representation of the rural states in the nation's Congress, and with a booming market in automobiles, this has led to the undervaluing of the critical importance of city-supportive passenger rail transportation.

Twentieth-century patterns of urban sprawl, now commonly emulated worldwide, were based on the assumptions of cheap fuel and cheap land, and on an almost exclusive reliance on the private automobile. The consequent proliferation of cars has come with major and long-recognized liabilities, including the copious consumption of fossil fuels, with its environmental and military implications, the major appropriation of space for cars within our cities and neighborhoods, and the simultaneous paving over of greenfields. Nevertheless, an eagerness for immediate profits has driven much anti-environmental decision making. A public policy of investing adequately in urban transportation infrastructure, other than car-oriented, which could create jobs in the short term and drive economic growth in the long term, has yet to materialize on a scale appropriate to the need.

Now with the unprecedented challenge of climate change, with heightened competition for, and volatile costs of fuel, food, and commodities of all kinds, and as the beauty and health of our once seemingly endless open lands are eaten away by suburbanization and by drilling for fossil fuels, it is abundantly clear that a deep and comprehensive commitment to more sustainable forms of land use and transportation is sorely needed. This priority is in turn exponentially heightened with an ongoing growth in population—local, national, and worldwide—and with urban mobility itself becoming increasingly problematic as our planet becomes ever more crowded with cars.

Specifically, the time is overdue to seriously question the central role of the automobile in our lives, as a relic of the twentieth century that was based on moving human beings in large metal containers weighing two or more tons. Envisioned is a release from the triple tyrannies of traffic congestion, dependency on petroleum, and an overwhelmingly paved environment—all of which derive from our commitment and addiction to the automobile. In an alternate scenario, residents of both urban and suburban areas would ultimately realize fluid mobility via extensive networks of public transport—including, most notably, rail—with walking, cycling, buses, and small, flexible, and shared vehicles serving as important distributors to and from regional transit stations and other local destinations. Petroleum-intensive intra-continental flights of between 100 and 500 miles (between 160 and 800 km) would no longer be justified or needed, having been replaced by high-speed rail—a vision already achieved in Japan, in many countries throughout Europe, and increasingly in China.

In the early part of the twentieth century, there existed impressive rail transit networks in the United States—in the electric streetcar systems around which cities and suburbs were built, in commuter rail lines that linked cities and their surrounding towns, and in the interurban railways, which in the most favorable cases served as convenient extensions of the streetcar lines. These networks formed a viable infrastructure for a truly democratic society, supporting mobility for all within the cities and making travel outside the cities both accessible and affordable for the ordinary citizen. Rail reinforced the cities as economic, cultural, and political centers.

In contrast, the scattering of population out of US cities and over the landscape after World War II has not only made car ownership a requirement for mobility. It has also drained the cities of much of the middle class, and with it much participatory democracy, fostering political passivity, even in the face of extreme income disparities. Costly car dependency has at the same time encouraged the habit and acceptance of borrowing as a way of life, leading to the weight of personal debt that dominates so many Americans.

This book necessarily concentrates on conditions in the United States, where, with less than 5 percent of the world's population, we are spending one-third of the planet's natural resources. Because this nation consumes more gasoline than the next twenty countries combined, meaningful efforts to reduce the carbon emissions generated by automobiles and aircraft must begin in our own country. What is needed is a major shift in priorities for investments from roads, highways, and new airports to passenger rail and other forms of public transport. While the preeminent economic position that our nation held in the twentieth century is in question today, our car-dependent lifestyle, aggressively promoted on multimedia around the globe, still serves as a much-imitated model. Automobile ownership has become *the* status symbol in less developed but fast-growing nations such as China and India, where burgeoning populations, multiplied by automotive lifestyles, portend unprecedented and truly massive climate change for the planet. Our challenge today is to nurture more sustainable development in our own country, while maintaining a desirable—even coveted—standard of living.

In fact, we seem already to be on the cusp of a change in attitudes away from the car-centric lifestyle. In much of the United States until recently, a tradition of aversion to high density has prevailed. It has long been assumed, and has been incessantly advanced in commercials since the mid-twentieth century, that the "American Dream" must necessarily consist of owning a single-family, detached house in the suburbs, a car for every motorist in the household, and the many purchases whose perceived needs are generated by these possessions. Our entire economy has been based upon this form of hyper-consumerism. But when the personal fortunes of individual families come into question or are devastated, as they have been for many during the deep economic recession that began in December 2007, aspirations for owning so much material baggage are sharply challenged and basically undermined.

Concern about the effects of hyper-consumerism on climate change and on the pollution of the planet is, at the same time, beginning to make its mark, particularly on the younger generations who will inherit the earth. Many young people with small households actually prefer the freedom and flexibility of renting or owning an apartment in a compact and walkable neighborhood, to the responsibility and permanence of owning a detached house, and many of them prefer the option of walking and traveling by transit, in lieu of the need to drive everywhere. Another demographic group to be considered is our growing population of the elderly. For them, the responsibilities of owning and maintaining a house and car can be overbearing, and as their driving skills gradually diminish, it becomes all the more important for their independence to live near public transportation. Indeed, since the mid-1990s, these groups have been increasingly migrating back toward apartment living in cities and toward more compact, walkable, mixed-use, and transit-served neighborhoods.

Most streetcars have been gone from our cities for more than half a century, and many of the people who currently oppose rail transit have never ridden it. But it appears that a more basic source of opposition to rail transit is that it can generate relatively high densities of development, and in fact typically requires these densities to justify its provision. Thus, anti-transit, and anti-rail arguments in particular, are quite closely linked to residual anti-urban sentiments about the higher densities of development that are associated with it.

It is worth exploring the components of this opposition, as done in chapter 1, since the potential economic and ecological savings of more compact development are vast, and make great sense for a future of growing populations and scarcer resources. As densities of urban development are increased, significant savings per dwelling unit can be realized in the costs of land, utilities, and construction materials; in the energy required for space heating and cooling; and particularly in the fuel, raw materials, and land consumed in transportation. These economic benefits for individuals, families, municipalities and nations are but a reflection of the most basic of benefits—the ecological ones—which are the survival issues for all of humankind.

Acknowledgments

The material in this book is derived from a lifetime of travel and study, and from the ideas, encouragement, and assistance of many individuals in interrelated fields.

I owe special debts of gratitude to Dr. Vukan R. Vuchic for his informative and inspiring books, presentations, and remarks on urban transit and on the true value of rail transportation for cities; Donald C. Shoup for his illuminating analyses of car parking practice in the United States; Robert Cervero for his perceptive and extensive writings on transit-oriented development; Professor John Pucher for his eye-opening talks and articles on the potential of bicycling in the transportation mix, as well as for the use of his photo of Freiburg's car-free center, where traffic is essentially limited to trams, pedestrians, and bicycles; Greg Thompson and Margarita Novales for their insights into the successes of light rail insertion into the cities of France and Spain; Andrea Broaddus for the use of material from her study of the eco-communities of Vauban and Rieselfeld, Germany; Lester R. Brown for his thoughtful books and articles on the earth's environment and climate; and the Institute for Transportation and Development Policy for its excellent report by Nicole Foletta and Simon Field, *Europe's Vibrant New Low Car(bon) Communities* as well as for the use of site plans of the eco-communities of Vauban, Germany, and Hammarby Sjöstad, Sweden.

I particularly thank Sam Schwartz for his firm's weekly e-newsletter on transportation developments in the United States and around the world; Ruedi Ott, director of traffic management for the city of Zürich, for his extensive discussion of that city's auto-free-street and transit policies; Gehl Architects of Copenhagen for sending photos of that city's famous Strøget, Europe's longest pedestrian street, which Jan Gehl's guidance was so pivotal in developing; Bernhard Gutzner of the Department of Circulation Planning of the City of Freiburg for use of the map of Freiburg showing its pedestrian and traffic-calmed area, as well as photos of Klarastrasse before and after traffic calming and of a typical neighborhood "home zone" in that city; Calthorpe Associates for the use of their theoretical site plan of "a constellation" of transit-oriented developments; the city of Minneapolis and Downtown Denver Partnership for sending photos of pedestrian streets in each of their respective cities; friends and colleagues Ron Shiffman, Tina Lund, and Daniel Sherr for the use of their photos of light rail in Strasbourg, Istanbul, and Barcelona, respectively; Michael King for his photos showing traffic calming in Dortmund and Heidelberg, Germany; Larry Fabian of Trans21 for his photo of Detroit's downtown people mover; and Mathieu Delorme, for his delightful Photoshop images of how the vision42 project could transform Midtown Manhattan.

I thank Bill Conis of Siemens Transportation Systems for his company's beautiful photo of Spain's Velaro high-speed rail; Bombardier Transport International for their photos of the light rail tram in Milan and the Vancouver Skytrain; Dan Schned of the Regional Plan Association for his organization's aerial photo of the Milford Shopping Center and for their map of eleven US urban corridors designated as potential candidates for high-speed rail; Craig Kuhner, photographer, and Sasaki Associates, Inc. for their photograph of the Dallas downtown transitway mall; William Lark Jr. and Ryan C. C. Chin of Smart Cities, MIT Media Lab, for their illustrations of the CityCar; Benson Chin of Translink of the greater Vancouver region for his photo showing easy access for bikes on Skytrain; and Steven Grover, president and CEO of eLock Technologies, LLC, and Bikelink, for the photo of their electronic bike lockers in use on the Bay Area Rapid Transit system.

I especially thank my friends and colleagues: civil engineer and transportation planner George Haikalis, for sharing his knowledge of light rail development around the world, and for his many years of collaboration with me on the vision42 proposal for Manhattan, as well as architect-planner Alfreda Radzicki and planner Nina Arron, who each painstakingly reviewed the manuscript of the book, and offered many helpful criticisms and suggestions. I would also like to thank Clay Morgan, my acquisitions editor, and Miranda Martin, acquisitions assistant at the MIT Press, for their helpful advice and encouragement in bringing this book to print.

I am blessed with a loving and understanding husband, Edgar Sonnenfeld, who has endured my multi-year obsession with the subject matter and writing of the text, and has contributed his invaluable insights as an architect and humanist. To him I dedicate this book with heartfelt thanks.

1

Perceptions of Cities and Rail, and a Changing Paradigm

It is natural for an architect to be immersed in issues of transportation planning, since transportation is a central component of urban planning and design—urbanism—which is the embodiment of architecture at the maximum scale. At the same time, it is essential that urbanism be conceived with deference to the much larger-scale environment of the planet.

This book had its beginnings in a theoretical urban design project for the reconstruction of the center of the small pre-auto-age town of Mount Vernon, New York. In the development of a program of space allocation for new office, retail, and residential facilities, it became immediately and abundantly clear that the area required for automobiles outweighed and dominated all other human functions. It was, in fact, a forgone conclusion that, if typical standards for roadways and parking were applied, the result would be an imposing concrete superstructure—a monument to the automobile—which would sacrifice all possibility of restoring the urban center at a personally interactive human scale. At the same time, most of the center's existing parks and green parcels of land would fall to the bulldozer.

Given the undesirable alternatives of either traffic congestion or a massive concrete edifice—that is, whether the town was to be re-tailored to the automobile or not—it seemed that its obsolescence and gradual abandonment were assured. This typical impasse, when replicated in countless other similar small-scale towns and cities all over the United States, has worked to impel the widespread decentralization of our population, the wasting of our older urban areas, the simultaneous consumption of virgin land for new development, and an enormous demand for petroleum to drive to and from these new spread-out locations. So a study that had begun with one small town broadened to encompass the larger issue of reconciling urban growth with local and global environmental concerns. Simultaneously, the study narrowed, to focus on alternative urban planning practices and technologies that could be suited to current needs.

Far-reaching decisions are often made by technical specialists who, no matter how gifted and erudite they may be in their own fields, approach the problem with a kind of tunnel vision, basing their proposed solutions only on impeccable mathematical formulae, and purposely avoiding a universalist approach. In contrast, this book endeavors to integrate these issues, and as such it is addressed to a wide range of readers.

The political scenario, current conditions, and ecological priorities

Cities as a central issue

With more than half of humanity now living in cities, and more to come, the inherent conflict between the automobile and the city needs to be addressed. For while the automobile has granted us unprecedented mobility, as its numbers multiply within a city, it creates immobility instead. This is essentially a product of the *space* that it consumes: even if the challenge of finding carbon-free, affordable, and abundant fuel for our cars is resolved tomorrow, the spatial problem will remain as long as ubiquitous automobility remains.

Climate change, which is poised to inundate our coastal cities worldwide with flooding, is integrally related to our dependency upon cars and the replication of this pattern across the globe—a pattern that is commonly expected to continue into the future. According to the International Energy Agency, emissions from transportation are the fastest-growing source of global greenhouse gases, and are projected to increase 300 percent by 2050. By then, 2 to 3 billion cars may be on the world's roads, compared with 800 million cars today.[1] Curtailing our use of private motoring, and, toward this end, supporting more viable and extensive public transportation infrastructure for our urban areas, which in the United States are already home to more than two-thirds of the population, will therefore be critical to slowing climate change—a subject that is further discussed in this book's final chapter.

In the United States since 1980, about one-half of suburban sprawl has stemmed from population growth, but the other half is the result of the per capita increases in space and land consumption that have occurred with the proliferation of single-family housing and a reliance on private motoring.[2] While both issues need to be addressed, it is the latter that this book explores.

It is especially relevant, and disadvantageous for our cities, that our dominant modes of transportation—automobiles and aviation—are, by their very nature, capacity constrained. In comparison with driving and air travel, a variety of types of rail transportation can smoothly accommodate *dramatic* increases in the numbers of people they can carry, thereby enabling the fluid functioning of cities even as their populations swell. This issue—the high value of passenger rail for cities—is further developed in chapter 3.

Cities are, and have been since antiquity, places of intellectual awareness and creativity. They are also the places where significant savings in land and fuel consumption can be realized—through more compact development, and through walking, cycling, and the use of public transportation. In light of our environmental challenges, these benefits cry out to be appreciated and supported with more enlightened, pro-city policies. As noted by architectural critic and educator Aaron Betsky:

Cities can only exist through the continual presence of a great deal of infrastructure that is visible. Mass transportation, cops on the beat, utilities, and everything that lets people live in such close quarters is necessary and in your face. Equally visible are both the rich and the poor, and thus the contrast between them. It is clear why government is necessary, and that we live in a society of contrasts in which we all have to get along—and perhaps even help each other.[3]

The fact that, in the United States, the primarily rural states, no matter how sparsely populated, are allotted two senators each, while the more urban, highly populated states are limited to the same number, makes it well-nigh impossible to advance an urban agenda—one that would adequately support, for example, educational and cultural institutions, sound urban infrastructure, and in particular, high-quality systems of public transportation. Yet given the current left-right divide, it will be virtually impossible to change this imbalance, because to do so would require a major amendment to the US Constitution, which the rural senators would be highly unlikely to sign on to. Perhaps a long-term solution to the problem might lie in the gradual conversion of our rural populations to appreciate these urban assets for their social benefits to humanity and their environmental benefits to the planet.

The clear alternative to widespread reliance on private motoring is a comprehensive and well-coordinated network of public transportation. If this sounds to conservative ears "a little too much like socialism," it is because there is considerable confusion about the very meaning of socialism. A socialist society is one in which the means of production and distribution—industry, agriculture, banking, and commerce—have been deprivatized. In a democratic society, in contrast, a rise in the well-being of the public-at-large through smoothly functioning public transportation, good public health and education systems, and the like, equates to social well-being, not socialism—as shown in the Scandinavian countries, which are among the most civilized on Earth, despite being monarchies.

For a democratic society to agree to substantial public investments in urban infrastructure, there needs to first be a sense of common public purpose, and for this the conversation ought not to be limited to narrowly economic terms. For example, the late historian and thinker Tony Judt pointed out that "The French and the Italians ... and most of continental Europe ... have long treated their railways as a *social* provision.... The railway station and the facilities it provides to even the smallest of communities are both a symptom and a symbol of society as a shared aspiration." But in the US and the UK, noted, Judt, "We too readily assume that the defining feature of modernity is the individual: the non-reducible subject, the free-standing person, the unbound self, the un-beholden citizen."[4] Little wonder that our favored mode of travel, the private car, directly reflects this self-image.

Suburbanization and climate change

Suburbanization in the United States was both anticipated and inspired by Frank Lloyd Wright's vision of Broadacre City, wherein each family would occupy a full acre of land. It has also been amply demonstrated by University of Chicago professor Robert Bruegmann that suburban sprawl is not a recent phenomenon, but has been a feature of life sought by wealthy individuals since the earliest times.[5] Nevertheless, with substantial population growth, its negative impacts take on disquieting dimensions, ranging from the global to the personal.

The extensive driving that is integral to suburban and exurban living feeds our oil addiction voraciously. Between 2007 and 2011, oil consumption cost the United States two trillion dollars, according to researcher David Greene at the Oak Ridge National Laboratory.[6] Even more to the point, together with air travel, it contributes heavily to climate change, which is now threatening the entire planet, having surpassed such albeit important issues as ground-level ozone and photochemical smog. It has been emphasized by Robert Puentes, senior fellow at the Brookings Institution, that climate change" … has quickly emerged as the main environmental problem linked to transportation … [which] is the single largest contributor to the nation's carbon footprint, causing more damage than industry, homes, or commercial buildings."[7] And land use strategist and developer Christopher Leinberger observes that households that are car-dependent emit three times the volume of climate change gases as those in walkable, transit-related communities.[8]

Clearly, truly meaningful measures to reduce the carbon emissions generated by transport need to be initiated in the United States. With less than 5 percent of the planet's population, our country accounted for nearly one-quarter of the world's petroleum consumption in the two decades between 1990 and 2010.[9] We are also near the top among nations in miles driven per vehicle, and near the bottom in fuel efficiency. Three-quarters of the petroleum used annually in the US is spent on transportation, and of this amount, approximately two-thirds is burned by motor vehicles.[10] The influence on our foreign (and particularly, military) policy of our voracious demand for petroleum should be a matter of especially grave concern.

Much excitement, as well as controversy, has been generated in the US over proposed new high-speed rail, with its huge potential for replacing domestic air travel and large numbers of personal vehicles on trips of up to 500 miles (800 km)—saving much time and petroleum, and greatly diminishing greenhouse gases and congestion in the process. However, local and intra-regional transit systems will need to be substantially upgraded and much better patronized than they are at present for sufficient numbers of passengers to be rationally conveyed to high-speed rail stations. Otherwise, these stations will need to be surrounded by vast car parking facilities, instead of compact, walkable urban development.

In these respects, the need to support our cities and our urban transit systems, and our need to conserve the earth's climate and resources are literally two sides of the same coin.

The currently low use of public transit ridership in the United States
Although public transportation ridership in the US has been rising by 2.5 percent annually since 1996, it is indeed starting from a low base.[11] In 2008 it accounted for less than 2 percent of all urban travel in the US.[12] According to the 2009 *Greendex* report by the National Geographic Society, only 5 percent of US residents surveyed reported that they use public transit on a daily basis, while 61 percent reported that they *never* use it.[13] Even for short trips—those of one mile or less—the automobile dominates in the US, accounting for 67 percent of these trips. This compares with only 27 percent in Germany, where incomes and auto ownership are also high.[14]

To encourage the wider use of public transit, it is not enough that job centers be served with reliable transit systems. For it is *compact, residentially based, mixed-use* development that holds the other key to the usefulness of public transit as an everyday alternative to private motoring—because of three simple truths: (1) the great majority of all kinds of trips either begin or end at home; (2) when a car is needed on either end of a trip, the natural tendency is to drive it all the way to one's destination; and (3) certain minimal residential densities are required to justify the provision of regular, frequent, and dependable public transit.[15] For this, the most obvious solution is multi-family housing. And it should be mixed-use development, since bundling residential development with convenience shopping and other amenities can serve as the bases for walkable communities, while cutting down on the need for much local driving.

But from the mid-twentieth century for at least six decades, the patterns of new housing development in the US were diametrically opposed to this imperative. US biases against high densities were reflected in, and institutionalized by, zoning laws that date from the early twentieth century. In 1916, planners in the city of Berkeley, California, established a new zoning category, the single-family zone, from which not only all business and industry were banned, but also any housing other than single-family.[16] Ten years later, legal barriers between types of land use were further reinforce, and the special status of single-family housing was further elevated, when the US Supreme Court, in *Euclid v. Ambler*, classified apartments as a commercial use, and declared them "alien and potentially destructive to single-family life."[17] Although there have been a number of inroads in recent decades to modify the exclusivity of these laws, allowing mixed-use zoning in specific areas, single-family zones in the United States more typically ban all other uses, and cover the largest single share of territory in every US metropolis.

At the same time, the largest investment that the federal government makes in housing goes to the home mortgage interest deduction, which happens to benefit the wealthiest homeowners, while serving as a major inducement toward suburban sprawl.

The scope of land consumption for low-density housing and some recent reversals

Thus, new housing in 1999 accounted for some 43 percent of the total land developed in the US, and most of this was single-family housing.[18] In the metropolitan area of Phoenix, new residential subdivisions were devouring land in 1996 at the rate of an acre an hour (0.405 ha per hour).[19] Between 1982 and 1997, while the US population grew by 17 percent, the area of land developed had grown by 47 percent. In the twenty years between 1982 and 2002, the average acreage per person for housing had nearly doubled; between 1994 and 2002, ten-plus acre (4.05-plus ha) housing lots accounted for 55 percent of the land developed.[20] As the land devoted to housing per person in the US expanded, enormous "McMansions" on large lots became all the fashion. Although the Great Recession that commenced in December 2007 has served to undermine this vogue, a vast inventory of oversized houses in outlying areas, in addition to more modest ones, remains.

Toward the end of the twentieth century, with the centrifugal momentum of development nearly unconstrained, we were depleting prime and unique farmland, forests and wildlife habitats for exurban construction at an estimated rate of 50 acres (20.23 ha) every hour, every day.[21] At these low densities of automobile-related development, we have been consuming land at a per capita rate unprecedented in human history. And as destinations have become increasingly dispersed, our inventory of cars has grown twice as fast as the human population, as have the average lengths of trips and the popularity of heavy, self-protective, but fuel-inefficient vehicles.

The years since 2000 have seen a shift of an appreciable amount of US residential construction back toward the cities and urban neighborhoods. As the 2008 housing bubble burst, the construction of single-family homes fell to 35 percent of its 2005 level, down from 1.7 million to 600,000 units, while multi-family residential construction retained its previous levels at around 200,000 units, despite the economic downturn. The share of residential construction occurring in central cities had more than doubled in twenty-six of the nation's fifty largest metropolitan areas. This centripetal trend has been a reflection of shifting market fundamentals, and has taken place even in the absence of formal policies and programs.[22]

But this is not to proclaim the end of suburban sprawl as we know it. These figures indicate that, in the three-year period between 2005 and 2008, there were still three times as many single-family homes built as there were multi-family residential units. It must be realistically assumed that this implies continued car dependency for growing numbers of households. Between 2005 and 2009, 70 percent of all new development took place on greenfields, thereby expanding the suburbs.[23] And despite significant growth in multi-family housing starts by 2012, there continued to be a critical undersupply of this type of housing.[24]

The extent of paving for cars

Since all of this suburban living requires car ownership and induces extensive solo motoring, it is not surprising that only 9 percent of households in the US owned no automobile in 2007.[25] During that year, a full 76.0 percent of US workers drove alone to work, and 10.4 percent carpooled, while only 4.9 percent took transit. Some 4.1 percent worked at home, only 2.8 percent walked, and 1.7 percent traveled by "other" means, including cycling.[26]

To serve this extensive driving, even more land has been consumed for roadways, parking lots, and garages than has been devoted to housing—in fact, the two have compounded each other. It has been calculated by Todd Litman, researcher at the Victoria Transport Policy Institute, that in typical suburban areas, about three times as much land is dedicated to roadways and parking as to housing.[27]

Opponents to the advocacy of more compact development object that traffic congestion rises and paving of the environment increases as a function of density. However, the underlying reality is that both depend very much upon transportation mode. Prior to the advent of the automobile, urban densities equivalent to 31 to 63 persons per acre (76 to 156 persons per ha) could be quite pleasantly accommodated. Indeed, most of the world's towns and cities were within this range.[28] The scenario now differs markedly when cars are included, as each "medium-sized" automobile commands about twenty-five times the space of a human being, and in motion requires even larger expanses—the higher the speed, the greater the space. And when not in motion (which is 95 percent of the time[29]), a parking space is need at both the origin and destination of every trip.

In fact, to meet the traditional guidelines of the lending institutions that finance development, we typically provide, when we build, not one, but two or three parking places per car—one at home, one at work or school, one at the shopping center, entertainment, or vacation spot, etc. This is true whether we are building in rural areas, in suburbs, or in cities, with the exception of only a few cities that are still served by regular, around-the-clock public transit systems. When access drives are included, at least 300 to 350 sf (28 to 32.5 m²) are allocated for each off-street parking space. So we are dedicating 600 to 1,050 sf (55.7 to 97.5 m²) to each private car for the purpose of its storage alone, even before streets and highways are counted.

Highways—which were intended to solve congestion, but have typically induced more of the very traffic they were built to relieve—are similarly land consuming. The space required on a highway for the safety of each moving car—some one thousand square feet at least (93 m²)—exceeds by a factor of fifty the space occupied by a public transit rider, and exceeds by a factor of more than one hundred the space a pedestrian needs. Even "high-occupancy vehicles," when carrying four persons per car, have been found to be far more space consuming than a quarter-full bus, especially when consideration is given to the parking space required at the destination.[30]

The scale of development is thereby grossly inflated, and a largely paved environment and traffic congestion are virtually guaranteed as densities rise. The resulting loss of greenery, and the severe economic penalties that these spatial requirements impose on compact development, have persistently helped to drive the impetus of development toward outlying areas, acting as a geographically divisive force to magnify all other decentralizing factors—be they poor city schools, crime in the cities, racial divisions, real estate speculation, competitive inducements among outlying municipalities to attract new commercial development,

Figure 1.1
Development overblown. Scattered development near the interchange of US Route 1 and the Connecticut Turnpike includes the Milford Shopping Center, a movie theater, three motels, four factories, and a trailer park, each of which requires its own parking field.
Source: Regional Plan Association.

or simply the relatively looser regulation of development in outlying areas.

Impacts on the ecosystem

This paving process is happening slowly enough that the average person notices only a small part of the picture. However, once virgin land is taken for development, the process is generally irreversible. It is also the choicest farmland, forest and scenic lands that are built upon, since those very qualities that make them desirable for one purpose, such as fertility, good drainage, natural beauty, and proximity to urban centers, make them similarly desirable for the other. An easily discernible negative result is the loss of fertile farmland close to urban areas; another is the destruction of the habitats of wildlife. As woods and grasslands are sliced up into housing developments, malls and highways, the whole complex fabric of the natural world has been gradually unraveling, leaving only isolated islands of "nature preserves," and rendering untold numbers of plant and animal species vulnerable to extinction. Largely because of loss of habitat, animal species worldwide are becoming extinct at a rate at least one hundred times their normal replacement levels. What was once a vast continuum of interrelated natural landscapes is being fragmented into isolated islands so small that they are unable to sustain viable populations of many flora and fauna.[31]

Not commonly appreciated, yet profound, are the massive losses of invertebrate life that occur as natural areas are degraded. These need to be recognized as truly catastrophic losses, for it is this myriad of tiny invertebrate creatures that serve as the very basis of every ecosystem, decomposing wastes, and maintaining the soil structure, pollination, and fertility upon which plant growth and thus all higher organisms depend.[32]

When new towns are located in outlying areas on the assumption of dependency upon private cars for mobility, which is our typical planning assumption, they are simply exporting these ecological ills to the countryside. The net impact is the same—it is only not concentrated so close to the metropolis.

The need to protect the quality of the water supply—sparing virgin watersheds

One of the most compelling reasons for curbing sprawl is the need to protect the quality of our water supply, many of whose persistent problems derive directly from sprawl-type development. The nation's leading threat to water quality is "non-point-source" pollution—the contamination of water runoff from widespread surfaces—as compared with "point-source" pollution, which comes directly from industrial drainage pipes and sewers. Sources of non-point pollution are normally harder to identify; they include agricultural and lawn fertilizers and pesticides, mining and logging operations, construction sites, large engineering projects, and urban runoff. Natural landscapes are typically porous; rainwater percolates slowly through them in a filtering and cleansing process on its way to underground aquifers, lakes, streams, and estuaries. But when forests, wetlands, and grasslands are replaced with impervious surfaces, such as parking lots, roads and rooftops, stormwater becomes trapped above these surfaces, running off in large volumes, often at high velocity, picking up pollutants along the way. There is consequently a strong correspondence between the percentage of land in a given area that is covered with impervious surfaces and the inability of our water systems to regenerate themselves. The degradation of streams begins, and fish begin to disappear, when impervious cover in a watershed exceeds 10 percent of the land area. A watershed is considered generally degraded at levels above 30 percent imperviousness. Residential subdivisions with one-acre (.4047 ha) lots typically result in 10 to 20 percent impervious surfaces, and industrial, commercial, and shopping center developments normally result in 75 to 95 percent imperviousness.[33] Therefore, for the vital purpose of protecting regional water quality, the very best direction for urban development, advocated by author/researcher Tom Schueler of the Center for Watershed Protection, is *to concentrate as much development as possible in high-density clusters within areas that are already developed and therefore biologically non-supporting*, allowing them to be degraded to as much as 100 percent imperviousness, in order to spare other watersheds from exceeding the 10 percent maximum threshold needed to protect the area's water quality.[34] *This recommendation is in direct synchrony with other ecological and economic reasons for concentrating future growth within existing urban areas.*

American perceptions about cities

Common suppositions about high densities

Resistance to building alternatives to sprawl for residential use has hinged in the first place on the issue of density—that is, on the question of whether the relatively compact development that is needed to support, and indeed to justify regular public transit service as an alternative to driving can be made both desirable and marketable. Especially for families with young children, a green residential environment is highly valued—a matter that must be explicitly and transparently addressed and resolved before fully popular multi-family and mixed-use alternatives to sprawl can be realized.

Peripheral growth stretching out toward ever cheaper land, cheaper housing, and less congested areas has continued relatively unabated in most of the US in the twenty-first century. An analysis of 2010 US Census data by Robert Lang, an urban sociologist at the University of Nevada at Las Vegas, revealed that, between 2000 and 2010, most of the growth of housing occurred on opposite ends of the suburban expanse. That is, while the suburbs closest to the major cities grew by some 11.3 percent (against a growth of 9.7 percent for the US as a whole), emerging suburbs and exurbs further out grew more than twice as fast—by 24.5 percent.[35] It is yet to be determined whether this trend will be substantially thwarted by increases in the cost of gasoline, particularly as people realize that their costs for transportation—typically a household's second-largest expenditure—are outweighing the advantages of lower housing costs.

It is not only cheaper land and housing that underlies this attraction to the exurbs. Pro-driving and anti-city sentiments have long prevailed in much of the United States—as well as aspirations to the tradition wherein a sense of respectability rests upon owning one's own detached house, surrounded by leafy private grounds, remote from the confusion, pollution and poverty that can be found in cities. This old aversion to cities, only now easing, was surely intensified with the advent and proliferation of the automobile in the twentieth century, as our cities were re-designed to accommodate cars, and simultaneously despoiled as compatible walking environments. For in a land where private automobiles, each bearing one person, are the dominant mode of travel, we have come to normally associate *any* form of high-density development—residential or commercial—with environmental blight, paving of the landscape, and traffic congestion.

It has also been commonly assumed in the US that high density in itself is responsible for generating high rates of crime. This supposition is actually disproven by the examples of such highly civilized, high-density/low-crime countries as Holland and Japan. Similarly, the high-density borough of Manhattan shows lower per capita rates of crime than the conurbations of Phoenix and Los Angeles.[36] Research indicates, rather, that when such elements as income, education level, and migration rate are factored out, there is virtually no remaining relationship between density and crime rate.[37]

People rarely complain about being crowded when they are seated in grandstands watching a football game, or standing at a closely packed cocktail party. In fact, if the subject is *expecting* to have a good time, that person is likely to have an even *better* time under crowded than uncrowded conditions.[38] This is a very meaningful finding for urban design, since with the design of the streetscape, we set the mood for the street life of the community.

A related notion, of older, basically xenophobic origin, is that the cultural diversity and flexibility of lifestyle that are commonly found in cities are in themselves inherently not conducive to a healthy, moral life. Such attitudes, together with a tradition of nostalgia for a long-lost agrarian ideal, appear to lie at the root of policies that have clearly undermined our cities, and of the nation's ambivalence regarding initiatives that could actually strengthen the cities.

Fiscal policies that have so disadvantaged most US cities, briefly alluded to in chapter 3, appear to be similarly grounded in a number of additional negative assumptions about high density—some of which are in fact very much open to question. One is that our older cities are irreversibly obsolete, an assumption stemming largely from their problems in accommodating auto traffic and trucking. It is certainly true that the compact, older cities are inefficient for many modern industries, whose needs for expansive space have drawn them toward less congested and cheaper land in outlying areas. Undeniably, certain types of development need lower densities for their optimal operation, including power and other industrial plants, sports facilities, and other enterprises that require large horizontal expanses.

On the other hand, many light industries with less demanding spatial requirements can truly benefit from proximity to a city's diversity of interrelated industries and the specialized skills and services of an urban workforce. For offices, retail shopping, and many other commercial functions, as well as residential ones, compact development can be ideal from the standpoint of convenient home-to-work access, personal contacts, and their economy of infrastructure and operations. One of the great values of compact development is that it can enrich the sphere of cultural, social, employment, and other opportunities within a small area, and in doing so, can reduce the number of miles (kilometers) that need to be traveled in the first place.

Perspectives on sprawl's "inevitability"
It is certainly a gross simplification to assume that sprawl is the inevitable outcome of technological progress, free choice and the free market. True, from the standpoint of the developer—with most Americans owning

cars—new homes, jobs, and shops no longer need to be built in close proximity; one location is nearly as good as another for the purposes of attracting a motoring public. There are also powerful incentives toward land speculation in outlying areas, where real estate investors typically buy large tracts of land at wholesale prices, then sell smaller chunks of it to home builders at retail prices, realizing profits that are frequently measured by a factor of five.[39]

Yet sprawl would have never occurred in its present and growing dimensions without the massive government and corporate investments and subsidies that have encouraged private motoring, and a tax code in which an agenda favoring suburbanization has played a central role. A report released in January 2013 by the organization Smart Growth America detailed how the federal government spends $450 billion every year on a combination of loans, mortgage guarantees, grants, and tax credits, which are heavily skewed through the suburbanization of the country.[40] The past and present influence of this largess, and the potential for shifting future public support toward different priorities, cannot be dismissed from consideration.

The most effective tool we could possibly use for curbing urban sprawl would be a shift of public investments in urban infrastructure—away from new highways and roads, and toward a variety of forms of public transit networks—particularly rail, for reasons that are elaborated on in chapter 3. If moratoria were placed on the construction of new highways and utility infrastructure on the urban fringe, sprawl would quickly begin to lose its momentum. Changes would also be needed in those zoning laws that literally *force* strip-commercial and large-lot residential development, as well as excessive off-street parking facilities. These would entail largely political decisions, for land speculation—particularly in concert with new transportation access—has long been one of the most lucrative and politically protected enterprises of the powerful. The so-called Iron Law of Urban Decay is a creation of political choice and not of nature.

Variable and constant factors at work against US cities

A number of elements have clearly played key roles in drawing new development and economic life away from US cities. These may be seen as falling into three general categories—variable factors, constant factors, and those that fall somewhere in between.

The *variable factors* are those that are the most amenable to change, given a consensus of human will and effort. Foremost among these are government and corporate policies and programs that have been strongly biased toward suburbanization, and have deeply subsidized the costs of private motoring. A prime example is the heavy investment of public funds in highways and parking facilities versus a stark underinvestment by government in public transportation. Equally basic is the fact that developers in the US have not been obliged to pay for the extension of water supplies and sewers to outlying areas, nor for schools and other social necessities for their exurban projects. If they had been, they might have been more inclined to build instead within existing urban areas. At the same time, an exclusive reliance on cars has been encouraged by an unwillingness to tax gasoline commensurate with its costs to society and by the free, and tax-free parking that is typically provided by corporations to their employees outside of the cities. Additionally, our federal income tax provisions governing capital gains and mortgage interest have been so designed that they strongly encourage the outward migration of potential homebuyers from the cities and inner suburbs. (In contrast, no such tax benefits have been granted to the renters of apartments.) Any or all of these factors are subject to change.

The *constant factors* are those that are uncontrollable from the standpoint of policy and planning. For example, lower land costs, lower taxes and lower-wage workers are normally found in areas of lower density. And it is considerably less costly, complex and controversial to develop virgin, outlying lands (as long as public moneys are providing the infrastructure for this). The constant factors also include our ongoing and open-ended revolution in communications technology—multiple electronic networks that have further loosened the ties that once bound a city together. Particularly with the common availability of high-speed broadband, an employment center can be as isolated as the entrepreneur sitting at home at a computer terminal.

Most of the other decentralizing factors fall somewhere in between the variable and constant; that is, each is amenable to change, but only if there is public clarity of purpose and perseverance in favor of such change, given the presence of other interlocking conditions. Thus, the loss of jobs in cities leads directly to the sequiturs of: poverty → poor schools → poor training of the workforce → loss of more jobs → more poverty → and crime—all of them compounding and compounded by the society's painful legacy of racial/economic division. If their mutual reinforcement is to be broken, the handicap of the variable factors must first be lifted.

The *divisive factor:* Also falling into this variable/constant and potentially amenable-to-change category, is the physical restructuring of our cities that has occurred since the building of the interstate highway network. In a culture tied to the automobile, the spatial demands of traffic congestion and parking, with their implications of urban obsolescence, have alone been enough to demagnetize our cities, and to reformulate the urban geography into "prosperous suburbs versus disadvantaged inner cities," dividing those who can afford long car commutes and detached, single-family homes in a clean, green environment from those who cannot. Our massive allocations of land for private cars have pervaded, reinforced, and formed the underlying physical basis for any and all of the other divisive and decentralizing forces. It has been an easy jump from there, for those so inclined, to find reason to turn their backs on the cities altogether.

Mobility issues and solutions for dispersed development

Social and practical limits of automobility
Not everyone has benefited from the geographic spread of development resulting from our automobile-based transportation system. One-third of the US population is not licensed to drive, whether by choice or circumstance; yet most communities around the nation are defined by roads that are inhospitable and dangerous to people traveling by foot or bicycle.[41] Non-motorists living in low-density areas unserved by mass transit—those too young, too old, or physically or financially unable to own and drive a car—are typically dependent on friends or relatives for getting around. The resulting social isolation was aptly described by Lewis Mumford more than a half century ago:

… the wider the scattering of the population, the greater the isolation of the household, and the more effort it takes to do privately, even with the aid of many machines and automatic devices, what used to be done often with conversation, song, and the enjoyment of the physical presence of others…. Instead of centering attention on the child in the garden, we now have the image of "Families in Space."[42]

Most significantly, the migration of job opportunities from cities to sub-urbs and beyond has made them inaccessible to many urban dwellers. Conversely, many low-income families who have been priced out of urban core areas have had to move into car-centric suburbs—where housing may be more affordable, but car ownership and driving are all but required. At the same time, faced with strained budgets, transit authorities are rais-ing fares, trimming routes, and cutting back on frequency of service. A 2011 report by the Brookings Institution found that *42 percent of US suburban residents without cars do not have access to public transit.* This problem is most serious in the Atlanta area, in Dallas–Fort Worth, Hous-ton, Phoenix, and Saint Louis, and somewhat less acute in Los Angeles, New York, San Francisco, Seattle, and Miami–Fort Lauderdale.[43]

In such spread-out areas as Atlanta, generation-to-generation upward mobility has become increasingly difficult, as job opportunities are physi-cally out of reach for many—an apparent inverse relationship between sprawl and social mobility.[44] This lack of mobility for people of low in-come has been exacerbated in recent decades as cars have become ap-preciably more complex and costly. In stark contrast, a comprehensive system of public transportation is a vital tool in reducing the adversities of economic disparity, as it affords to all, regardless of income, the pos-sibility of moving at least cost.

Buses and rail—competing or complementary? The French example

There have been bitter struggles and lawsuits about the social equity of spending on rail in lieu of buses, since low-income residents rely heavily on buses, which can serve more dispersed locations than rail on limited transit budgets. In the Los Angeles region, the Bus Riders' Union has been challenging the Metropolitan Transportation Authority since 1994 over its high expenditures on the construction of rail projects and its simulta-neous neglect of bus service. According to bus advocates, some 92 percent of Los Angeles County's bus riders are people of color, with median household incomes of only $12,000, and bus service cuts and fare hikes are hurting them disproportionately. Similar grievances and lawsuits have occurred in the San Francisco Bay area, Atlanta, Memphis, and many other US metropolitan areas.[45]

Part of the problem derives from the way transit is financed in the US. Particularly because buses can be stalled in mixed traffic, the bus riders do not come close to paying for their service through the farebox. So each additional passenger increases the amount of subsidy needed, and the transit managers are inclined to view new bus riders as a fiscal drain.[46]

It is often assumed by advocates for each mode that bus and rail transit alternatives are competing for the same pot of money—that spending on buses and rail is a zero-sum game. However, recent research by Jonathan Levine, professor of urban planning at the University of Michigan, indicates instead that spending on one of these modes is normally positively associated with spending on the other. This occurs because of the necessary interaction between the modes, as with feeder buses to rail.[47]

Thus, investment in rail transit does not necessarily have to come at the expense of investment in the local bus network. A case in point can be found in France, where the insertion of new light rail trams has been accomplished in twenty-seven cities since 1985, and where the trams have been carefully coordinated with extensive pre-existing bus systems. In each of these cities, the light rail now serves as the backbone of the transit system, while the buses function as critical feeder systems to the light rail. As a result, gains in *overall* transit ridership have been impressive— typically between 30 and 60 percent, while farebox recovery, averaging 48 percent, has been excellent, despite moderate fares and union drivers, and despite the fact that on some lines, heavily discounted students' fares make up over half of the riders.[48]

The small car solution and its limitations

Since the mid-1980s, the fuel economy of our automobiles has been improved, but much of that efficiency has been lost in making vehicles heavier (by 29 percent) and more powerful (by 86 percent), so that the resulting fuel economy for average automobiles had, by 2010, actually been lowered by 5 percent.[49] Then in 2012, when the US standard for fuel efficiency was only around 29 miles per gallon, the government mandated that this standard be gradually raised by 2025 to 54.5 miles per gallon.

Given the markedly low base of public transit ridership in the US, there is an assumption among many transportation planners that even a doubling of the country's mass transit riders would net relatively small gains in the conservation of energy, by comparison with the savings that might be realized through the conversion of passenger cars to smaller, lighter, and more energy-efficient vehicles. This appears to be an appropriate strategy for short trips within existing cities and inner suburbs. However, the average length of commuter trips has, at least until very recently, been increasing every year, and longer trips call for travel at higher speeds. The very lengths and speeds of many of these trips are ill-suited to, and tend to discourage the use of, small, energy-efficient cars, which afford less power in propulsion and less protection in accidents, especially in competition with far heavier cars, SUVs, buses, and trucks.

Markets are emerging for gas-electric hybrid cars, plug-in hybrids, rechargeable electric cars, and battery-powered cars. Toyota scheduled the introduction of a vehicle to be powered by a hydrogen fuel cell in 2015. General Motors has come out with an electric car—the Chevy Volt—that promises to deliver the equivalent of 230 miles per gallon (97.6 km per liter) and is able to travel 40 miles (64.4 km) on its battery alone.

An automobile was developed in the 1990s by energy analyst and inventor Amory Lovins of the Rocky Mountain Institute, which incorporated a very light, ultra-strong, totally aerodynamic shell, using fiber-reinforced molded plastics. The vehicle was supposed to provide the same crash protection as a steel car, but would permit a smaller engine for the same power. The "Hypercar," renamed in 2004 as "Fiberforge," would incorporate a new carbon fiber "superflywheel" to store the car's braking energy, and re-use it for acceleration and hill climbing. It was predicted that, in combination, these innovations would increase the energy efficiency of today's cars some three- to five-fold.[50] Whether and when this project will be economically realized remains an open question.[51]

If any or all of these cars were to sweep the market in the near future, they could, as quickly, end our dependence on foreign oil, and would immediately reduce the magnitude of today's air pollution and greenhouse gases. Alternatively, this could also be the case if and when direct algae-to-fuel-grade ethanol is achieved inexpensively and commercially. Still present, however, would be the space-related problems of traffic congestion and parking that are integral to a primarily private automobile-based transportation system (although smaller-sized vehicles would help alleviate these problems somewhat). But neither the small car solution nor the hypercar would adequately address the issue of which kinds of transportation would be the most beneficial to foster in conjunction with *compact* development, or within walkable communities.

For whatever the relative energy savings of smaller cars and cleaner, more locally obtainable fuel may be, it should not be forgotten that it is the higher-capacity (shared, public) transit modes which, because of their much more efficient use of space, will enable the uncongested functioning of more compact forms of development—thereby reducing, as previously noted, the travel required and the fuel and space consumed in the first place.

Electric cars—some second thoughts

While electric vehicles will emit fewer pollutants into the urban environment, the actual *production* of each electric vehicle emits about twice as much carbon dioxide equivalent as its internal combustion counterpart—87, as compared with 45, grams. These are the findings of researchers at the Norwegian University of Science and Technology, who took into consideration the electric car's reliance on rare minerals, the complexity of its batteries, and overall labor and production factors, in assessing its greater "environmental intensity." The researchers also took note of the obvious fact that it will be counterproductive to promote electric vehicles where the electricity is primarily produced from burning coal, lignite or oil.[52]

And again, there is the space issue—there will be no less urban space consumed by a population of electric cars than by cars of the internal combustion variety.

"Intelligent Transportation Systems"—easing, and perpetuating private motoring

This simple truth is not even part of the equation in an ongoing effort by at least eleven major auto manufacturers and the US Department of Transportation to develop an "Intelligent Transportation System," (ITS), which is strongly oriented toward easing private motoring and making it safer. With ITS, private cars can be outfitted with on-board navigational equipment and guided by satellite tracking, to enable motorists to anticipate and avoid congested roads.[53]

As the ITS program was originally conceived, the navigational equipment onboard personal vehicles would have been matched with highways that would also be automated—with magnets or wiring embedded in their surfaces, which would allow appropriately outfitted cars to speed along them at very close headways, either individually or in platoons. But it ultimately became apparent to the inventors of these systems that it was more practical to put all of the "intelligence" into the vehicle itself instead of into many miles of highways.

Self-driving vehicles have been in the making for several decades, dating back to the introduction in 1956 of General Motors' Firebird II, which included a system that worked with an electric guidance wire embedded in the highway. In 1959, a rocket-like "Cyclone" car was introduced, which had an autopilot to steer the car, and a front nose cone that warned of collisions and automatically applied the brakes.[54]

A technology known as "adaptive cruise control" can now automatically maintain set distances between a vehicle and those in front of and behind it—key to avoiding crashes and relieving congestion and traffic jams. Vehicles can employ sensors to parallel park on their own, and to alert drivers to vehicles approaching in the driver's blind spot.[55] Google has a fleet of a dozen computer-controlled vehicles that has logged more than 300,000 miles (482,700 kilometers) without an accident. And regulations were passed in 2012 in both Nevada and California that have established safety and performance requirements to test and operate autonomous vehicles on state roads and highways.[56]

Additional autonomous features now include lane-keeping systems. In January 2013, four major European manufacturers announced that they would be offering models with sensors and software to allow a car to drive itself in heavy traffic at speeds of up to 37 mph (60 km/h).[57] While self-driving vehicles are close to being technically ready for market, and hold the promise of safer driving for an aging population, it has been cautioned that, even if autonomous vehicles win the hearts and minds of most drivers, and if the price can be brought down to an affordable level, the infrastructure to support self-driving cars must also be established—not only the technology, but also the legal and liability frameworks—which may take many years to put in place.[58]

The ITS programs incorporate a number of features that are benefiting public transport and cycling systems as well, such as preempting traffic lights in favor of light rail and buses, informing passengers by cell phone when the next train or bus will be arriving, matching riders to vanpools and carpools, and supporting car-sharing and bike-sharing systems.[59]

The concept of self-driving cars appears to have been inspired not only by safety concerns, but may also derive from the industry's understandable fears that the currently increasing paralysis of traffic brings the public within danger of disenchantment with their cars. But while promising the benefit of relieving traffic congestion and making driving safer, the technology's most obvious other accomplishment, where it is oriented toward the private automobile, would be to squeeze even more cars into a given area—thus promoting the continued ubiquity of private motoring.

Economies with recycling older urban areas and buildings

To accommodate new population growth, the recycling and restoration of existing cities and their environs, in lieu of building in more remote areas, not only saves open land, but greatly reduces personal travel needs and avoids the need for new spread-out utilities and other public services. Abundant opportunities exist in the United States for infill development and adaptive reuse of older buildings, where the required infrastructure is already in place. This is true even in the densest region of the nation—the Northeast urban core—the contiguous metropolitan areas of Boston, New York City, Philadelphia, Baltimore, and Washington, DC. These areas include many urban "gap" sites—former industrial land, underused commercial strips, parking fields, and closed or dying shopping malls.[60]

There are also compelling ecological and economic reasons to recycle old buildings, in lieu of demolition. The adaptive re-use of existing buildings enables the recycling of materials and significantly diminishes the climate change impacts generated in the process of demolishing and rebuilding anew. Studies show that it can take between 10 and 80 years, and most commonly 20 to 30 years, for *even a new energy-efficient building* to overcome, through efficient operations, the initial carbon impacts that are created in the process of demolition and replacement.[61]

And while the costs of new construction are about 50 percent labor and 50 percent materials, the costs of rehabilitation are some 60 to 70 percent labor. The latter therefore has the benefit of creating more jobs, while saving materials that would otherwise end up in landfills.

Additionally, there is this basic benefit in recycling buildings: without massive subsidies, it is not normally possible to build anew and rent cheaply. As observed by the visionary journalist/urbanist Jane Jacobs, both old and new buildings ought to be combined on the same city block, since this will allow a good mix of incomes and help retain the area's social and economic diversity: "The district must mingle buildings that vary in age and condition, including a good portion of old ones, so that they vary in the economic yield they must produce."[62]

Not incidentally, new infill buildings judiciously located among the old can also enrich the historic authenticity and visual variety of a district, particularly when they are designed "true to their time," rather than imitative of a previous period.

As for building on greenfields, new "growth" in suburban areas can be especially costly to a metropolitan region when people and businesses move from already built-up areas to previously undeveloped areas within the region. The costs of providing new public services for such development—including roads, utility lines, schools, police, and fire protection—which are all more expensive when the development is spread out—contribute to growing fiscal stresses on the municipalities responsible for them. These costs could be appreciably reduced if the growth were directed instead toward areas where the required infrastructure already exists. Municipal governments often aggressively court new commercial developments with generous financial incentives, under the assumption that because they don't require new schools, they may be able to subsidize existing residential areas—only to be disappointed when the commercial developments have themselves attracted new residential development.[63]

Concentrating new development within existing metropolitan areas, rather than scattering it on the outskirts, can also have the important advantage of locating people within useful proximity to public transportation, vastly improving their resiliency to rising oil prices—a benefit not only global but personal. A report released in 2011 by the American Public Transportation Association indicated that habitually using public transport instead of driving, and owning one less car, can save the average US household some $9,656 per year—calculated as an average of $805 per month, based on the January 5, 2011, average gasoline price of $3.08 per gallon ($0.815 per liter) and on the national average fee for unreserved parking rates.[64] These savings are more than the average household spends on food in a year, and are only expected to increase if gasoline prices increase.

Another 2011 report, by the Center for Clean Air Policy, found that cities that have invested in public transportation and downtown redevelopment have been enhancing the prosperity of their communities—generating economic benefits for local businesses, increasing property values, and growing tax revenues. After a new light rail system in Dallas, Texas, began operations, retail sales in the city's downtown grew by 33 percent. A $100 million investment in streetcars in Portland, Oregon, helped to attract $3.5 billion in private investment. Denver, Colorado, has also benefited from its new light rail network: between 2006 and 2008, home values within a half-mile of the light rail stations rose by 18 percent, while those in the rest of the city were declining by 8 percent. And in Sarasota, Florida, development costs in the downtown were only half the costs of suburban development, while generating four times as much in tax revenues.[65]

A changing paradigm

A shift toward rental housing and walkable communities
The one bright aspect of the Great Recession that began in December 2007 is that it helped to put a damper on suburban sprawl. On the other hand, as the housing bubble burst, it brought with it an ongoing foreclosure crisis. It also led to such serious uncertainty in the job market that the demand dried up for single-family homes, and, unlike in previous cycles, single-family house construction became a strong drag against an economic recovery. The public began turning increasingly to the option of renting, most typically in multi-family buildings.[66] And developers who once dealt only in suburban housing began undertaking urban projects.[67]

As remarked by Richard Florida in *The Great Reset*, "Mobility and flexibility are key [survival] principles of the modern economy. Home ownership limits both…. [It] ties people to locations, making it harder for them to move to areas of economic prosperity."[68] A pent-up demand for urban living is reflected in the fact that in fifteen out of twenty major US housing markets, higher housing prices now correlate with proximity to city centers. And, while housing values have plunged in many of the far-flung suburbs, housing in walkable urban communities has tended to hold its value.[69]

This demand for urban residential location is in part due to the changing composition of today's households. According to an analysis of the 2010 Census by the Brookings Institution, only one-fifth of US households that year were comprised of married couples with children, down from 43 percent in 1950.[70] For the so-called "Generation Y," comprised of 85 million people in their late teens to early thirties, the meltdown of the housing industry has had a significant impact on their perceptions of home ownership. As observed by John McIlwain, president of the Urban Land Institute, "As they watch millions of Americans lose their homes to foreclosure, the allure of buying real estate has become less powerful. They will be renters by necessity and by choice rather than homeowners for years ahead. They have lost the confidence of prior generations that homeownership is a way to develop wealth." McIlwain also notes that many members of Generation Y tend to actually *prefer* urban settings to the suburbs, prefer walking to driving, and are willing to live in smaller spaces in order to afford an urban lifestyle.[71]

Baby Boomers are themselves becoming empty nesters, and many have voiced a preference for urban living. Consequently, while twenty years ago, housing within most US cities was a bargain, it can carry a sizable premium today. Housing in the urban neighborhoods of cities as diverse as New York, Washington (DC), Denver, Portland (Oregon), and Seattle can now cost 40 to 200 percent more than suburban space for the equivalent area. Suburban towns that were built in the nineteenth and early twentieth centuries, especially those built around rail stations, have also seen a considerable amount of infill development in response to a growing demand.[72]

Living in *small* cities and towns has held a special attraction. As pointed out by author, professor and architectural critic Witold Rybczynski, while the populations of many major US metropolitan areas have steadily declined since 1970, the portion living in small cities with between 25,000 and 250,000 inhabitants has been growing.[73] And according to the national community development advocacy organization Smart Growth America, between 2010 and 2011 the city centers of small US metropolitan areas (those with under one million people) were growing faster than their suburbs.[74]

The National Association of Realtors found in 2011 that a full 47 percent of US households were looking for urban, rather than suburban living, which was a big change from ten or twenty years before. Real estate advisors Robert Charles Lesser and Company similarly found a massive imbalance in US housing supply and demand: among the generation moving into the housing market in 2011, some 88 percent preferred to live in an urban setting, where there was an acute shortage of rental units.[75] The building industry was gearing up to meet this demand: in early 2012, work was scheduled to begin on about 260,000 apartment buildings and townhouse units within that year, up by 45 percent from the previous year and the most since 2008.[76]

From the late 1990s onward, cities across the United States have been gradually experiencing this demographic shift. A complementary trend has been the redevelopment of older suburbs into denser, mixed-use communities. Affluent citizens of all ages are choosing to migrate toward more compact, walkable neighborhoods—mixed-use developments that combine residences, retail, offices, and public transportation. In some cases these are rehabilitated and/or gentrified downtowns, as in Chicago, Washington, Atlanta, Fort Worth, Houston, Denver, Minneapolis, Salt Lake City, and Charlotte (North Carolina). They also include altogether newly created suburban walkable "town centers" built on the sites of no-longer-profitable shopping malls. Prime examples are Belmar in Lakewood (Colorado), Mizner Park in Boca Raton (Florida), and Sunnyvale (California).[77] The trend has attracted not only young singles and married couples but unmarried and gay couples as well as exurban empty nesters—singles and small families of all kinds—who are looking to escape high fuel costs and long commutes in traffic, and seeking the cultural endowments, convenient shopping, and sense of community that can be found in town centers.

The movement of people and jobs from suburbs back to the cities has been dubbed "The Great Inversion" by author Alan Ehrenhalt. Higher rates of population growth in cities than in suburbs in a majority of US metropolitan areas have been documented by Brookings Institute demographer William Frey. Additional evidence of this residential shift to urban areas has been documented by Jed Kolko, chief economist at the real estate agency Trulia. Kolko has tracked the annual change in housing prices for both suburban and rural neighborhoods, and has found that housing prices had their greatest rise—14.3 percent—in racially and ethnically diverse urban neighborhoods, as compared with an annual rise of 10.2 percent in less diverse suburban neighborhoods. The negative side of this phenomenon is that these urban areas have been getting pricier, potentially pricing out the very diversity that has made them attractive in the first place.[78]

Another Brookings study, released in 2012, found that, in the metropolitan area of Washington, DC, which includes surrounding suburbs in Maryland and Virginia, commercial and residential real estate values are increasing as neighborhoods become more walkable, and where everyday needs, including commuting, can be met by walking, cycling and/or taking transit. Similar findings appear to apply to much of the rest of the nation. For example, in the metropolitan areas of Seattle, Denver, and Columbus (Ohio), people are now willing to pay more for homes that allow them to walk rather than drive. Again, the one negative result is gentrification—that is, that the increased prices in these neighborhoods make them unaffordable to non-affluent households—a challenge that may ultimately be met long-term through the building of many *more* walkable communities, to increase their availability.[79]

A shift toward the greater use of public transit

Coupled with this resurgent urbanism, the use of all kinds of public transit in the US has, since the early 1990s, been increasing more than twice as fast as the population, and 2008 saw the highest level of ridership on US public transit systems in more than fifty years. From its initially low base, transit patronage grew by 38 percent between 1995 and 2008—a figure nearly triple the 14 percent growth of the population.[80] In particular, all types of passenger rail, including streetcars, light rail, rail rapid transit, and commuter rail, have proven highly effective in attracting discretionary riders—those who have a car and could drive, but choose to take transit instead.

It is noteworthy that much of this growth has been occurring in the western United States, around cities that have grown up in the age of the automobile. A number of new metros and expansions of metros, including modern (light rail) versions of streetcars, have been planned and built in the US since the mid-1990s in cities such as Portland (Oregon), Minneapolis, Dallas, Denver, Phoenix, Salt Lake City, and Charlotte—and dramatic surges of development have occurred around the transit stations.

Dallas has developed an extensive light rail network, and has seen a 32 percent increase in residential property values within a quarter-mile of its transit stations.[81] The town of Irving, Texas, located in Dallas County, dynamited its forty-year-old Texas Cowboys Stadium in April 2010 in order to lease the site, much more profitably, to the Texas Department of Transportation for new high-density transit-oriented development (TOD), to be served by the Dallas light rail network.[82] Houston is adding 30 miles (48 km) to its current 7 miles (11.2 km) of light rail in the anticipation that, as in Dallas, the extension of rail will catalyze new development.[83] And Washington, DC, is building a 37-mile-long (60 km-long) streetcar line that will place 50 percent of the area's residents with walking distance of rail transit, as compared with the current 16 percent.[84]

In the late 1990s, few people lived in Denver's downtown near its historic Union Station. However, the Union Station Neighborhood Company has embarked on a $1 billion restoration of the station, and on a 30-acre (12.14-ha) transit district surrounding it, which includes more than 4 million sf (371,612 m^2) of mixed-use commercial and residential development. Denver's light rail system is scheduled for a $4.7 billion expansion, which will add 122 miles (195.2 km) to its length by 2017. Along the light rail network, a number of mixed-use, walkable communities have sprouted—and fifty more new transit-oriented developments are anticipated over the next decade. Already the rail lines bring a lively public to populate Denver's downtown shops and restaurants long after the workday has ended.[85]

California has been at the forefront of progressive planning legislation with its Senate Bill 375, or "SB 375," passed in 2008. The state's population is expected to increase by around 10 percent in each coming decade, and this bill takes account of the anticipated environmental pressures. SB 375, which is complex but fairly balanced, directs each of the state's metropolitan planning organizations to coordinate transportation investments, housing, and other land use in a way that minimizes greenhouse gas emissions (GHGs) and other environmental impacts. It was the nation's first law to link the planning of transportation and land use with GHGs.[86]

The law directs the California Air Resources Board to assign transportation emissions targets for each region, and requires each region to develop a detailed strategy to meet these targets. SB 375 includes significant legal protections to land developers who follow the new plans; it also contains safeguards to provide an adequate supply of affordable housing. At the time of its passage, it enjoyed tremendous support from a diverse group of real estate, housing, commercial, government, and environmental interests, which had worked long and hard together to reach a consensus. Targets for housing types, for example, include increasing multi-family housing from 27 percent of the total (in 2008) to 53 percent (by 2035). A 2012 report on the progress of SB 375 found that the law was being implemented in three of California's four largest metropolitan regions—Southern California, Sacramento, and San Diego, comprising two-thirds of the state's population. In the fourth region—the San Francisco Bay area—the challenges to meet the goals of the plan have been found to be more complex, primarily because of the high pressures for and high costs of housing there, and the consequent dispersal of low-income families toward outlying areas, and away from public transit.[87]

Nevertheless, there is a growing attraction among many in the United States toward truly urban living. This has been insightfully described by architect and urban designer/planner Mark L. Hinshaw in his book *True Urbanism: Living In and Near the Center*. Hinshaw notes that the densities associated with downtowns—in excess of forty units per acre and as high as several hundred—are more than sufficient to justify frequent public transit service.[88] Yet it has been considered controversial by the US Congress to provide funding adequate to the task of building and maintaining viable and comprehensive public transportation infrastructure to support and further stimulate this trend. Resistance persists among much of the electorate and many of our governing bodies to truly effective measures that would curb our driving habits.

Affording the needed transit infrastructure

It is often claimed by advocates for highways that roads "pay for themselves" through gasoline taxes and other charges to motorists, and that these cover nearly the full costs of highway and street construction and maintenance. On the contrary: according to a January 2011 report by the New Jersey Public Interest Research Group, the money that had been spent on highways and streets since 1947 had actually exceeded that collected through taxes and user fees by a full $600 billion in 2005 dollars, and this had occasioned an enormous transfer of general funds into highways and streets.[89]

And while the public's demand for transit, and especially rail transit, is clear, it is less obvious how this might be paid for—particularly under conditions of economic downturn, while our cities and states are struggling to maintain public services that are at least as crucial—such as schools, hospitals, fire and crime fighting, and the maintenance of bridges and water systems. Schemes for the funding of transit through revenues collected from raising the gasoline tax, congestion pricing, and the tolling of bridges—which have been so successful in Singapore, Stockholm, and London—have met with fierce resistance from motorists in the US where the car is still "king."

One answer can be found at the community level. Jason Jordan, director of the Center for Transportation Excellence, which supports initiatives to fund public transportation, has remarked that "in one of worst economies in a generation, people have actively chosen to raise their own taxes to support transportation." Jordan points out that, while normally, only 35 percent of such ballot initiatives pass, in 2008 and 2009, 76 percent of them did. In 2011, about 79 percent of twenty-eight referenda on transit met with local approval.[90]

In Denver in 2004, voters approved a 0.04 percent sales tax increase, which has been funding the $4.7 billion expansion of the transit system.[91] In light of the fact that Los Angeles contains six of the seven most congested highways in the nation, that city has chosen to embark on the largest expansion of its mass transit system in decades.[92] Through sheer persistence, Los Angeles' then-mayor Antonio Villaraigosa managed to set in motion plans to double his city's rail infrastructure. In 2008, Los Angeles voters approved by a two-thirds majority a half-cent sales tax surcharge to finance the expansion of the rail network, a surcharge that is expected to raise $40 billion over the next thirty years.[93] Eager to accelerate the pace of investment so that benefits to the community can be realized sooner, Villaraigosa advocated for the federal government to provide a series of loans that would be paid back using projected sales receipts. In this way, what would have taken thirty years to accomplish could potentially take only a decade. This idea has been dubbed the

America Fast Forward Financing Innovation Act program, and as such has been gaining currency around the nation as a way for the federal government to work in partnership with local governments and the private sector.[94] Thus, the same city that led the way into the automobile-oriented era has come to the recognition that to continue to be livable and functional despite its tremendous growth, it needs a balanced, multimodal transportation system.[95]

Throughout the United States, there were, by January 2013, some 721 fixed guideway transit projects in various stages of planning and construction, including commuter rail, subways, and streetcars. The major barrier they face is that they require $250 billion in funding, at a time when the federal funding pot is very small.[96] As for US infrastructure as a whole, it is estimated by the American Society of Civil Engineers that a failure to invest at least $1.1 trillion in it by 2020 will result in mounting annual job losses, employment cutbacks, and seriously declining business activity.[97]

There are major concerns in the US among members of both major political parties, including labor and business leaders, about the nation's crumbling infrastructure and its need of heavy investments—in public transportation lines, the highway system, water and sewer systems, power grids, roads, and bridges. Creation of a federal infrastructure bank, or "I-bank," that leverages private funds to finance these investments has been a method that has worked successfully internationally for decades, and has begun to gain traction in the US. By lending out seed money at currently low interest rates, an I-bank can profitably attract capital from private equity and pension funds that are searching for stable ventures in which to invest.[98] It is estimated by at least one seasoned investor that six to seven times as much private money as public seed money can be leveraged through an infrastructure bank.[99]

Not to be underestimated is the potential of infrastructure construction for creating jobs and stimulating the economy in general. In 2011, it was calculated that there was a $2 trillion deficit in the infrastructure of the United States, at the same time that there were an estimated nineteen million people unemployed, in the US with the construction, manufacturing, and retail trades having been particularly hard hit. With interest rates at an historically low level, the tremendous potential of the I-bank method for meeting simultaneously these needs for both infrastructure and jobs has become increasingly obvious. This potential has galvanized erstwhile rivals on both sides of the political divide—the presidents of the AFL-CIO and US Chamber of Commerce—to band together and vow to "take their show on the road" as the new "Odd Couple."[100]

Fortunately, private capital for infrastructure appears to be abundant. A 2011 report by Sphere Consulting, LLC, indicated that there was an estimated $250 billion in private funding globally that was available for infrastructure public-private partnerships ("P3s")—a 40 percent increase from just one year before. The report estimated that this amount could be leveraged to a value of $650 billion and could create 1,875,000 jobs over ten years. Sphere also identified forty-nine pension funds that have expressed an interest in infrastructure investment, and have $38 billion in available funds for this purpose.[101]

There will be no profit motive in the I-bank itself, but the private investors will of course be looking to make money. Therefore, any such public-private partnership must be transparently constructed and operated in a way that ensures that the serving of public purposes will take precedence over private profit. That is, for the ultimate good of society, private sector incentives must be aligned with public sector goals, and the public sector must retain control over key transportation decisions.[102]

Once an infrastructure bank has been set up, its projects can be insulated from the unpredictabilities of the political scene. But contrarians in Congress have blocked the initiation of an I-bank on the federal level, and federal funding has been limited to the support of state-level I-banks. Some thirty-three states have set up such entities since 2005, when Congress granted them the authority to do so; these have proven their worth in helping to finance transportation projects around the nation.[103] Yet when funding is limited to state boundaries, it is unable to encompass big, regional projects that cross jurisdictions—which happens to be the very nature of many transportation projects.

Alternately, or additionally, the United States might be more receptive to a suggestion made in 2011 by Chen Deming, the commerce minister of China, to convert some of our mountain of debt to that country into investment by the Chinese in the renovation and construction of our nation's roads and rails. Not only would this create jobs in the US, but such new economic cooperation could also help defuse fears that Beijing might use its approximate $1.15 trillion in US reserves as a political weapon. This could be a mutually beneficial arrangement, for it would be to China's advantage to invest more abroad—in the United States, in Europe, and elsewhere—to reduce that nation's reliance upon exports.[104]

In 2011, former senator Bill Bradley, former governor Tom Ridge, and former US comptroller David Walker compiled a report on US transportation infrastructure for the Carnegie Endowment for International Peace. They warned that, since the completion of the interstate highway system more than two decades ago, the nation's transportation investment decisions "have become increasingly unfocused, short-term, and highly politicized, [and that while] states and metropolitan areas have cobbled together their own project and investment plans for highway, transit, and rail ... this piecemeal approach prevents the smooth integration of local, state, and federal policies and hinders potential synergies across projects."[105]

With more than two-thirds of the country's population living in urban areas, much higher levels of federal commitment to metro-wide, intercity, and interstate systems of public transport are vital. But for this to happen, what is first needed is a consensus and commitment among a sizable portion of the public that construction of transit and, in particular, *the compact development that it will engender* are indeed worthy goals for society. In the words of the former mayor of Bogotá, Enrique Peñalosa, "First you have to decide what type of society you want to live in, before you discuss transportation."[106]

2

The Parking Challenge to Compact and Affordable Transit-Oriented Development

If space for the parking of cars can be diminished as the main design challenge, then endless possibilities will open up for more environmentally friendly, people-friendly design. The results can also be appreciably more affordable for those living on limited budgets.

Social equity in housing

The potential beneficiaries of transit-oriented development

Noted in chapter 1 were the relatively high densities of development that are needed to justify and sustain regular, high-quality systems of public transit—a subject that was explored in depth by Boris Pushkarev and Jeffrey Zupan in their 1977 book, *Public Transportation and Land Use Policy*.[1] Compact, mixed-use development can at the same time allow a large portion of daily *local* trips to be made virtually cost-free, by walking or cycling. But given the strong new market demand for housing near public transit, and the high costs of building in high-value urban areas, the construction of new transit-oriented development in the US is most typically targeted toward *affluent* households.

At the same time, when new fixed guideway transit is inserted into existing neighborhoods, the predominant pattern is one in which housing becomes more expensive, and the residents attracted to the neighborhood are wealthier and more commonly own cars. This can create a cycle of unintended consequences, in which core transit users—particularly low-income households, for whom good transit can be an essential service—are priced out of the market in favor of higher-income, multiple-car-owning households, who are in fact less likely to use public transit on a regular basis.[2] This is one reason for much of the resistance of many low-income communities to the investment of public moneys into new rail systems, as mentioned in chapter 1. It also runs, in effect, contrary to the intent of reducing greenhouse gases through increases in the public's use of transit.

More than 40 percent of the future demand for housing near transit is expected to come from households that earn less than 80 percent of the area's median income, according to the Center for Transit-Oriented Development.[3] Yet as also noted in chapter 1, many low-income households must elect to live instead in car-centric suburbs, only because housing there may be more affordable. Clearly, where public endowments of transit service are primarily benefiting the affluent rather than those most in need, an obvious social injustice comes into play. While some jurisdictions have inclusionary zoning ordinances requiring a minimum percentage of affordable units in all new residential development near transit, these ordinances will often allow the affordable units to be located off-site—and thus, not near transit.

A "toolbox" for maintaining affordable TOD, including revisions to parking policy

The Dukakis Center for Urban and Regional Policy published a report in 2010, "Maintaining Diversity in America's Transit-Rich Neighborhoods," which describes a comprehensive strategy that can be used to preserve existing affordable housing in these cases. For example, low-income tax credits can be allocated by state housing agencies to developers to provide money for affordable housing. The building and/or preservation of affordable housing may also be partially financed through tax increment financing districts, using revenue from higher property taxes in the surrounding area. Before transit projects come in and drive up land prices and property values, TOD acquisition funds can be used to build or preserve affordable housing—as has been done successfully in communities in Denver, Charlotte, and the Bay Area. And as mentioned above, inclusionary zoning ordinances that require some proportion of new housing to be affordable (usually 10 to 25 percent, and sometimes more) is another commonly utilized tool.[4]

But one of the most important levers in both preserving affordable housing near transit and assuring the increased use of transit, while discouraging driving, is parking policy. The Dukakis Center report recommends providing only one parking space per condo or rental unit, unbundled (priced separately) from the living unit, while supplying some *shared* parking spaces in the same garage, so that people can make their second car a shared one. An annual transit pass can then be provided by the developer, who would have spent more on building a second sub-surface parking spot for each unit than the annual transit pass would cost.[5]

It should be noted that compact, multi-family housing is not necessarily cheaper per unit *to build* than single-family housing (although it has the capacity to save enormously per unit on land and on energy for space heating and cooling). In fact, where it is higher than three stories, such housing can actually be *more* expensive per unit to construct because of the more complex materials and designs required to meet building codes.[6] Therefore, every major component of new multi-family housing design, particularly where it is to include affordable units, should be scrutinized with respect to its true necessity. Car parking in such development is one element that can add significantly to its costs—both monetarily and in terms of a degraded urban design and environment. The generous provision of parking for both existing and new multi-family housing should certainly be questioned, particularly where the option of traveling by transit exists, and certainly in the case of transit-oriented development.

There are, in any case, significant challenges to building mixed-income housing near transit. For example, land prices can increase because of speculation when a new transit line is planned. And developers of affordable housing—often nonprofit organizations—may lack the capital to acquire the needed land before its price goes up, and to hold it until development can go forward. Mixed-income projects can also require complex financing structures. Additionally, community opposition to high-density and affordable housing can be both a barrier and time consuming for the developer.[7]

But underlying and augmenting all of these barriers is often an assumed requirement for abundant car parking. And this requirement itself needs to be challenged.

Spatial and cost implications of parking provisions

Parking as a determinant of location
It was remarked in chapter 1 that the average automobile is parked 95 percent of the time, and that each off-street parking space occupies, when

access drives are included, some 300 to 350 square feet (28 to 32.5 square meters) of paved area. The gross area required per vehicle is greater when the parking is located in a multilevel structure, because of the need for stairs, elevators, and ramps between levels.

The costs of providing this parking are a major determinant of what gets built and where. Even for simple surface parking, there is no way to estimate the cost per space without knowing the cost of the land that it sits on. Thus, according to Donald C. Shoup, parking expert and professor of urban planning at the University of California at Los Angeles, a surface parking space may cost almost nothing to provide where land costs are low, or more than $100,000 where land is priced, for example, at $300 per sf—experiences vary widely. While each parking space within a structure may cost $10,000 to $30,000 or more, this also depends very much upon the type of structure it is in, the city, and the year of construction. In 1999, underground parking beneath a shopping center in Seattle actually cost the city $61,000 per space to build, including land costs, and this is not the most expensive example.[8]

Above-grade parking in a free-standing, multi-level parking structure can cost more than three times as much to build as surface parking, and above-grade parking in a multi-use structure nearly six times as much. Below-grade structured parking, normally built only where land costs are high, can cost more than seven times as much as surface parking. There can also be significant annual operating and maintenance costs for these parking spaces.[9]

It naturally follows that open lots are by far the most common solution for parking, and their sheer size requirements are enough to draw developers and business owners toward outlying areas, where land in large tracts is more available and affordable—thereby giving added impetus to sprawl. Vast parking fields then result in the relentless monotony of so much of our built environments. Not incidentally, they also enable the owners of businesses and shopping centers to provide "free" parking to their employees and customers, the real costs of which are added into the prices of goods and services for motorists and non-motorists alike. Over 90 percent of US workers now park for free at work—a fringe benefit that makes solo commuting almost irresistible.[10]

Shoup has cast a perspective on the enormous subsidies that we as a nation pay to provide this "free" parking:

In most U.S. cities, planners assume most people will travel everywhere by car and thus require each site to provide enough off-street parking spaces to satisfy the expected peak demand for parking. As a result, most new commercial buildings have parking lots or structures bigger than the buildings themselves, and almost everyone drives wherever they go: 87 percent of all trips in the U.S. are made by personal motor vehicles, and parking is free for 99 percent of these trips. Requiring all new buildings to provide ample off-street parking reduces cruising for free curb parking, but it also creates many new problems. It increases the cost and decreases the density of urban development, leading to faster sprawl; it fosters excessive reliance on the car, contributing to greater air pollution, traffic congestion, and energy consumption; and it degrades the transportation system for other modes than the car, including buses ..., cyclists ..., and pedestrians.

All this free parking is charity for cars. In 2002, the total subsidy for off-street parking was somewhere between $127 billion and $374 billion a year. If we also count the subsidy for free and underpriced curb parking, the total subsidy for free parking would be far higher. In the same year, the federal government spent only $231 billion for Medicare and $349 billion for national defense.... Because parking costs so much and motorists pay so little for it, the hidden subsidy is truly gigantic.[11]

Impacts on cities—minimum versus maximum parking requirements

The Institute of Transportation Engineers (ITE) in its parking guidelines manual specifies precisely how much parking "should" be supplied in association with each building type.[12] These specifications are based on isolated suburban sites and ubiquitous driving; so for more urban sites they are overly generous. But in the US the ITE standards have been adopted unquestioningly by most municipal authorities who write the codes. Thus, parking for cars in cities has been massively over-provided, and a good deal of paved area, including expensive garage space, lies empty for much of the day. In many cases, the standards adopted are decided arbitrarily, can vary enormously from municipality to municipality, and may be diametrically opposed from city to city.

In downtown Los Angeles, for example, the zoning calls for a stated parking minimum, while the San Francisco central business district has a stated maximum. Los Angeles requires a minimum of fifty times more parking for a concert hall than San Francisco allows as a maximum.[13] San Francisco's more restrictive approach to parking is thereby reflected in the more human scale of its streets and their much more exciting and pleasurable walking environment.

A number of US cities, including Portland (Oregon), Washington, Boston, and Seattle, have begun to adopt the San Francisco approach of imposing parking caps.[14] San Diego, Houston, and Atlanta have also reduced their minimum parking mandates in areas that are well served by transit.[15] Columbus, Ohio, realizing that most of its parking lots were half empty, reduced the parking requirement at its shopping malls (but only by 20 percent). Shoup had deduced that, to minimize wasteful "cruising" for parking, on-street parking should be sufficiently highly priced to result in an ideal 85 percent occupancy level, a formula that now defines San Francisco's on-street parking policies. That city, in 2010, pioneered an advanced on-street parking management system with electronic sensors—small unobtrusive discs that lie flat on the pavement—which track the availability of parking spots and match drivers with vacant spots. In facilitating the search for on-street spaces, this is enabling San Francisco to significantly decrease its needs for off-street parking.[16] Dubbed SFPark, similar "intelligent" parking systems are going forward as pilot projects in the cities of Los Angeles, Boston, Fort Worth, New York, and Washington.[17]

Manhattan's core—the area south of West 110th Street and East 96th Street—has parking maximums in place. However, most of New York City is still governed by parking minimums—even the inner ring of neighborhoods surrounding the core that are right on top of subway stations. Since freely available parking is an obvious generator of traffic, this is not at all in accord with any recent mayor's stated goals for a more sustainable city. The NYC Department of City Planning has been considering reducing—but not eliminating—minimum parking requirements in this inner ring, while dense and transit-rich neighborhoods just a little farther from the center may not receive any reforms at all.

By comparison, Washington, DC's approach has been, for the first time in fifty years, to do away with parking minimums entirely for most downtown buildings that are near transit. This has been done in response to "hard experience." The director of Washington's Office of Planning, Harriet Tregoning, found that when the district cut parking requirements in half, only half of the remaining parking spaces were being used. Tregoning has even offered her advice on parking reduction as a resource to New York City, in case New York should ultimately decide to pursue more progressive parking reforms.[18]

Sadly, in cities across the United States, the downtowns were carved up in the twentieth century in a futile attempt to compete with suburban shopping centers with a superabundance of parking. In most US cities, roadways and parking lots consume over 30 percent of the developed land, and as much as 70 percent of the downtown surface areas.[19] One half of the land in downtown Buffalo, New York, is devoted to parking, and in Albuquerque, New Mexico, more land is claimed by parking than all other land uses combined.[20] *Along with the erasure of perfectly good buildings, this has meant the radical expansion of the distances between destinations, so that these cities have become utterly deprived of their convenience and appeal as walking environments. Simultaneously, there has been a major loss of land value—since car parking is perhaps the least economically productive of all land uses.*

Reclaiming paved land for urban use

Massive parking provisions have been the natural accompaniment to the bulldozing of cityscapes for limited-access highways. Figures 2.1 and 2.2 illustrate the transformation of the downtown of Hartford, Connecticut, that occurred between 1957 and 1995, with the construction of a highway and extensive parking facilities that now dominate the city's core.

Figure 2.1
Aerial view of downtown Hartford, Connecticut, in 1957.
Source: University of Connecticut Libraries Map and Geographic Information Center (MAGIC).

Figure 2.2
Aerial view of the same area of downtown Hartford in 1995, after the demolition of many buildings, the construction of an interstate highway running through the heart of the city, and the building of vast parking facilities.
Source: University of Connecticut Libraries Map and Geographic Information Center (MAGIC).

That highway, which physically divided the city, and for which entire neighborhoods were razed and hundreds of people displaced, is now slated for demolition. It will not be a simple matter to restitch those bulldozed neighborhoods back together. But in cases where this has been accomplished, such as upon demolition of New York's West Side Highway and San Francisco's Embarcadero, the results have been exhilarating.

Other US cities are acknowledging and attempting to rectify similar past mistakes. Baltimore, Providence, and Milwaukee are now engaged in massive highway demolition projects.[21] So are Oklahoma City, Trenton (New Jersey), New Haven (Connecticut), and New York City. In New York, community organizations are keen to free up the land currently occupied by the Sheridan Expressway for much-needed housing and parks.[22] In Dallas, as part of a large revitalization of that city, planners envision restoring Elm, Commerce, and Main streets as the shopping boulevards that they once were, before their conversion decades ago into

Box 2.1

On the other side of the planet, we see occurring the very same car-centric planning mistakes as those from which the US is beginning to recover. China's 1.3 billion people are "simply wild about cars," and with increased prosperity, there is a frenzy among the Chinese citizenry to buy them, strongly encouraged by government tax breaks and subsidies. Beijing has consequently experienced a phenomenal growth in its car population—in 2009, there were 46 percent more cars purchased there than in the previous year. The resulting severity of the city's traffic congestion is matched only by that of Mexico City. Beijing's government has unveiled an ambitious plan to address the problem. This includes, on the positive side, 348 miles (557 km) of new subway track—but, on the negative side, 125 miles (200 km) of new downtown roads and *280,000 new parking spaces*. There are already five ring roads that girdle the city, and eight more highway spokes from the suburbs to downtown.[a]

It is regrettable that China is repeating some of the worst mistakes in US urban planning and design, and alarming in its implications for climate change, but there is no dampening the enthusiasm of the Chinese for cars. Ironically, it is projected that, given the city's current congestion, the average speed of cars in Beijing by 2015 will be as slow as 9 mph (14 km/h).[b] This is approximately the speed of a bicycle, which was the predominant mode of travel in China only thirty years ago.

By 2012, Beijing had finally faced the sorry truth: that access to more highways and dedicated parking spots leads invariably to more driving and even heavier traffic. In August of that year, the government announced plans to build a system for imposing congestion charges on motorists in the city. Caps had already been placed on the number of new vehicle registrations, as well as limits on the use of private vehicles on designated days, based on license plate numbers.[c] At roughly the same time, Guangzhou, a sprawling metropolis that is one of China's largest car manufacturing centers, began license plate lotteries and auctions intended to cut in half the number of cars on the streets.[d]

Notes

a. Michael Wines, "Cars Multiply, But Chinese Still Can't Find a Fast Lane," New York Times News Service, *Taipei Times*, December 23, 2010, A6.

b. Ibid.

c. Ying Tian, "Beijing Plans to Levy Congestion Charges to Ease Traffic Jams, *Bloomberg News*, August 20, 2012, http://www.bloomberg.com/news/2012-08-21/beijing-plans-to-levy-congestion-charges-to-ease-traffic-jams.html.

d. Keith Bradsher, "A Chinese City Moves to Limit New Cars," *New York Times*, September 5, 2012.

Box 2.2

India is facing problems very similar to those in China. With rising incomes, that country is currently experiencing the automobile revolution that the US underwent sixty years ago. In what is still a primarily agricultural nation, some 80 percent of India's passenger traffic and 65 percent of its freight moves on a network comprised mainly of two-lane roads, and congestion is costing the country $5.5 billion per year. Thus, India plans to build about 1,000 miles (1,600 km) of highways with at least six lanes. In the countryside, the biggest challenge to this plan is the acquisition of land, since farmers are understandably refusing to leave their land for fear of losing their livelihoods. As a result, a quarter of the 226 roads that have been commissioned by the government are behind schedule.[a]

In the cities of India, road widening is meeting with more organized resistance by the urban citizenry than the country's farmers have been able to muster. Bangalore, for example, is still known as the "Garden City" for its beautiful, tree-lined streets. But to accommodate the city's roughly four million vehicles, s and to alleviate its estimated $3 million daily congestion costs, Bangalore's government has adopted a policy of widening the streets, paving more land for parking, and cutting down many beautiful old trees in the process. These measures, which have been tried in the past and failed, have been met with increasing opposition from local residents, and at the same time have been (fortuitously) slowed by a lack of funds. Of 216 roads that had been scheduled for widening in Bangalore, only 20 projects had broken ground by September 2012.[b]

But rising incomes are not a prerequisite for traffic overload. In Cairo, although poverty and unemployment remain extensive since the 2011 uprising—more than 40 percent of the people are thought to live on less than $2 per day—vehicles have been multiplying twice as fast as the population, creating intractable problems of congestion and environmental misery.[c]

Notes

a. Karthikeyan Sundaram, "India Plans $5.3 Billion of Highways as Jams Sap Growth," Bloomberg.com, June 28, 2012, http://www.bloomberg.com/news/2012-06-28/india-plans-5-3-billion-of-highways-as-jams-sap-growth.html.

b. Mark Bergen, "India's Cities Risk Repeating America's Congestion Mistakes," *Atlantic Cities*, September 7, 2012, http://www.theatlanticcities.com/commute/2012/09/battle-bangalores-soul-comes-down-its-streets/3186.

c. Scott Sayare, "Traffic and Congestion Unmoved by Uprising," *New York Times*, September 11, 2012, http://www.nytimes.com/2012/09/11/world/middleeast/for-egyptians-no-relief-from-cairos-infamous-traffic.html?pagewanted=all.

high-speed arterials.[23] Syracuse, Buffalo, Louisville (Kentucky), Cleveland, New Orleans, and Seattle are all considering removing highways and vast parking lots from their downtowns and restoring pedestrian life to the streets. This is occurring just as the interstate highway network has aged to the point where it will require major repairs to maintain its useful life—costing, in some cases, twice as much as the demolition option.[24]

Parking minimums as inhibitor to building new compact and affordable housing

Parallel to their negative impacts on entire cities, blanket parking directives have been similarly deleterious for individual buildings in the United States. For a new multi-unit apartment building, the ITE parking standards can be especially costly. Harvard professor of real estate development Richard Peiser and real estate development consultant Anne Frej have detailed how—given a zoning requirement of two parking spaces per apartment, which is common in the US—the parking footprint for a modest-sized apartment can be at least twice that of the apartment itself. This is because if the building is three stories high and contains apartments of 900 sf (84 m²), each unit will have a footprint of 300 sf (28 m²) or 900 divided by 3 stories. Each parking space will then occupy at least 300 to 350 sf (28 to 32.5 m²) of land, and two spaces will occupy twice that area.[25]

In light of actual parking demands, this need not be the case where transit is a viable option. For example, a 2010 survey of the utilization of parking facilities in twelve TODs in California's Santa Clara County concluded that there was a gross oversupply of parking spaces for the need in these communities. Whereas the zoning for some of these developments called for more than 2.5 parking spaces per dwelling unit, it was found that the actual need was on average only around 1.3 spaces, and that some 26 percent of the spaces that had been provided were going unused.[26]

Many US zoning ordinances require a substantial 2.25 parking spaces per dwelling unit (two for the residents, plus one guest space for every four units). If a one-acre (0.4047 ha) piece of property is already zoned for 30 units per acre (74 units per ha), it should normally be a simple matter to build a 30-unit apartment building on that land. But with a 2.25 to 1 parking ratio, there is also a requirement to build 68 parking spaces. Because of land constraints, at least some of this parking would need to be provided within or underneath the building itself. But if the zoning also limits the building height to three stories, there is not enough space on the lot to provide the parking except underground—which can double the cost of construction. The developer may thus find that it is simply too costly to build the largest project permitted by zoning, and that it is necessary to reduce the size of the project in order to cut the cost of providing the parking. The project size will have been driven by the parking requirements, rather than by the allowable density or setback constraints. *In this way, parking repeatedly squeezes out the kind of multi-unit housing that is so vital to the convenient use of transit.*[27]

This significantly affects affordability, since when parking requirements restrict the supply of housing, they inevitably raise its price. In a study on the conflict between parking provisions and housing affordability by Wenyu Jia and Martin Wachs at the University of California at Berkeley, it was found that 24 percent more San Franciscans would have been able to afford to buy a dwelling if the required on-site parking space had not been included.[28]

Similarly, the Bay Area Rapid Transit (BART) *TOD Guidelines* state that "parking provisions can account for 20 percent of the cost of a typical apartment in Silicon Valley ... [and that]each additional parking space provided per unit in a residential building reduces the overall number of units that could otherwise be provided by up to 25 percent."[29]

In another example, in Palo Alto, California, of how parking provisions dramatically increase the cost of building low-income apartments, it was found that by reducing the parking requirement, $10,500 could be saved per apartment for very small (260 sf 24.15 m^2) single-room occupancy units that cost only $32,000 each to construct. But even with the reduced requirement, the parking spaces increased construction costs by a full 38 percent, and thereby increased the rents.[30]

And although low-income households tend to own fewer cars, there are few US cities that reduce their parking requirements for low-income housing. Some municipalities, in fact, deliberately set high and rigid parking requirements as a means of excluding low-income housing, and as a means of reducing the practicality of dense development.[31]

According to five different studies that separated out the costs of parking from the costs of the associated buildings, excessive parking requirements substantially raise rents, reduce land values, reduce density, and encourage sprawl. Sometimes the cost of structured parking will even exceed the cost of land for multi-family housing. *And this parking is frequently being provided for households that cannot afford a car.* This includes 22 percent of renter households, according to the 2000 census.[32]

Notes Amit Gosh, chief of comprehensive planning for San Francisco:

Parking requirements are a huge obstacle to new affordable housing and transit-oriented development in San Francisco. Nonprofit developers estimate that they add 20 percent to the cost of each unit, and reduce the number of units that can be built on a site by 20 percent. We're forcing people to build parking that people cannot afford. We're letting parking drive not only our transportation policies, but jeopardizing our housing policies, too.[33]

The irony is remarked by Shoup:

Planners everywhere are concerned about housing costs and urban sprawl, but they have not attempted to evaluate how parking requirements affect either housing costs or urban density.... Scarce land and capital are shifted from housing for people to housing for cars. Zoning requires a home for every car but ignores homeless people.... People sleep in the streets, but cars park free in their ample off-street quarters.[34]

Parking minimums as inhibitor to the adaptive re-use of buildings
The adaptive re-use of older buildings for new types of use was cited in chapter 1 as an important means of retaining the economic and visual diversity of cities. However, adaptive re-use is frequently precluded by minimum parking requirements. Since adding new parking spaces within most older buildings is normally unfeasible, zoning laws that mandate them can freeze a building in its existing use or even prevent any other practical use. In many municipalities, a building that has remained unoccupied for a specified period of time—perhaps one or two years—and is being considered for a new use, may have lost its grandfathered rights, and hence be required to meet the *current* parking requirement for the new use. Even if a potential owner would *like* to keep the building in its previous use, it will be mandatory to provide all the parking spaces that are currently required for that use. Thus, a building that has been vacant for more than a year or two may—only because of parking requirements—become extremely difficult to reuse.[35]

A very gradual erosion of such off-street parking requirements is fortunately beginning to occur in California. In 1999, Los Angeles adopted an Adaptive Re-use Ordinance (ARO), which allows for the conversion of historically significant or economically distressed downtown office buildings into residential units—with no new parking spaces. Between 1999 and 2008, this made it possible for developers to convert 56 largely vacant, fine Beaux Arts and Art Deco office buildings on Spring Street into some 7,300 new housing units. Instead of the 2 or more parking spaces per unit that the city would have required without the ARO, the developers were able to limit the parking to an average of only 1.3 parking spaces per unit, with 0.9 spaces on site and 0.4 spaces off-site in garages or lots.

A number of benefits resulted from the adoption of this ordinance. Not only were more housing units built than would have been otherwise, but these units were constructed in beautiful and unique buildings and in neighborhoods that had been underused and commercially stagnant. And since almost half of the parking was unbundled from the residential units, *the project targeted an underserved population—people without cars.* Although the ARO applied only to downtown when it was first adopted, its benefits became so quickly apparent that, by 2003, it had been extended citywide.[36]

Parking minimums as inhibitor to providing landscaping and pedestrian amenities

Overly generous parking requirements can also preclude the provision of landscaping and amenities that business owners may want to include in their projects. For example, on a lot with a permitted floor/area ratio of 1.0, an entrepreneur might choose to build a one-story restaurant with a floor area of 1,000 sf (92.9 m^2). However, the parking requirement may well be 10 spaces per 1,000 sf of restaurant area, which will occupy an area of at least 3,000 sf (278.7 m^2), or three times as much area as the restaurant itself. Including all the required parking, the restaurant will then need a site of 4,000 sf, or four times as much land as it would have without the parking. The parking will be consuming all of the land except for that occupied by the restaurant, leaving no room for outdoor dining or landscaping.[37]

The sheer bulk of a parking garage can, at the same time, inhibit pedestrian circulation. The functional failure of the renovation of

Philadelphia's Independence Mall has been attributed to a large garage that dominates the mall's middle block. It includes long access ramps that monopolize the frontage on Fifth and Sixth Streets, and blocks pedestrians from flowing naturally into the park and toward a very elegantly designed new café. Camouflaging the garage with landscaping has proven an insufficient solution, as the garage roof pokes above street level.[38]

Certainly, in designing urban streets, US planners have been unduly dominated since the mid-twentieth century by the prescriptions of the traffic engineering profession. Streets have been widened and driving lanes increased, typically at the sacrifice of sidewalk widths and street trees—all in the interests of faster motoring, and ignoring the potential of the streets as pleasant spaces for walking and social gathering. In effect, city streets have been converted into speedways—dubbed "traffic sewers" by their detractors. There is no way to measure the effect of these losses of space, peace, and greenery on people's decisions to migrate from cities toward suburban and exurban locations, but it may be assumed to be considerable, especially for families with young children.

Transit-oriented development—walkability on both ends of transit trips

The original concept
Clearly, the greatest environmental and economic benefits of public transportation occur when people can walk directly to its stations. Transit-oriented development (TOD), or the clustering of compact communities around transit stations, is basically the contemporary name for a phenomenon that occurred quite naturally prior to the advent of the automobile. We have long had TOD in such cities as New York, Chicago, Philadelphia, Boston, San Francisco, and Los Angeles as well as in smaller cities and suburbs all over the country that were developed around streetcars. We just didn't call it TOD.

But in the late twentieth century, the concept of TOD was reintroduced, coincident with the reintroduction of streetcars and their updated versions as light rail in many places that had hitherto become overwhelmingly auto-centric—cities like Dallas, Fort Worth, Houston, Austin, Phoenix, Denver, Los Angeles, Seattle, Atlanta, and Charlotte.

In the early 1990s, architect and TOD pioneer Peter Calthorpe redefined TOD: its purposes should be to provide a viable transit alternative to automobile dependence, within walkable neighborhoods, while achieving the densities needed to sustain transit infrastructure. Calthorpe envisioned TODs as a constellation of interdependent communities, linked throughout a region by a trunk line transit network, which:

... typically consists of either light rail, heavy rail, or express bus service, with at least a 15-minute frequency of service and a dedicated right of way. Providing a dedicated right-of-way ... serves two important purposes: 1) It ensures expedited and free-flow transit travel; and 2) it represents a long-term transit commitment that allows developers to make similar investments.[39]

He spelled out critical criteria for the internal design of a TOD:

Very simply stated, it's an area, a walking shed, around a transit station that should be mixed-use and very, very walkable. The idea is that people are more likely to use transit if they can walk to the station than if they have to drive, park, and then get on the transit system.... And you need walkability at both ends! If you arrive at the end of a transit trip and you're stranded, you can't walk to your final destination, you're not likely to use transit.[40]

Calthorpe defined two general categories of TODs, as shown in figure 2.3:

• *Urban TODs* are located directly on the trunk line transit network: at light rail, heavy rail, or express bus stops. They should be developed with high commercial intensities, job clusters, and moderate to high residential densities.

• *Neighborhood TODs* are located along a local or feeder bus line within ten minutes transit travel time (no more than 3 miles [4.8 km]) from a trunk line transit stop. They should place an emphasis on moderate density residential, service, retail, entertainment, civic, and recreational uses.[41]

Realization of TODs

Since the mid-1990s, construction of TODs in the US has been advanced by planners, developers, architects, and public transit agencies, typically acting in public-private partnerships—with the public sector providing transit, parks, and other infrastructure, and offering financial incentives and zoning law revisions in return for the private developer taking the risk of building in an unproven area. Many state, regional, and local programs have been formed that have provided tax credits, grants, loans, and direct financial incentives to TOD projects for planning, property acquisition, and implementation.[42] By 2006, there were more than one

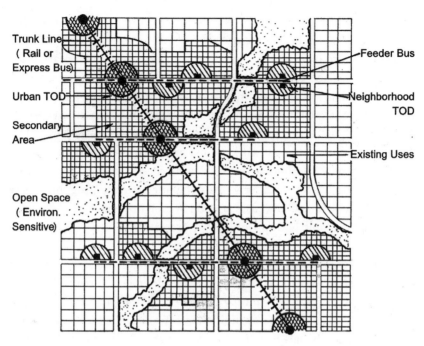

Figure 2.3
Theoretical site plan: "a constellation" of transit-oriented developments (TODs),
including both urban and neighborhood TODs. The TOD site should be located
on an existing or planned trunk line, or a feeder bus route within ten minutes'
travel time from a stop on the trunk line.
Source: Calthorpe Associates.

hundred "transit villages" operating in the US, and at least one hundred
more in planning, according to Robert Cervero, TOD expert and planning professor at the University of California at Berkeley.[43] TOD corridors (series of TODs) were beginning to take form along the Rosslyn-
Ballston axis in Arlington, Virginia, and in the Vermont/Western district
in the Hollywood area of Los Angeles.[44] Between 1996 and 2009, the
Rosslyn-Ballston area experienced the development of more than 7 million sf (650,300 m²) of commercial space and nearly 11,000 new dwelling
units. Yet the number of cars on the major arterial roads in the area had,
by 2013, actually declined by an estimated 45,000 car trips per day. This
has been attributed to a robust "mobility-management" program that
encourages residents, workers, and visitors to these TODs to make use
of the options of walking, biking, and using transit. Arlington's successful

"road diet" program, whereby the number of driving lanes have been decreased, has also been a factor.[45]

In 1999, the New Jersey Department of Transportation spearheaded a "Transit Village Initiative" to create incentives for municipalities to redevelop or revitalize the areas around transit stations, using design standards that create pedestrian-friendly neighborhoods where people can live without relying on automobiles. New Jersey does not force TOD on municipalities; rather, it works to maintain the integrity of the Transit Village "brand." Localities must meet firm criteria and commit to developing around transit in order to be designated for the program. These criteria include mixed land uses, station area management, and commitments to affordable housing and to the preservation of the architectural integrity of historically significant buildings.[46]

By 2012, some twenty-four transit villages had been designated in New Jersey and were in various stages of development. Three of them—in New Brunswick, Rahway, and Cranford—were the subject of a tour in December 2012, sponsored by the Tri-State Transportation Campaign for state and local officials from Connecticut, a state where interest in TOD is high and growing. It is noteworthy *that the critical element that all three of these successful New Jersey TODs have in common is frequent rail service; in fact, this is what makes them truly viable.*[47]

Cervero cautions that, in a society already provided with an extensive roadway network that allows for ubiquitous driving, TOD is not something that the market creates automatically:

When transit is limited to one or two branch lines, it cannot begin to compete with the car for the majority of origin/destination combinations. It is premature to be passing judgement on our transit investments, particularly rail investments, until they can start achieving some of the spillover benefits of the chief competitor to transit: the highway/freeway system. I believe that with every additional link we add to our transit networks, we will see synergistic spillover network effects that will begin to produce proportionally bigger mobility benefits.[48]

Cervero points to the proactive planning that has made TOD so successful in Stockholm, where development around rail transit has been leveraged with an assortment of tools, such as density bonuses, as-of-right zoning overlays, and supportive investments and amenities.

In the US as well, municipal governments have played essential roles in assisting with land assemblage, in modifying zoning regulations to allow higher densities, and where feasible, in relaxing parking requirements for TODs. Zoning overlays have been successfully used in cities such as San Diego, Seattle, and Atlanta, to increase permissible densities, to diversify land uses, and to prevent automobile-related uses from preempting walkable environments and degrading the quality of pedestrian circulation in TODs. The most successful of these developments emphasize "place-making" and human-scaled civic spaces; they contain an assortment of restaurants, public plazas, art shops, and other cultural offerings and entertainment venues. Vibrant examples of TODs can be found at Portland's Pearl District, Dallas's Mockingbird Station, and Chicago's Arlington Heights.[49]

By 2012, TODs were no longer as tough to sell to institutional and private investors as they once were, since a much better understanding of mixed use had evolved among these critical groups. As observed in 2012 by prominent Seattle land use lawyer John Hemplemann, lenders are increasingly recognizing proximity to transit as a benefit. He notes that

> ... we are seeing remarkable investments in TOD despite the recession, and now that we are coming out of the recession, we see it happening at an accelerated pace. It's happening very quickly here in Puget Sound. We have more developers, both local and from around the country, trying to buy parcels that are within a quarter mile [400 m] of a light rail station.[50]

Nevertheless, because transit investments are typically made at the regional scale, often across jurisdictions—while most housing and community development investments are made at the project or neighborhood scale—it is especially challenging to align the planning processes for TOD.[51] Moreover, considerable perseverance on the part of the developer is required because of the complex and exceptionally long and drawn-out nature of the development process. This can involve many entities, including cities, counties, states, and transit authorities, as well as such factors as zoning variances, hearings, other developers, and neighborhood groups. It is therefore vital to line up legislators, the municipality, and the transit authority at the beginning of the process, so that they "buy into" the project, and may even become champions for it. TODs can take up to a decade or more to complete, so maintaining continuity with the public sector is often a special challenge, as a decade is longer than many at the government level stay in office.[52] Construction costs for TOD can also be some 10 to 12 percent greater than for conventional construction, in part because the work has to be performed with a minimum of interruption to the transit system. Thus, the only hope that the developer has of making money on a TOD project is to create enough density to compensate for the extra costs.[53]

The densities and sizes of TODs, and the length of a walk to transit

The BART TOD guidelines call for densities of rail-related TOD that are moderate to high—at least 40 units per acre (99 units per ha), or 80 to 100 residents per acre (198 to 247 residents per hectare)—high enough to justify and sustain the provision of rail transit—with the highest densities located closest to the transit station. BART's guidelines advise that the TOD should be concentrated within a half-mile radius (0.8 km) of a rail transit station, or a 10-minute walk, and may cover around 500 acres (202 ha)—an area that may be larger if the walking environment is favorable.[54] Cervero and colleagues Christopher Ferrell, and Steven Murphy note that the boundaries of a TOD are likely to be firm only if it is part of a legally defined development district; otherwise its borders may be loosely defined. They find a general consensus in the manuals of four

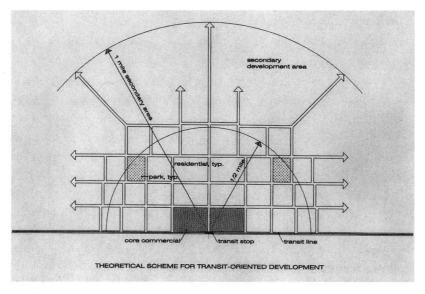

Figure 2.4
Theoretical site plan for a TOD. Planning guidelines advise that ideally, the development should be concentrated within a five- to ten-minute walk to the transit station, and with commercial and retail facilities closest to the station.
Source: Roxanne Warren.

different transit agencies that the planning area for a TOD should extend to between a quarter and a half mile from the transit station (0.4 to 0.8 km), or the approximate distance of a 5- to 15-minute walk.[55]

Regarding the willingness of people to walk to transit, Michael Bernick and Cervero refer to a study by Richard Untermann, an urban designer from the University of Washington. Untermann, who upon closely examining walking behavior in the United States, found that

for non-work and casual trips, most Americans are willing to walk 500 feet, 20 percent will walk 1,000 feet, and only 10 percent will walk half a mile [152 m, 305 m, and 0.8 km, respectively]. For more crucial trips, such as to work, acceptable walking distances are farther, with nearly half of middle-aged Americans willing to walk up to half a mile.[56]

Acceptable walking distances can certainly also be affected by necessity and by the safety of the path, as well as by weather, topography, the walker's physical condition, and the destination. (For example, people are less likely to want to walk long distances for retail shopping, from which they may be carrying heavy packages.) However, these distances may be stretched where the walking corridors are safe, interesting and pleasant. As an integral part of its design, a walkable neighborhood can be enriched and enlivened with street trees, interesting building entries, and recycled older buildings. Ideally, the shops should be a series of small retail establishments, rather than "big-box" stores, which tend to lure shoppers in their cars, not on foot.

The mixed-use character of the TOD should also satisfy much of the public's need for short-range travel. For conventional suburban development, most driving already *is* of a local nature—more than 80 percent of it takes place within 10 miles (16 km) of home, in the process of commuting, shopping, visiting and casual entertainment.[57] With enlightened planning, a mixed-use TOD can meet much of this demand within the walkable neighborhood. TODs should feature retail commercial spaces prominently at their core, including shops, restaurants, offices, medical services, and cultural and entertainment facilities. Guideline manuals also typically call for day care centers to be located near the TOD core for the convenience of transit-commuting parents.[58]

Calthorpe advises that, if the TOD is in a redevelopment area, it should encompass at least 20 acres (8.09 ha) in order to produce sufficient numbers of residents, workers and shoppers to make investments in rail transit more feasible; whereas if it is on a greenfield site, it should comprise at least 40 acres (16.2 ha) to meet this transportation threshold.[59]

The issue of density immediately raises the issue of car parking—whether it will be generously and freely provided—which with high densities, will bring a flood of cars and the near-total paving of the site—or whether, given the presence of a transit system, some restraints on car parking will be seriously considered. Chapter 6 contains a description of how these concerns have been amicably resolved in a number of European "eco-communities," where a strong emphasis is placed on the environmental benefits of reducing private motoring. In the US, in contrast, with a public accustomed to driving everywhere, developers and their lending institutions are particularly wary about the market acceptability of any limits on cars.

Distinguishing between TOD and transit joint development

Related to TOD, although the distinction is not always clear-cut, is transit joint development (TJD), which is also normally carried out through a public-private partnership. A transit agency and a real estate developer may work together to produce a "win-win" outcome, most commonly involving the joint sharing of capital and construction costs. The transit agency benefits through the sharing of construction costs and potential gains in ridership, while the developer gains because the adjacency to a transit station can be capitalized into greater occupancy and higher rents. The TJD is project-specific, often occurring within one city block—as compared with TOD, which typically encompasses multiple blocks. As such, the introduction of a new TJD is normally less controversial among adjacent communities than is TOD. The Washington Metropolitan Area Transit Authority has aggressively pursued the development of TJDs, and has realized impressive profits from them. New York City has also been a leader in developing TJDs.[60]

These projects have typically included high-rent office buildings and sometimes high-priced residential condominiums. But proximity to transit is not necessarily a guarantor of success for residential TJDs. Cervero, Ferrell, and Murphy note that, while San Diego's Barrio Logan project has succeeded at building residential units near transit, Atlanta has had difficulties in doing so. Near its Metropolitan Atlanta Rapid Transit

Authority (MARTA) stations, there is a high demand for office development, partly as a result of density entitlements provided by the zoning code. This has boosted property values so high in the station areas that only high-end office and retail developments are financially feasible. As a result, most of the dense development around MARTA stations is "suburban-style office towers *with lots of parking and poor pedestrian connectivity to nearby stations.*"[61]

TODs and TJDs are not limited to rail-based transit systems. As was suggested by figure 2.3, neighborhood TODs can be served by feeder buses that lead toward higher-capacity transit trunk lines. In other cases, bus rapid transit (BRT), described in chapter 3, may function as the principal transit system.

Two very successful TJD developments have occurred abroad since the mid-1990s in and around rapid-bus stations in Curitiba (Brazil) and Ottawa. Bus-based TJDs exist in Denver at the southern end of the Transitway Mall, at the Corpus Christi Staple Street Transit Center in Texas, and at the Santa Ana Transportation Center in Orange County, California. A bus-based TOD has also taken form in San Diego's Uptown District.[62] It has nevertheless been found that people are typically willing to walk farther to a transit line that offers a truly high quality of service such as rail.[63]

Distinguishing between TOD and New Urbanism

While the advocacy of TOD and New Urbanism has often overlapped, the two terms should not be conflated. New Urbanists have certainly had a good deal of well-deserved success in popularizing their ideas about walkable streets, while evoking a sense of continuity with the past. But, while *aspiring* to transit-orientation and walkable communities, New Urbanism is in reality a basically suburban town concept that has failed to dynamically engage the issue of public transit. New Urbanist developments have typically been built on greenfields far from existing urban centers and planned with essentially unconstrained accommodations for the automobile. With these communities' conventional relationship to cars, it has been difficult for developers to obtain permits to build them at densities much above around 7 units per acre (17.3 units/ha), which is generally too low a density to justify the provision of high-quality, regular transit service.

Furthermore, the retail in these communities has had some difficulty in surviving financially. Without sufficiently high densities there are too often simply not enough customers.[64]

In its albeit laudable aim to revive the lost art of "place making," the New Urbanist movement often addresses stylistically, through the application of retro-design, the public's aversion to modern mega-scale and loss of community—but largely ignores public transportation complexities, issues of population growth, income disparities, and the fundamental changes that have occurred since the nineteenth century to the world's statistical conditions. Humanity cannot retreat from these concerns to a relatively few select, nostalgic and homogeneous, pre-industrial-style villages.

It has been remarked by architect and urban designer/planner Mark L. Hinshaw that:

Many new urbanist communities are the product of a single developer and sometimes, only a handful of architects. Most are developed in phases, with each phase fixed in time to offer a pleasant, complete, photogenic quality.

Not so with places exhibiting true urbanism. They are constantly evolving, infilling, and redeveloping, and have a broad mixture of styles and sensibilities.... They have a gritty urbanity that values variety over uniformity. Rarely are they subject to a highly prescriptive set of design standards; rather they thrive with the idea that everything need not fit an ideal.[65]

The influence of TODs on transit ridership and the issue of free parking

Unfortunately, proximity to rail does not necessarily guarantee a level of patronage adequate to support it. Exploring this issue in 1992 and 1993, Bernick and Cervero surveyed the travel habits of 885 households in 27 residential projects that were within walking distance of one of California's rail systems. These included the BART system, the Santa Clara County Light Rail, the Peninsula CalTrain, the Sacramento Regional Transit, and the San Diego Trolley. In analyzing more than 2,500 trips, they found that an average of only 15 percent were by rail transit. In the case of BART, which offers extensive mobility on a regional scale, rail use was somewhat higher, having been used for more than 25 percent of all trips, and for 32 percent of commuting trips. Among the 27 housing projects surveyed, they found rail shares of travel as high as 79 percent, but as low as 2 percent.[66] These were disappointingly low percentages for the use of these costly rail systems.

In truth, free parking has in all likelihood contributed to the continued heavy use of private automobiles by TOD residents in the US. So has the fact that parking is typically bundled financially and physically with housing. For example, some of the new apartment complexes that have been built as TODs along Denver's light rail network devote their lower floors to bundled parking, which makes it all too easy for residents to drive everywhere, in lieu of taking the light rail.

The Orenco Station development, located about 15 miles (24 km) from downtown Portland, Oregon on the Westside light rail line, has won a number of awards for epitomizing the very best in transit-oriented development. Surveys have nevertheless found that, because its parking is bundled with housing so that the parking *appears* free, two-thirds of Orenco's residents actually commute by car. This is occurring despite the fact that they do use transit, biking, and walking for non-work trips to a greater extent than their neighbors in nearby conventional suburbs.[67]

It seems that the Orenco Station development, with its conventional accommodations for cars, and its reliance on retro-architectural design to create a "village" image, is rather a prime example of New Urbanism. Orenco compares starkly with straightforward TOD, such as one finds in the eco-communities of northern Europe that are described in chapter 6. For example, the community of Hammarby Sjöstad in Sweden (while comprised of buildings of thoroughly contemporary architectural design) has achieved a goal of 80 percent of its residents' trips being completely car-free—made by walking, cycling, ferry, or other transit. As long as these two concepts—New Urbanism and truly transit-oriented development—are conflated and confused with each other, US efforts at developing TOD may be subject to well-deserved criticism.

As an aside, the initial Orenco Station development is not to be confused with the nearby Orchards at Orenco Station, a 57-unit affordable housing community that was scheduled to begin construction in 2014, by a nonprofit developer, REACH Community Development. Through passive building design, superior insulation, triple-paned windows, and air ventilation systems, REACH is managing to reduce energy consumption by about 90 percent. Proximity to transit, lower housing costs, and much lower energy costs will enable truly lower living costs for a low-income population.[68] REACH plans to eventually build 150 apartments on 6 acres (2.43 ha).[69]

Compromising away the benefits of rail and TOD

BART's *TOD Guidelines* note that "charging employees for parking has been found to reduce [parking] demand by between 7 [and] 30 percent, depending on the charge and the availability of other transportation options."[70] At the same time, it has also been found that *a TOD may have little effect on travel behavior if parking remains free and transit remains expensive.* One study of a TOD in Mission Valley, San Diego, revealed that 83 percent of the TOD resident commuters were offered free parking by their employers, while only 17 percent were offered a transit subsidy. Of that 83 percent, only 5 percent took transit to work, while 45 percent of those whose employers did *not* offer free parking *did* commute by transit. The TOD was embedded in a region where free parking was the norm, and this also had a major influence on the TOD residents' choice of transportation mode.[71]

With TOD's intended emphasis on creating compact, walkable neighborhoods, one should expect that there would be a reduction in its legally required parking. Yet zoning regulations in San Francisco's Bay Area, for example, often require the provision of more than one parking space per dwelling unit, even given the excellent region-wide mobility offered by the BART system. This is occurring despite surveys that have shown a demand for "carless" housing.[72]

In a survey of TODs in California, it was found that, at seven of the eleven sites studied, there was no reduction at all of parking requirements, but rather adherence to ITE parking standards. Furthermore, when parking spaces at an existing park-and-ride lot are built upon with TOD, there is a common rule that an equal number of replacement spaces must be provided. Additionally, the goal of providing a good walking environment with compact development means that the TOD's parking must also be compact—that is, provided within decks or garages rather than in lots, and therefore far more costly. The costs of this parking are most often borne by the TOD itself, and so can heavily impact its financial viability.[73] Fortunately, the BART system has recently modified this requirement, a change that should eliminate some major financial hurdles for its future TODs.[74] BART has also abandoned its policy of providing free parking at many of its East Bay stations.[75]

Research by TOD planner and designer G. B. Arrington, together with Robert Cervero, has confirmed that the common adherence to conventional ITE parking standards has meant that fewer TOD projects have gotten built, and that those that have been built have contained far fewer dwelling units than originally planned and are less affordable to households of moderate income. Their report also pointed out that developers are being charged environmental impact fees for non-existent auto trips, while being required to pay for expensive parking spaces that are not needed. A specific objective of their research was to help prepare the way for the ITE and the Urban Land Institute to update their guidelines on parking for TODs to better reflect actual conditions. The case studies that Arrington and Cervero examined helped to confirm that lowering parking ratios by 50 percent in station areas with high-quality transit will allow increases in residential density of between 20 and 33 percent, as well as savings in the costs of building residential parking of between 5 and 36 percent. Such reductions in parking requirements should result innot only reduced traffic impact fees, but potentially greater developer profits and/or improved housing affordability.[76]

Arrington and Cervero's study helped to underscore what must have been intuitively obvious—that TOD households produce considerably less car traffic than is generated by conventional auto-related development. They also found that households in TODs are almost twice as likely as average US households to not own *any* car, and when they do own cars, to own approximately *half* the number of cars as other households.[77]

Erick Guerra and Robert Cervero examined the net capital and operating costs in 2008 for fifty-four recently constructed heavy and light rail lines in the US, and found that these costs ranged from $0.22 to $4.17 per passenger-mile, and in just one case, over $10. Their purpose was to identify job and residential densities that can support more cost-effective fixed-guideway transit service. They found that, while higher capital costs were entailed in constructing rail in high-density areas, these higher densities (not surprisingly) tended to improve rail's operating cost effectiveness. But only 25 percent of the heavy rail station areas they examined, and 19 percent of the light rail areas surpassed the minimum thresholds for transit-supportive densities that were recommended by Pushkarev and Zupan in 1977. Guerra and Cervero concluded, "We suspect that the barriers to development are often regulatory, not just market-driven, and that restrictive zoning and parking requirements are major obstacles to increasing transit efficiency."[78]

Clearly, the mixed uses, high densities, and reduced parking requirements that ought to characterize TODs are actually still illegal in most US cities and transit districts, and this creates an obvious obstacle to affordable TOD development, as well as to creating transit-supportive densities. Nearly $75 billion in public dollars was invested in rail transit between 1997 and 2008. However, many of the anticipated dividends of this investment, such as lower housing and transportation costs and less time stuck in traffic, have not yet been realized. It is largely because of overly generous parking provisions and restrictions on density, that our heavy investments in rail and many of TOD's hoped-for benefits have been compromised away.[79]

Reducing the parking requirement

For employer-provided parking, the "cash-out" option

In Donald Shoup's early work, he emphasized that if one can park free at work, it is an invitation to drive to work alone. This simple revelation led to a 1992 California state law that requires employers to offer cash to workers in lieu of a parking space. Shoup conducted a study five years later, and found that where this "cash-out" program had been implemented, solo driving to work had dropped by 17 percent, carpooling had grown by 64 percent, walking and biking had risen by 33 percent, and transit ridership had increased by 33 percent. These results occurred in spite of the fact that the cash-out program was not well known, and therefore not widely used.[80] In the future, adequate publicity and promulgation of this simple program might reap great benefits.

Car sharing, unbundling parking from housing, and modifying parking ratios

Car-sharing systems have quickly gained popularity throughout the US and Europe as a means of saving the expense and aggravation associated with car ownership, including the search for parking space. With car sharing it becomes more feasible and attractive to not own a second car. Typically, car-sharing systems are accessed by signing up online for membership, and then for usage as needed. Fees normally cover both gasoline and insurance. The cars are parked in numerous locations throughout cities, and, unlike rental cars, can be rented for short periods—for as little as half an hour. In the US there are national car-share companies, such as Zipcar, Hertz, and Enterprise, as well as numerous smaller companies operating in limited areas.

The use of car-sharing systems can cut down considerably on the total space required for parking. The BART guidelines note that car-sharing services in the Bay Area have shown that one shared vehicle can replace between five and six privately owned vehicles. [81]

It can be a challenge to find locations in cities where car-share vehicles can be parked between uses. These locations tend to be of three types: within residential developments, in off-street commercial garages, and directly on the street. When constructing new residential buildings, developers may seek out car-share agencies for collaboration. It is also important that any city that is planning to encourage car sharing update its zoning codes to allow car-sharing vehicles to be parked within new residential buildings.[82]

A car-sharing system has been developed in the small town of Hoboken, New Jersey (population approximately 50,000), which is part of the New York City region and contains the major transportation hub of Hoboken Terminal. Approximately 56 percent of its residents already use public transportation regularly. In 2010, the politically delicate decision was made to sacrifice just forty-two of the city's roughly nine thousand on-street parking spaces for the car-sharing system. Two years later, the new system, dubbed Corner Cars, had attracted some three thousand members, of whom nearly a quarter said that they had either given up their own cars or decided against buying one because of the convenience of car sharing. Hoboken's experience has attracted the interest of city officials from Buffalo to San Francisco, who are curious as to whether their residents can be nudged from car-owning to car-sharing to no cars at all. Hertz, which operates Corner Cars, has used Hoboken's success as a model for similar programs in Miami Beach and San Antonio. Robert J. Pirani, a vice president at the Regional Plan Association, has remarked that this program appears to be transferable to New York, or to "any city that has limited parking and access to transit."[83]

As noted above, when the costs of parking are "bundled" together with the costs of leasing or purchasing residential or commercial space, these costs are "sunk" and cannot be avoided regardless of the actual need for parking. In contrast, in a highly successful effort to reduce the space consumed by car parking, the founders/residents of the German eco-community of Vauban, on the outskirts of Freiburg, Germany, have succeeded in completely unbundling the costs of constructing parking from the costs of constructing housing, thereby clarifying the actual costs of the parking, so that residents can knowledgeably choose whether to purchase it. The result has been to minimize its provision. Chapter 6 contains a description of how this was accomplished.

Not incidentally, when a TOD is designed with minimal parking, and car use is de-emphasized, it can provide an ideal environment in which children can grow up and flourish, while their parents can be more relaxed about their safety. Not only are small children safer in neighborhoods where cars are less dominant, but as they grow, they can discover independent mobility with the use of nearby public transit. To date, splendidly functioning examples of such child-friendly TODs are found in Sweden, the Netherlands, and Australia, as well as in Germany, where they have been specifically designed as child-friendly TODs.[84]

It must be acknowledged that a number of agencies in the US are now allowing parking ratios to be less than one car per dwelling unit, but it will often cost the developer dearly to prove the adequacy of such plans.[85]

An innovative program in California, combining all of these strategies

An especially creative and promising new approach has been taken by a non-profit organization, TransForm, based in Oakland, California, which serves the San Francisco Bay Area with a program called GreenTRIP. Funded by the Rockefeller Foundation, two banks, a community foundation, and the Bay Area Air Quality Management District, this system is engaged by housing developers who would like to reduce the amount of parking that they are required to provide. The developers approach this organization for special certification, for which they pay a fee.[86]

Concerns about a new influx of traffic appear to be the major reason why existing communities oppose proposed new development nearby. Opponents generally do not trust city staff when they claim that a development will have "low traffic" and be a good neighbor, and they tend to trust developers even less on this issue. As an independent nonprofit entity, GreenTRIP's great advantage is its ability to clearly and credibly explain to the public why a project will have low traffic. TransForm has convinced developers to make commitments to donate free or deeply discounted transit passes for each new housing unit for a period of forty years as well as free car-share memberships for that same period, and to unbundle the costs of parking from the costs of housing. Another feature of this program is to limit parking ratios to no greater than 0.75 to 1.5 spaces per unit, depending on the location.

The developer gains substantial benefits by being able to eliminate a lot of expensive extra parking, and the tenants gain very deep discounts in both their transportation and housing costs—in other words, *deep discounts in the two major living expenses for most households of limited income* Between 2010 and February 2013, this organization had certified ten proposals for development in the Bay Area, and by February 2014, there were an additional ten projects in the pipeline. The benefits of GreenTRIP are exceeding expectations, and the group is considering ultimately going national. In particular, they would like to release the concept from their own proprietary control—that is, to see GreenTRIP principles ultimately embedded into the building codes. Toward this end, the nonprofit is involved in community engagement and education.[87]

Other challenges and opportunities in developing TOD

Elements of NIMBY versus TOD and theory versus reality

It is commonly the case that, when high-density development is proposed in the US, the rallying cry of "not in my backyard" (NIMBY) is heard from surrounding communities. A frequent fear is that TOD will bring an influx of lower-income residents, and with them a burden on the local school system.

An equally important, related component of NIMBY resistance is a nearly universal assumption that TOD will have a negative effect on housing prices in surrounding residential neighborhoods. However, a study of this issue performed in the San Francisco Bay area revealed very little empirical evidence that such fears are well founded. On the contrary, it found that, in the case study, suburban TODs either "had no impact or had a positive impact on the surrounding single-family home sale prices."[88]

Similarly, MIT's Center for Real Estate published a study that looked at eight communities across the Boston metro area in which large, mixed-income, multi-family developments were being built in neighborhoods of single-family homes. When the values for the single-family houses that were the most impacted by the new developments were compared to the home values of comparable control areas, it was found that movements in their sales price indexes were essentially identical. The report concluded that "large, dense, multi-family rental developments ... do not negatively impact the sales price of nearby single-family homes."[89]

Nevertheless, regardless of any impacts on housing prices or school systems, prominent and persistent NIMBY barriers to development typically include the additional traffic and paving over of the landscape that are anticipated with a higher-density project. Note Cervero, Ferrell, and Murphy:

NIMBY opposition has stopped mixed-use, infill development near rail stations in Oakland, Miami, and most likely every U.S. city that has built rail systems over the past half century. Made weary by the prospect of additional traffic generated by the planned mixed-use development at Atlanta's Lindbergh station, a neighborhood group has filed multiple suits against MARTA to block construction. While the project is moving forward, these suits have set the project behind schedule. Because of community pressures, the 512 housing units recently built near Santa Clara County's Whisman light rail station—representing the largest housing development in Mountain View in at least 20 years—contained no rental units and were built at less than half the density originally proposed.[90]

Thus, with NIMBY resistance aggravated by the prospect of an influx of more cars, the component of rental housing was eliminated from this project, with the result that, for individuals and families who were unable to afford home ownership, or would have preferred the convenience, flexibility, and economy of renting an apartment close to a transit line, this option was discarded.

While the abstract concept of TOD enjoys broad appeal in the US, there is in fact a huge gap between theory and reality. For example, economic downturns and tepid real estate markets have been associated with little development around the light rail stations in Buffalo, Pittsburgh, and Saint Louis. TODs that have been realized to date have come about only as the product of committed and arduous efforts on the part of developers, architects, planners, and public agency professionals. It is primarily where TODs have been actively championed by the public sector that they have had a real chance of success. Such success has occurred most dramatically in Montréal and Toronto. In these cities there is a tradition of regional governance, which has been highly instrumental in orchestrating the co-development of land use and transportation infrastructure—particularly through the aggressive application of the transfer of development rights.[91]

Bernick and Cervero advise that, given conservative lending practices and the lingering doubts of the US investment community about the marketability of higher-density housing, some degree of risk sharing between the private and public sectors will be vital if TODs are ever to proliferate. They name a number of mechanisms which can be helpful in stimulating this market: "The public sector can help absorb risks through such actions as writing down the costs of land assemblage, covering the costs of supportive infrastructure, and providing loan guarantees in the event of a market downturn. Relaxing zoning codes to allow fewer park-ing spaces, high densities, and more mixed land uses near rail stations would also help, as would tax abatements and credits against impact fees."[92]

Most rail-based households do own only one car and are twice as likely as most other US residents to not own *any* car. Requiring only one parking space or less per household will also allow more compact and walkable development, and reduce the environmental impact of the whole project. TOD developers could be rewarded through the more expeditious public review of their proposals and processing of their building permits.

Bernick and Cervero make note of another tool that was proposed by Sierra Club transportation chair and Natural Resources Defense Council consultant John Holtzclaw—which is for banks to grant "location-effi-cient mortgages," or LEMs, for home purchases to people buying condo-miniums near rail transit. A LEM increases the amount of money that a homebuyer is able to borrow, based on the savings that can be realized by not having to own more than one car.[93] LEMs can, at the same time, help to offset the higher costs of housing that are typically found in high-density areas.

The trade-off between commuter parking and TOD—and opportunities
One of the most challenging issues in planning for walk-to-transit com-munities has been the competition for space around stations between com-muter parking facilities and transit-oriented development. Whether the

land around transit stations is better used for building communities or for providing more commuter parking is an issue that plagues transit systems all around the nation. As observed by Cervero, Ferrell, and Murphy:

In many typical suburban locations, park-and-ride lots are essential to rail rider-ship success, especially at terminal locations that draw customers from a large, sometimes exurban/semi-rural catchment. The Puget Sound Regional Council (1999) recommends park-and-ride lots only in areas where immediate develop-ment is not expected. [Reid] Ewing ... indicates that park-and-ride lots are only appropriate where there is a long commute to downtown.... The city of Seattle has opted to limit park-and-ride lots planned for the LINK light rail network to terminal stations to maximize development potential and encourage TODs. Park-ing lots need not preclude TODs, at least in the long term. Indeed, they can serve as an interim use, banking land for eventual infill conversion if and when market conditions are ripe.[94]

Thus, having an abundance of surface parking associated with a rail sta-tion is not an entirely bad thing during a down market, as it preserves TOD opportunities for the future. Often, in fact, a developer will wait until a rail system is built or at least under construction, before getting started on TOD.

But while it has been possible in some cases to convert existing park-ing lots into TOD, the collective voices of existing park-and-ride patrons are normally louder than those of the potential residents of a proposed TOD. Furthermore, the regulations that require the one-to-one replace-ment of any parking spaces that are lost to TOD are still common—for example, with Washington, DC's Metrorail and with Maryland's Transit Authority. The financial burden of this replacement is severe, and falls on the TOD, which must generate enough revenue to replace surface parking for the commuters with more compact, but much more expen-sive structured parking. And where land costs are high, this has all but precluded TOD.[95]

Effective strategies—shared parking, mini-cars, and shifting TOD park-ing locations

It is without a doubt that the bloating of TOD with excessive parking provisions has made it less affordable, less compact, and less successful in weaning its residents away from private motoring. In summary, both the generation of heavy traffic, and some of the high costs of providing structured parking at TOD may be ameliorated by means of a number of strategies.

Maximum rather than minimum parking requirements should be adopted in high-density neighborhoods such as TODs, as well as in cities. And unbundling the costs of parking from those of housing—separating the costs of parking from the lease or sale of housing—will mean that tenants or homeowners will pay only for what they really need, thereby reducing the overall space required for parking. Any excess parking space can then be leased or sold to others. Landscaped reserves can also be specified, which can be converted into parking in the future only if and when they are needed.

The successful cash-out program in California for employer-provided parking was already mentioned above. Similarly, charging for residential parking in lieu of providing it for "free" can be one of the most effective ways of changing travel behavior, and can reduce the overall parking demand by 10 to 30 percent. Pricing may also be structured to advance specific objectives, such as supporting retail shopping with charges that favor short-term over long-term parking by commuters.[96]

Parking spaces can be shared between complementary uses. For example, office-related parking, which is most in demand during workweek daytime hours, can be complementary with entertainment-related parking, for which the greatest demand occurs on evenings and weekends. A transportation management association may also be formed to act as a "broker" of underutilized parking facilities. These measures can all significantly reduce the required off-street parking space.[97]

Another strategy for shrinking the space required for parking, which is used occasionally in Europe, is to charge proportionately smaller parking fees for smaller vehicles as an incentive for motorists to purchase or rent smaller vehicles. This idea is further developed at the end of chapter 4.

Yet another recommended means of alleviating the competition for space around transit stations is to locate the parking in structures that are some distance away from the stations, decoupled physically, as well as financially from the other TOD buildings. For the Dallas Area Rapid Transit (DART) system, for example, the parking is now permitted to be 700 feet (213 meters) away.[98] Parking spaces in these structures might then be leased according to individual demand. As residential and commercial development fills out, additional parking facilities may be added as well—but only if they turn out to be truly needed.

3

Transit Options and the Unique Features of Rail

When railways were first introduced in the streets of New York in 1832, it very quickly became obvious to the operators of horse-drawn omnibuses that with the extremely low rolling resistance of steel-on-steel contact, their horses could pull heavy loads of passengers much more easily over rails than over rough pavement. From that day forward, rail technology, in its various forms, has proven to be uniquely qualified as the transportation infrastructure essential to the fluid functioning of cities.

A very brief history of passenger rail in the United States

The evolution and spread of urban rail

As remarked by urban transportation expert Dr. Vukan R. Vuchic, the invention of the first railway by George Stevenson in England in 1825 represented a major breakthrough in transportation. This new mode vastly stimulated the growth of cities and industrialization, as it possessed capacity, speed, comfort, and reliability that were many times greater than any mode previously known. The benefits of railways were found to be so great that construction of their networks proceeded rapidly after their introduction in the western countries in the 1830s. The ease and economy with which materials and goods could now be transported by rail virtually eliminated previous limits on the sizes of cities, and by the end of the nineteenth century, the economic functioning and growth of nearly all North American and European cities depended upon rail transportation.[1]

The evolution of streetcars proceeded at a similarly swift pace. In US cities in the 1850s, many of the most heavily traveled horse-drawn omnibus routes began to be converted into horse-drawn rail tramways. Grooved rails that were flush with the pavement were introduced, and since these did not protrude above the street surface, they helped to ease the widespread acceptance of street railways. Horses, however, were quickly worn out by street work, and in 1872, thousands of them died in a great equine influenza epidemic. Then in 1884 and 1888, electric motors were introduced on streetcars in Cleveland, Ohio, and Richmond, Virginia, respectively. With the development of technical improvements, electric traction gradually replaced horsepower, so that by 1902, virtually all of the 16,645 miles (26,782 km) of streetcar lines in the United States had been converted to electricity. Electric operation was not only considerably cleaner but much less costly than horsepower, and this made it possible to reduce fares and attract more passengers, which in turn led to the building of more streetcar lines. By 1912, the total length of streetcar lines in the US had nearly doubled to 30,438 miles (48,975 km).[2]

This remarkable proliferation of streetcars prompted the dramatic expansion of cities outward toward formerly remote areas, creating "streetcar suburbs." In fact, the extension of these rail lines was eagerly financed by real estate developers, who were strongly motivated by the profits to be made by purchasing outlying lands and making them easily accessible by rail. As noted by author Sam Bass Warner Jr., "The simple procedure of placing a coach on iron rails seemed a miraculous device for the promotion of out-of-town property."[3]

Parallel with the development of streetcars, large cities were beginning to build higher-speed rail lines both for commuting between the cities and suburbs and later, for intra-urban travel—via rail rapid transit (metros) on fully separated rights-of-way (ROWs). These trains were initially run by steam, but were ultimately converted to electric traction, as a more environmentally acceptable power source. By the early part of the twentieth century, there existed quite extensive rail networks within and outside many US cities. In addition to substantial streetcar networks within the cities, commuter lines linked the cities with surrounding towns, and rail metros were serving the major cities of New York, Boston, Chicago, and Philadelphia.[4]

Toward the end of the nineteenth century, a new application of rail had been developed throughout the United States—the very popular interurban electric railways. While these existed in virtually every state in the nation, more than 40 percent of the interurban network was concentrated in the central states of Indiana, Ohio, Michigan, Illinois, and Wisconsin.[5] These were large vehicles, operating at high speeds between cities and towns, and could run both in the street and on separated rights-of-way. In New England, they often actually functioned as continuations of urban streetcar lines, and were so extensive that it was once possible to travel from Boston to New York by transferring among interurbans and streetcars without paying a fare of more than five cents. The US had a national network, at its peak in 1913, of 16,000 miles of interurban railways (nearly 26,000 km), and a number of other countries around the world were developing similar networks. Today, only two interurban lines have been permanently retained in the US, the Norristown Line in Philadelphia, and the South Shore Line in Chicago. However, several other countries still benefit from this mode, including Germany, Belgium, Switzerland, Italy, France and Japan.[6]

All kinds of rail transit were simultaneously being developed around the globe. Nevertheless, notes Vuchic, "During the first decades of the twentieth century, rail transit in US cities was in many respects more advanced and more extensively used than in any other country."[7]

How did we lose these valuable assets?

In the middle of the twentieth century, many US cities still had comprehensive networks of streetcars; however most of them did not survive much longer. In fact, they were literally starved for cash: while the costs of labor and operation had been rising, regulatory bodies had not allowed corresponding increases in transit fares. In some cities these were still limited to five cents through the end of World War II. Nor was there any significant public assistance to public transit, either financial or in securing reliable rights-of-way on city streets.

The unprecedented freedom and flexibility offered by the automobile were not the only reasons for its dramatic ascendancy, nor for the corresponding decline of rail and other public transit systems in the US. Rather, the country's conversion to an automobile-based transportation system was heavily influenced by industry lobbying and a concerted and fiercely fought battle on the part of interested corporations. Between 1936 and 1949, National City Lines—a company backed by the Big Three automakers, major oil companies, tire manufacturers, and the trucking and construction industries—succeeded in buying up and closing down more than one hundred electric trolley lines in forty-five US cities and replacing them with buses. Their interest was not in selling buses; it was in selling cars, rubber tires and gasoline, and this they accomplished on a stunning scale. By 1949, when National City Lines was convicted of this conspiracy, and fined a mere five thousand dollars, critical damage to US urban rail transit had essentially been achieved.[8] Remnants of the country's streetcar systems survived only in San Francisco, New Orleans, Boston, Philadelphia, Pittsburgh, and Newark.

Meanwhile, the 1938 US federal planning guidelines for new residential neighborhoods, which had to be followed thereafter by anyone receiving federal mortgage insurance, were based on the premise that the transportation mode of the future *would* be the automobile, and so this became a self-fulfilling prophecy. The guidelines mandated that new residential roads be laid out along circuitous routes, which are typically unfeasible to serve with transit.[9] The trend was strongly reinforced by the federal Housing Loan Program that was established after World War II, which required that its loans be used to buy only new homes—most of which were available only outside of the cities.

Then in 1956, passage of the Interstate Highway Act committed the US federal government to fund 90 percent of a new 44,000-mile (70,800-km) network of toll-free expressways, which effectively "ensured the complete triumph of the automobile over mass transit alternatives in the United States and killed off, except in a few large cities, the vestiges of balanced public transportation systems that remained in 1950s America."[10] What naturally followed was the dispersal of large numbers of the population out of the cities and all over the landscape. Advance knowledge of where the new highways were being constructed, and particularly the locations of their entrance and exits points, instigated extensive real estate speculation and highly profitable new development of all kinds, further spurring relocation outside the cities. The "factor of five" profits that can be realized in this way were described in in an endnote of chapter 1. Where the highways were brought directly into the cities, they were most typically located in a way that eviscerated urban neighborhoods.

A modest correction to government policies

More than a decade later, as the population had become increasingly dependent on cars for mobility, civic leaders and public officials began to realize that the need for public transit had actually been *increased* by the flood of private automobiles into the cities. Construction of rail rapid transit, which had been intensive until the Great Depression, had ceased altogether in the US prior to World War II, and there had been no federal assistance to transit between 1950 and 1964.

But in 1964, the Urban Mass Transportation Act of Congress was signed into law, and renewed in 1970, which provided cities and states with capital grants for up to 50 percent of the capital costs of transit improvements. This was parsimonious in comparison with the 80 percent of construction costs that were then being granted for highway projects, but certainly a step in the right direction. In 1974, the transit grants were extended to cover operating costs as well. Gradually increasing financial resources led to the acceleration of construction of heavy rail metros. While in 1970, only 5 US cities had metros, by 2007 there were 12 such systems. Worldwide, there had been an unprecedented growth in the number of metros, from 17 in the early 1950s to some 110 by the beginning of the twenty-first century.[11]

Critical attributes of the major urban transit modes

Performance versus levels of expenditure

There is commonly much confusion among the public about the assessment of transit modes and appropriate levels of expenditure on them, versus their quality of performance. To clarify these issues, Vuchic has classified ground transit modes by their three basic characteristics:

- *Right-of-way (ROW) category* (i.e., the degree to which the transit system is separated from other traffic)
- *System technology* (i.e., mechanical features—type of support and guidance, propulsion and control)
- *Type of service* (i.e., type of trips and routes, stopping schedule, and time of operation)[12]

Of all of these characteristics, it is the first—the right-of-way—that has by far the greatest influence on both the costs and performance of a mode. Vuchic defines three basic ROW categories, distinguished by their degree of separation from other traffic. Beginning with the least costly and least predictable in their speed, these are:

- **ROW category C**—includes transit vehicles operating on surface streets *in mixed traffic*. Examples are regular buses and streetcars, with or without preferential treatment, such as reserved lanes or special traffic signals. (Paratransit, including taxis and such systems as dial-a-ride and car sharing, are specialties within this category.)

- **ROW category B**—includes transit vehicles with significant portions of the ROW that are *longitudinally physically separated* from other traffic by such devices as curbs, barriers, and grade separations, but have grade crossings for pedestrians and other vehicles, and can include street intersections. This category is very frequently used for light rail transit, and is also commonly used for semi-rapid bus transit.

- **ROW category A**—includes only transit vehicles with a *fully controlled* or *exclusive* ROW for the entire route, without any grade crossings or legal access by other vehicles or people. The ROW may be on an aerial structure, in a tunnel, or securely fenced off at grade level. ROW category A is essential for true rapid transit, as well as for the automation of a system.[13]

Light rail vehicles can utilize all three ROW categories on the same line, and so can buses. The initial capital cost of a transit system increases sharply with its degree of separation of ROW. But with ROW category A, its *operating* costs may be decreased substantially through automation.

Emergence of intermediate-speed transit modes

The public has long been familiar with buses, streetcars (trams), cable cars, metros, commuter rail, and intercity rail. But the mid-1970s saw the emergence of new types of intermediate-speed transit systems that bridge the gap between metros and local buses.

Light rail or trams—relationship to the urban street
Light rail transit (LRT) is the upgraded version of streetcar technology, whose vehicles have been redesigned to be more spacious, often with low

floors. The low floor meets the accessibility needs of seniors, parents with strollers, and people in wheelchairs, while allowing faster boarding/deboarding, so that the system can perform almost like a moving walkway.

Light rail can serve as either a streetcar-like component of a larger transit system, or as the metro-type backbone of a smaller transit system. Thus, for many medium-size cities that are too small to qualify for a full rail metro, light rail has become the basic transit mode—a kind of mini-metro—typically including some separated rights-of-way for at least suburban portions of their routes. For example, LRT systems in Denver, Dallas, and Saint Louis have long stretches of separated rights-of-way in outlying areas, where speeds are very high—these are systems that attract many commuting motorists out of their cars.

Light rail can also run as multiple-unit trains, depending upon demand. This has been a very fast-growing transit mode worldwide since the early 1980s, with both new and upgraded systems being developed in Europe, Asia, Oceania, and the Americas. There are at least 175 streetcar/light rail/tram/systems throughout Europe, ranging from genuinely antique to thoroughly modern. After World War II, Germany not only retained its fifty-six streetcar networks but began upgrading them to light rail by separating their rights-of-way from other forms of traffic and procuring new updated vehicles.

In contrast, France had allowed its streetcar networks to decline between 1945 and 1973, at which point they remained in only three cities, Lille, Saint Etienne, and Marseille. However, since 1985, France has been redeveloping light rail tramways as a major and integral part of the mobility and aesthetic transformation of urban centers.[14] France now has sixty-five light rail routes with 435 miles (700 kilometers) of double track in thirty cities.[15]

Combining pedestrianization with light rail has been an important ingredient in this transformation of French cities, and toward this end, transportation professionals have worked in close partnership with urban planners. One important reason for light rail's popularity within cities in general is that, being above ground, it allows the enjoyment of the cityscape. Very beautiful light rail vehicles such as those in Milan, Barcelona, and Strasbourg (figures 3.1–3.3) are designed to maximize this advantage—they are highly transparent, with large windows, so that the passengers don't feel boxed in or strictly separated from the pedestrian

Figure 3.1
Low-floor light rail tram in Milan, Italy. This is the updated version of streetcars, redesigned to allow easy access by seniors, parents with strollers, and wheelchair users. The low floor permits reduced boarding time, and therefore shorter travel time, allowing the system to perform almost like a moving walkway.
Source: Bombardier Transport International.

Figure 3.2
Low-floor light rail in Barcelona.
Source: Daniel Sherr.

Figure 3.3
Low-floor light rail in Strasbourg.
Source: Ron Shiffman.

life of the street. The careful insertion of light rail into the French cities, for example, has enhanced, rather than detracted from the urban fabric. Where a building has preexisted in the transit path, the track has typically been simply skirted around the building; no buildings are demolished for the sake of the tram, as this would be counterproductive to the purpose of restoring and revitalizing the city. Nevertheless, because the trams in France have priority over other forms of traffic, they provide steady, reliable, and usually uninterrupted mobility, even at relatively low speeds. As noted in chapter 1, the tram lines form the backbone of the transit system in each of the smaller French cities, with feeder bus networks coordinated with all of the stations.[16]

The term light rail was first adopted in the US in 1972 by the Urban Mass Transportation Administration to define the streetcar evolution that was occurring in Europe; US interest in this mode was further ignited with an LRT conference in Philadelphia in 1975. North America's first light rail system, in Edmonton, became operational in 1978, and was followed by installations in Calgary, San Diego, Seattle, Galveston, and Memphis. By the end of 2008, there were thirty-three LRT systems operating in the United States.[17] Two years later, this had increased to thirty-five systems, with thirteen more under construction, and many more in the planning stages.

Bus transit types, with varying degrees of separation from other forms of traffic

Another intermediate-speed system that has emerged is known as bus rapid transit (BRT), or select bus service (SBS), which can improve upon the speeds of regular buses when provided with varying degrees of separation from other traffic, as well as a system of passenger payment before boarding.

Bus rapid transit, because it needs no rails or power installations, can have a clear capital cost advantage over light rail. Its use has therefore spread widely throughout the world. These systems have proven extremely popular and productive in speeding mobility in countries and cities where the capital costs of rail rapid transit or light rail have been unaffordable, where there is a low percentage of private car ownership, and where drivers' wages are also low—notably in Bogotá, Mexico City, and São Paulo and Curitiba, Brazil. The Insurgentes BRT line in Mexico

City now carries 260,000 passengers daily, and the city was scheduled to have ten more BRT lines in operation by 2012. In early 2008, Tehran launched its first BRT line, and the city is developing several more, all to be integrated with the city's new subway lines.[18] New BRT systems have been developed in Delhi and Ahmedabad, India; in Guangzhou, China; in Johannesburg; and in Jakarta—which at sixty miles (ninety-six kilometers) is the world's longest BRT.[19] In 2011, the Institute for Transportation and Development Policy named five BRT systems as the most effective in the US—those in Cleveland, Eugene (Oregon), Los Angeles, Pittsburgh, and Las Vegas.[20] Other successful BRT systems are operating in North America in Ottawa, Toronto, Minneapolis, Chicago, and between New Jersey and New York City.

The Great Recession that began in December 2007 has caused much belt-tightening, inducing New York City to experiment with an especially inexpensive form of BRT on Manhattan's transit-deprived far east side, on First and Second Avenues and on the 34th Street crosstown route. This system has been dubbed "Select Bus Service" (SBS) to distinguish it from full BRT. Grade separation was of course out of the question in a crowded, built-up city like Manhattan, but SBS has provided New Yorkers with a radical improvement over the slow service that they endure on other routes.

As in Curitiba and Bogotá, time is saved on SBS by requiring passengers to pay before boarding at outdoor ticketing machines that issue time-stamped receipts. These are randomly inspected by transit agents, who issue summonses with heavy fines for noncompliance. As with classic BRT, passengers board and debark through all doors without involving the driver. There is wide spacing between the stops, and it is intended that the buses will ultimately travel in interior lanes, pulling up to stop at "bus bulbs" (protrusions of the sidewalk,) thereby avoiding the need for the bus to veer in and out from the curb to pick up and let off passengers. Bus-mounted cameras are employed to record violations of the dedicated bus lane by non-transit vehicles. With SBS, the buses still have to share space sometimes with street traffic, including delivery trucks and right-turning passenger vehicles, often causing frustrating delays. But the time savings for passengers in New York are dramatic: it can now take less than twenty minutes to travel more than fifty blocks, from the South Street Seaport to 42nd Street.[21]

Enforcement of the bus-only lanes has been a problem. But significantly, the costs for SBS have been extremely modest—only around one million dollars per mile, excluding the costs of buses and bus bulbs.[22] If the buses are of the low-pollution type, such as diesel hybrid, they may also cost some half a million dollars each. This compares with standard diesel buses, which cost around half as much as diesel hybrid.[23]

New York's initial testing of the SBS concept began in the Bronx in 2008 on the Fordham Road crosstown route, on which service now runs 25 percent faster than on the old express buses. The city is moving forward on the expansion of SBS throughout its five boroughs, starting with Brooklyn and Queens, to include as many as sixteen of the most heavily congested corridors.

BRT lines have the benefit of being able to branch out in mixed traffic on outer portions of their routes to pick up and drop off passengers, which under certain conditions is more useful than total separation. They also have the significant advantage of lower capital investment on those segments of their routes. Even the extensive bus system in Curitiba (with stations beautifully designed by architect and former mayor Jaime Lerner) is not separated over its entire length. But the system has been highly effective: while the city's population tripled between 1974, the year the BRT was installed, and 2007, car traffic had been cut by a remarkable 30 percent.[24]

Nevertheless, branching out in mixed traffic for part of the route, even if there is an exclusive ROW for other portions of it, will classify the bus system as "semi-rapid transit"—ROW category B. It may be wishful thinking that BRT "allows buses to function like subways." If a sizable portion of the route is in mixed traffic, the very flexibility of buses becomes their weak point with respect to predictable speed.

The same principle of rapid and semi-rapid transit applies to rail as to buses. There are many light rail systems that have extensive sections of track that are fully separated from other traffic—either aerial (San Diego and Cologne), at-grade (Saint Louis and Calgary), or in tunnels (Boston and Frankfurt). Yet these systems have portions of their track that are not fully separated, and therefore qualify as semi-rapid transit.[25]

Automated guideway transit

Also in the intermediate-speed category is automated guideway transit (AGT)—most of whose systems are rubber tired, others having steel wheels on steel rails. AGT is 100 percent computer-controlled, with driverless vehicles, and therefore must operate on completely separated guideways for the entire route (figures 3.9–3.10). The city of Lille, France, opened an AGT in 1983 primarily on an elevated guideway, and has been cited as the world's first automated guideway system that was installed to serve an existing urban area. With AGT in Lille, the automobile remained as the primary user of the street, but in the French cities that chose surface-running light rail instead, it was pedestrians and trams that were given street priority.

Basic reasons for rail's practicality and popularity

The unique design of rail—combining suspension and guidance
Vuchic has highlighted features of rail's external guidance that contribute to its safety, its compact operations, its popularity with the riding public, and its stimulative effects on urban development:

[Because] ... rail vehicles are externally guided by their way (track), the driver's only function is to control its speed. The external vehicle guidance gives rail modes the following characteristics: they require *minimum ROW width*; they have *superior riding quality*, as compared with non-guided modes, *greater permanence*, and *stronger identity*, which are particularly important factors in *high passenger attraction* and *impact on urban development*....

as a result of external guidance, rail modes are characterized by high performance and level of service and by low operating costs per unit of capacity in high-capacity ranges.... most of the investment cost difference between various rail and bus systems in specific cities is caused by different ROW types, performance, and level of service characteristics; only a fraction of these cost differences is caused by the guideway itself.... Most of the operating costs in favor of guided modes in high-capacity ranges ... are caused by the economies of train operations made possible by the external guidance.[26]

Certain technical characteristics of rail transit help account for its stability and attraction for passengers and urban development, and ultimately, the reinforcement of cities. A common discomfort of buses, especially where they are articulated, is that they can lurch unpredictably from side to side as they move from the traffic lane to the curb lane to pick up and drop off passengers. This is especially an issue for standees, and generally does not happen with guided systems. Vuchic draws this distinction between guided and steered modes:

Highway vehicles are *steered* (by the driver) and their lateral stability is provided by wheel/support adhesion. Rail vehicles are *guided* by flanges and the conical form of the wheel surfaces. A distinct feature of rail technology is that its wheel/rail assembly combines both support and guidance. Externally guided rubber-tired vehicles in all forms must have additional wheels and surfaces for guidance.[27]

Thus, in the case of automated guideway transit (AGT) vehicles, where these are rubber-tired, and with rubber-tired metros like those in the Paris Metro, the vehicles typically need to be furnished with a second set of wheels for lateral stability, adding another degree of complexity. Vuchic further details why the combination of steel wheels on steel rails is the logical choice for ROW category A:

Flanged steel wheels running on two steel rails provide both support and guidance in a unique, extremely simple manner. Because of the flanges and the conical shape of their riding surfaces, each wheel is guided via a single contact point (actually a small area) with the rails.... guided technologies are superior to steered ones for operation on ROW category A; buses are less suitable for such lines because their most important advantage—ubiquitous mobility—is irrelevant; in most other characteristics, such as capacity, speed, safety, and so on, they are inferior to guided modes.[28]

Practical and aesthetic advantages of rail for surface transit in the city

There is ample evidence that streetcars, light rail, and heavy rail are likely to stimulate economic development around their stations, whereas documentation is lacking that the same is true of buses. For real estate developers, the fear with buses, whether local or BRT, is their lack of permanence.[29]

Rail also has some operational advantages. In countries where auto ownership is high and drivers' wages are also high, light rail can have lower operating costs than buses on heavily traveled routes, since one driver may carry many more passengers in an entrained, multiple-unit line of vehicles. For this reason, light rail should be at least considered for routes serving more than twenty thousand passengers per weekday.[30] With buses, as passenger demands increase, and buses are needed more frequently, not only can bus bunching occur but labor costs can grow very quickly, to a point where light rail can become the more economic option operationally.[31]

Within heavily populated city centers, light rail certainly has a lower spatial impact than buses. For example, much of Bogotá's famous BRT system requires four-lane busways to accommodate passenger flows and provide capacities equivalent to those of light rail. Such a broad swath of pavement running through the center of a city is spatially undesirable, in that *it runs exactly counter to the goal of creating a pleasantly walkable city*. Light rail has far more compact operations for the same capacities.

In this regard, it must be noted that Bogotá's TransMilenio BRT system, inaugurated in 2000 and widely emulated throughout the world, has already become a victim of its own success. Since it was built to carry only half of the 1.7 million daily passengers that it now handles, it has become difficult to manage during peak travel hours. In March 2012, commuter frustration with its overcrowded buses and stations turned violent, and this nearly paralyzed the city.[32]

Figure 3.4 illustrates the compactness of the right-of-way required for rapid rail, compared with that required for bus rapid transit. In summary, these multiple attributes of rail—its lateral stability and safety, its compactness and economy in high-capacity ranges, its high passenger attraction, and its ability to attract and serve dense development—uniquely qualify it as an ideal transportation framework for our cities and our increasingly urbanizing future.

Where light rail is operating in mixed traffic, it is also easier to enforce separation from other traffic than it is with buses. That is, the rails, particularly when embedded in rough pavement, create a commanding and

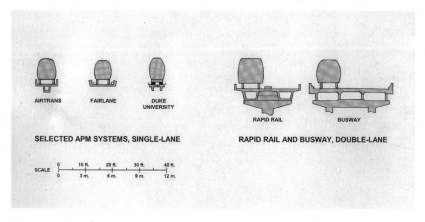

Figure 3.4
Comparative cross-sections of automated guideway transit (AGT), rapid rail, and a BRT busway.
Source: US Department of Transportation.

self-enforcing path. Motorists like to avoid driving along rail tracks, as their wheels can be pulled from side to side in the tracks. With busways, in contrast, except where they are protected by high curbs, it is all too easy for non-transit vehicles to enter the transitway. Other methods of ongoing enforcement are typically necessary for busways, such as policing and/or surveillance cameras and a system of ticketing.

Where there are aesthetic or practical objections to the overhead catenary wires of light rail/trams, the power for the system can be delivered by one of several catenary-free systems, such as special long-lasting battery packs, or, alternatively, by subsurface conductive metal power segments that are only activated when the tram passes over them, thereby protecting pedestrians. Both types of power delivery have been developed and successfully deployed by major international light rail vehicle manufacturers. Battery-operated light rail also has the potential for both capital and operating cost savings, because the need for installation and maintenance of the catenary is eliminated.[33]

A relatively inexpensive method of avoiding conflicts between surface transit and other forms of traffic, while avoiding the expense of grade separation and creating an appealing walking environment, is to take the French approach and establish a pedestrian-transit shopping street. Operating in pedestrian streets is of course possible for either buses or light rail, but light rail has certain advantages. Its electric propulsion is not only clean and quiet within the populated area, but the distinct image of the rails and the fact that the vehicles are reliably guided by their tracks provides a much more predictable and therefore safer presence for pedestrians.

The relatively narrow footprint of light rail and streetcars allows them to be inserted more discreetly into dense urban areas. In pedestrian streets, they travel at low speeds, being typically limited to a maximum of 15 mph (24 km/h) for pedestrian safety. It was noted above that, in the nineteenth century, when grooved rails that were flush with the pavement were introduced, they helped to ease the widespread acceptance of streetcars. The same is true today—when the rails are flush with the street surface, light rail can be well-integrated with the shopping street, and pedestrians can cross the street freely, as shown in figure 3.5. This can be a compatible model for both existing cities and transit-oriented development. In contrast, in outlying areas, where higher speeds are typically

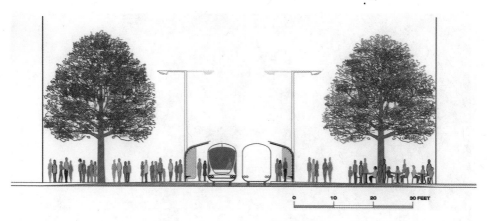

Figure 3.5
Prototypical cross-section of light rail operating on a pedestrian/transit/shopping street. Eliminating cars allows space for cafés and landscaping and allows the transit line to be well integrated with the shopping street.
Source: Roxanne Warren.

needed, so is a protected, segregated right-of-way, and there this simple model would not apply.

Light rail vehicles, as compared with streetcars, are built for more speed and power, and can travel at up to 70 mph (113 km/h) in outlying areas, while slowing to streetcar speeds when entering more densely populated areas, particularly where these are pedestrianized. This combination of light rail/streetcars and pedestrianization is popular in numerous cities in Europe and in the US as well, in the downtowns of San Diego, Sacramento, Minneapolis, Portland (Oregon), Dallas, and Houston. Dallas's light rail/pedestrian street, which forms the hub of the city's entire light rail network, is shown in figure 3.6.

Productivity in transit—not all travel time is created equal
While cost is always a concern, a cost/benefit evaluation of transit modes should factor in the *quality* of time spent on the transit vehicle. In this regard, time spent on rail is more *usable* than the time spent on buses; one can more comfortably read, write, and process work with electronic devices when riding a train or light rail. This is especially relevant for commutes and intercity travel. One study by Norwegian researchers Mattias Gripsrud and Randi Hjorthol at the Institute of Transport

Figure 3.6
The Transitway Mall in Dallas is at the heart of a $2.3 billion light rail network, whose lines all pass through this one-mile segment. The network has had an economic impact of $4 billion and has resulted in the creation of 32,000 jobs.
Sources: Craig Kuhner, photographer, and Sasaki Associates, Inc.

Economics in Oslo confirmed this to be the case. It found that, because information and communications technology have now expanded the ability to work from anywhere, train travel in particular is no longer considered "dead time," and that only one in ten work-related travelers considered their train trip to be "wasted." Gripsrud and Hjorthol's study indicated that 43 percent of business travelers worked on the train, and that their ability to do this was so reliable that half of them were able to have their train time approved as office hours. Since this study was completed in 2008, it probably understates the current prevalence of working on trains, as mobile devices have meanwhile become more powerful and pervasive.[34]

Permanence—a simple advantage of rail and other fixed guideway systems

To review: the bus and the minibus, while they are vital components of a balanced transportation system, can only adapt to, rather than influence patterns of land use. Rail systems, in contrast, should be appreciated by the public-at-large for their value over the long term in enabling the effective functioning of ecologically sustainable, compact development—in other words—*fluidly functioning cities.* As emphasized in 1977 by Pushkarev and Zupan, a primary value of fixed guideway transit is that it creates the preconditions for reversing the trend toward far-flung dispersal of development. Investments in rail should be regarded as "a downpayment on a more resource-conserving urban future."[35]

Flexibility in time, vesus flexibility in space

In addition to this essential quality of permanence, a fixed guideway system has vital operational advantages which greatly enhance its quality of service and appeal to passengers, even while making its operation more economical:

Whether manually operated or automated, a guided system has the capability of expanding and contracting its carrying capacities in response to the wide fluctuations in travel demand that normally occur during the course of a day. Thus, the vehicles can be entrained at peak hours to handle large increases in capacity without a corresponding increase in congestion or a corresponding increase in drivers; *this has been an economical practice of long standing in the operation of rail systems of all kinds, and is key to their role as the essential functional "spine" of any large city.*

This ability of rail and other fixed guideway systems, both manually driven and automated, to accommodate varying volumes of passengers as needed, and in particular their ability to absorb without congestion the high peak-hour demand, represents a *flexibility in time* rather than in space. By comparison, the bus and minibus—those systems that afford more or less unlimited *flexibility in space*—not only begin to create congestion at relatively low volumes of traffic, but are also rather rigidly limited in their peak-hour carrying capacities by the number of drivers that the system can afford to hire. The smaller the bus or minibus, the greater the problem, because of lower passenger-to-driver ratios. At the same time, when large buses (which are very destructive to roadways) must maintain their own rights-of-way, and when this expense is added into cost comparisons with fixed guideways, buses cease to be so economical.[36]

Yet another vital advantage of the fixed track or guideway is that a steady source of electrical power is provided within the guideway itself; thus it doubles as a kind of "long electrical cord," meeting the ideal criteria of cleanliness and quiet. Electric power, *generated away from the populated area*, not only satisfies these standards, it will also allow future flexibility in the choice of fuels, and a reduction of dependency upon petroleum.

Status of urban rail development

Funding priority given to non-rail modes in the US
There has been a fundamental misunderstanding in the United States about the strengths and value of passenger rail, and we have had a notorious history of underfunding it. As a result, despite a growing demand for it, our passenger rail network in the US today is shrinking, not growing. While cars, buses, and airlines have been the beneficiaries of copious, ongoing support in the form of many billions of public dollars spent on highways, parking facilities, airports, and petroleum subsidies, train travel of all kinds—intra- and intercity—has been expected to somehow be self-sustaining. The truth is that there is *no* mode of transportation, other than walking or cycling, that is self-sustaining.

Amtrak was established in 1971 as a government-owned corporation assigned to provide intercity passenger rail service in the United States. It began operations with a fleet of hand-me-down locomotives and cars, most of which were some twenty years old, and these became increasingly uneconomical to maintain as they aged. Except in the Northeast Corridor, freight railroads owned most of the track used by Amtrak and served only as a reluctant host, giving low priority to the passenger trains, although they were legally required to offer Amtrak trains top priority. This has resulted in unreliable passenger schedules—US trains are not just slow, they are late—which has discouraged their patronage.

Decades of chronic underfunding forced Amtrak to cut forty-two routes in 1996, and brought it to the brink of collapse in 1997. That year, Congress told Amtrak that it would be shut down if it did not turn a profit by 2002. The shutdown never happened, due in large part to the fact that the public began to view train travel with renewed appreciation after the terrorist attacks of September 11, 2001, had resulted in making air travel so cumbersome. As Amtrak's funding levels have improved somewhat, there has been a steady increase in train ridership since 2002.

Increases in fuel prices have hit Amtrak hard, but not as hard as the less energy-efficient modes—automobiles and aircraft. While Amtrak had received no reauthorization since 2002, this finally occurred in 2008, for a five-year period. Amtrak then received $1 billion in the American Recovery and Reinvestment Act of 2009, a a bill that also included some starter funding for high-speed rail.[37] Yet, as pointed out by Amtrak CEO Joseph Boardman in his September 2012 testimony to the US Congress, highways had received nearly 30 percent more emergency assistance in the previous four years—$53.3 billion from the general fund of the US Treasury—than the total federal expenditure on Amtrak since its inception in 1971.[38] Nevertheless, in the fiscal year that ended in September 2012, Amtrak had carried 31.2 million passengers, which was the highest annual ridership since the railroad's creation. As a result, its operating loss was the lowest in fifty years, and down 19 percent from the previous year.[39]

By 2013, Amtrak was carrying more than three times as many travelers between Washington, DC, and New York as all airplanes combined. This is especially significant in light of the fact that the New York area airports account for one-half of the nation's flight delays.[40]

While buses provide a flexible and affordable transportation option, they remain constrained by the limitation of the highway system—namely, congestion. But intercity bus systems in the US are at a great competitive cost advantage over intercity rail, because unlike rail, they do not have to construct and maintain their own rights-of-way. This has allowed the enormous growth of intercity bus travel. Private bus companies have been gaining market share from Amtrak, which is hardly surprising, since they can offer cheap travel deals, such as a $25 fare between New York and Washington, DC.

However, the resulting bus congestion, noise and pollution on city streets can be extremely disadvantageous and unpleasant for the cities. Long-distance charter buses, for example, have proliferated on the streets of Manhattan. Although the buses are not legally allowed to idle their engines in the city for more than three minutes, they often do so because of poor enforcement. Dan Biederman, president of Manhattan's 34th Street Partnership and the Bryant Park Corporation, notes that they tend to idle noisily and block pedestrians' view of street-level stores and restaurants, and that "The noise is overwhelming when you're standing within 10 or 15 feet. It's not that different from being at La Guardia [Airport]."[41]

These conditions have worsened appreciably as a result of the cancellation in October 2010 of the Access to the Region's Core (ARC) trans-Hudson rail tunnel project by New Jersey's governor. The difference that this decision will mean to the quality of life on Manhattan's streets well into the future should not be underestimated. According to calculations by New Jersey Transit, trans-Hudson commuting between New Jersey and Manhattan is expected to increase by 25 percent by the year 2030. The ARC project would have shifted 11,530 daily bus trips and 31,590 daily car trips to rail. But in light of the commuting demand, the absence of ARC is expected to cause an additional 1,230 daily buses to be packed onto Manhattan's already overcrowded streets.[42]

Granted, building new rail rapid transit in New York City poses a major funding challenge, as recent subway projects in that city have cost three or four times as much per mile as, for example, London's Jubilee Line. US union work rules are often given much of the blame. But as pointed out by former Manhattan borough president Scott Stringer, European capitals often provide similar benefits to their workers, and it may be that regulatory requirements and bureaucratic issues are the more likely culprits. Stringer also points to New York's vast and partly unknown network of public utility lines, water tunnels, gas mains, and wiring that make underground work increasingly unpredictable and costly, and notes that an accurate map of these facilities needs to be created.[43]

Growing demands for rail in the US and worldwide

New York's and New Jersey's relative paralysis in building a new trans-Hudson rail tunnel contrasts sharply with current efforts in London, where builders are tunneling a length of 13 miles (20.9 kilometers) directly under the city's intensively developed center for the eight-station, $25 billion Crossrail line—a project that has remained unaffected by Britain's extreme budget cutting.[44] Similarly, in India, the significant growth of cities is stoking a demand for public transportation, and that nation is planning to spend an estimated 960 billion rupees (US$22 billion) over the next seven years on new urban rail systems. In 2008, after winning a contract to provide New Delhi's subway operator, Montréal-based Bombardier opened a factory there.[45] And anyone who has traveled in Europe or Japan should be familiar with the excellent passenger rail systems in those countries, and the seriousness with which the importance of rail to the cities is appreciated and ongoing upgrading is undertaken.

But it is in China that the most remarkable new rail metro building program has been occurring. Rapid urban growth with sky-high commercial and residential towers is being supported by a plethora of rail rapid transit projects. With mass migration from rural to urban areas and the burgeoning population of the cities, investment in urban passenger rail in that country increased by 70 percent between 2000 and 2010, aided by a major stimulus package in 2008. And future construction that was approved by 2011 exceeded all of the passenger rail systems in North America.[46] Severely congested with cars, Beijing, at a cost of 61 billion yuan (some US$9.2 billion), opened five new suburban subway and light rail lines in December 2010. This brought the total length of metro lines in that capital city to 208 miles (336 kilometers).[47] Shanghai's metro, at 261 miles (420 km) long, is still growing and preparing the way for massive anticipated future population growth.[48] Between 2010 and 2015, twenty-eight cities in China are scheduled to build 1,554 miles (2,500 km) of subway lines at a cost of at least one trillion yuan.[49] In addition to the truly immense Chinese stimulus campaigns of 2009 and 2010, a much smaller stimulus package of around US$156 billion, focused on new subways, highways, and other infrastructure projects, was approved in September 2012, to counteract the more gradual economic slowdown of that year.[50] A network of more than 64,360 miles (40,000 km) of railway is in planning, which will ease access to and from the economic centers for China's enormously increased densities in population.[51]

After years of relative neglect, investments in infrastructure are finally being viewed by many Americans as a high priority. Frustrations with traffic, added to concerns about climate change and the high costs of gasoline, have increasingly soured the public on their long commutes by auto, and there is now a growing public demand for more and better transit.

It was noted above that the smooth ride and predictable travel time that normally characterize rail of all kinds are major reasons for its relative appeal. Thus, a free bus line into downtown Tacoma, Washington, attracted fewer than 500 riders a day, but when it was replaced with a light rail line, daily ridership increased to more than 2,400 [52] Similar phenomena have been experienced throughout the US, as new light rail lines have been built in such cities as Portland, Charlotte, Salt Lake, Denver, Phoenix, Jersey City, Dallas, Houston, and Minneapolis. Light rail had the highest rate of annual growth in ridership of all modes in 2008, with an 8.3 percent increase over the previous year.[53] Because of rail's popularity and the permanence of its tracks, these systems have proven to be enormous stimuli to development.

The growth of light rail in Los Angeles, a city famous for its car culture, has been particularly impressive. While light rail didn't even exist in that city e as recently as the late 1980s, by 2010 it was serving the third-highest number of passenger boardings in the nation, just behind Boston's light rail and San Francisco's MUNI. Los Angeles' then-mayor Antonio Villaraigosa, while also chairing the city's Metro Board, was the leading force behind this growth. Under his leadership, the city was at the cutting edge of forward thinking on transportation. In 1990, the city's light rail consisted of a single line to Long Beach but by 2012 transit service in Los Angeles had been expanded to a 106-mile (66-km) network of light rail, subways and a dedicated busway.[54] This includes the extension of the $2.4 billion light rail Exposition Line from downtown Los Angeles all the way to Santa Monica on the Pacific Ocean, for a total of 15.6 miles (25 km).[55] In 2008, the Los Angeles voters approved a half-cent sales tax increase, which is expected to garner $40 billion for transportation over the next three decades. The city's Metro organization has also been very strategic in building coalitions with real estate developers and institutions that stand to benefit from the new rail lines.[56]

New rail transit of various types has entered operation in numerous US cities, particularly across the West and Southwest in cities that were previously auto-dependent. Just in the year between 2008 and 2009, these included: an extension of New Mexico's Rail Runner commuter rail; Metro light rail in Phoenix; the Westside Express Service in Portland (the state's first commuter rail line), the new light rail MAX Green Line in Portland; in Seattle, Sound Transit's Central Link Light Rail; and the Dallas Area Rapid Transit's Green Line light rail. Two more rail lines were scheduled to open shortly thereafter: the Metro Gold Line light rail extension in Los Angeles, and the Northstar commuter rail in Minneapolis–Saint Paul. By December 2009, even in the face of the Great Recession, there were at least forty-five North American cities that were in the embryonic stages of planning for new streetcar networks, and the federal Department of Transportation was planning to make sufficient funds available to fund at least six of these projects.[57]

In June 2004, after twenty-five years of debate, the first phase of Minneapolis' 12-mile (19-km) long Hiawatha Light Rail Line was opened, connecting downtown with the Minneapolis–Saint Paul International Airport and the Mall of America in nearby Bloomington. In the first two months after its opening, ridership was actually double what had been projected, and after fourteen months of operation, was 64 percent higher than anticipated. The construction of residential condominiums has consequently flourished near its stations. The vehicles incorporate low floors, wide doors, and level platforms, making for ideal boarding/deboarding conditions.[58]

In Detroit, the original home of the US automobile industry, plans for an 8-mile (12.9-km), $450 to500 million light rail line have been reduced to a 3.3-mile (5.3-km) $140 million streetcar line. Nevertheless, and despite the city's current bankruptcy, the streetcar is to be built by a coalition of private sector philanthropists and business leaders, which has contributed more than $100 million toward its construction, and it is expected, with additional contributions from the federal, state, and local governments, to be running by late 2016.[59]

And despite its location in car-loving NASCAR country, initial public opposition, and cost overruns, a new light rail system in Charlotte, North Carolina, has turned out to be a national model for success. The city's conservative mayor lobbied relentlessly for light rail as an economic development tool, and managed to convince the electorate to tax themselves to pay for it. The light rail has outstripped ridership projections, triggering millions of dollars in high-density development. This project certainly benefited from very lucky timing—opening in November 2007, just after the decade-long real estate bubble, and just before the financial crash and 2008's record-breaking high gasoline prices.[60]

In Washington, DC, the Department of Transportation has proposed a 37-mile (60-km) new streetcar system to serve all eight of the city's wards, which will include a 22-mile (35-km) priority route between Union Station and Georgetown. Companies from the US, Spain, the UK, China, and Japan all responded to the request sent by the Department of Transportation in June 2012 for expressions of interest in the engineering, rail construction, vehicle manufacturing, operation, and financing of the system.[61]

Since the mid-1970s, the city of Portland, Oregon, has built five light rail corridors, a streetcar line, and an aerial tramway, and there are significant rail developments still to come. Prior to the decision to build the light rail lines, detailed comparisons were made with the option of buses. Four basic factors were named in favor of the choice of light rail:

• *Operating savings:* Each light rail car can carry over two hundred passengers, doing the work of four buses. Therefore, operating in two-car units, on eight-minute headways, each would do the work of eight buses, while driven by one operator. The equivalent buses, traveling at one-minute intervals, would create bus bunching, while requiring eight operators.

• *Long-range capital costs of vehicles:* Although a light rail vehicle costs far more than a bus ($4 million in 2008, as compared with $300,000 for a bus)—in doing the work of four buses, the light rail vehicle would actually save some $3.2 million in bus purchases over its thirty-year life.

This is because the bus will last only fourteen years at most, and fourteen years of inflation between bus purchases must be considered.

• *A public preference for rail* was revealed in surveys, and generally attributed to a smoother and faster rid, and to rail's permanent presence—a preference that has since been reflected in increased property values around the light rail stations.

• *Rail helps to structure/restructure the community* by creating a permanent framework to support development and a sense of "place."[62]

As succinctly stated by Lester R. Brown of the Earth Policy Institute:

A rail system provides the foundation for a city's transportation system. Rails are geographically fixed, providing a permanent means of transportation that people can count on. Once in place, the nodes on such a system become the obvious places to concentrate office buildings, high-rise apartment buildings, and shops.[63]

High-speed rail—existing worldwide, and envisioned in the US

Definition and potential

While the future of public transport *within* cities and metropolitan areas lies with a mix of metros, light rail, and buses, the future of travel *between* cities for distances of 100 to 500 miles (160 to 805 km) belongs to high-speed rail. HSR. This fact has been acknowledged in more than thirty countries around the globe (including even Mexico and Morocco) that have built, or are in the process of building new HSR lines. A high-speed train is one that is capable of reaching speeds of over 124 mph (200 km/h) on upgraded conventional track, and of at least 155 mph (250 km/h) on new track specifically designed for such speeds. By 2009, trains running on the most recently constructed lines in Europe were reaching speeds of 224 mph (360 km/h).

For trips of up to 500 miles (805 km), HSR has a clear advantage over either automobile or air travel, in terms of space, fuel consumption, air pollution, greenhouse gas generation, and usually, the time spent and costs to passengers. HSR lines also cost less per mile to build than interstate highways.[64] They are an ideal alternative to expanding airport capacity, which requires large expanses of land that is typically unavailable in and around cities. If automobile travel is inefficient in its use of space and generation of congestion, air travel is exponentially more so, and is increasingly difficult to accommodate close to dense urban areas. This is evidenced by the fact that over the past five decades, only one new green-field airport has been built in the United States—Denver International—and that was located practically in Kansas and required a land area twice the size of Manhattan.

The HSR mode has tremendous potential for reducing carbon emissions, especially considering the fact that aviation is a major consumer of petroleum. Short-haul air flights are much more energy-intensive per mile than long flights, since the great surge of energy required to get the plane up in the air is roughly the same whether the plane is traveling between Chicago and Detroit or between Chicago and Europe. Therefore, the airlines lose more money on short flights when jet fuel prices are high. It will be ideal to replace many of these flights with high-speed rail, and especially ideal where the HSR is powered with renewable energy. [65] Sweden has achieved an admirable goal climate-wise: it now powers 55 percent of its HSR entirely by renewable energy.[66]

Asian and European high-speed rail
Japan pioneered HSR in 1964 with its 340-mile (547-km) long Shinkansen bullet train from Tokyo to Osaka. Japan now has a HSR network of some 1,360 miles (2,188 km) interconnecting nearly all of its major cities. Until the tragic earthquake of March 11, 2011, these trains were routinely operating at speeds of up to 190 mph (306 km/h), safely moving hundreds of thousands of passengers every day, while measuring any delays in seconds.[67] HSR has, in many cases in Japan, as well as in Europe, nearly completely displaced short-haul air travel. In Japan, the bullet trains run as frequently as three minutes apart, with delays that average only six seconds. It is therefore possible to travel on them quite conveniently without a schedule. As high-speed trains enter the cities, they merge with existing rails and operate at conventional speeds.[68]

(Critical damage from the earthquake to Tokyo's high-speed network was averted due to the prudent installation of seismometers and anti-seismic reinforcement works, and the Tohuko Shinkansen bullet trains were able to restart operations only forty-nine days after the quake. However, many of the coastal railways and stations, together with coastal towns and their populations, were swept away completely by the tsunami that followed the quake. The towns will likely take years to rebuild.)[69]

Japan's HSR engineering skills are of a high order: the newest bullet trains on the Tokaido Sinkansen line have reduced energy consumption by some 32 percent and have improved energy efficiency by 51 percent compared with older models. China, Taiwan, and England have been adopting Tokyo's HSR technology, and it is currently being marketed to Brazil, Vietnam, and the US.[70]

And beyond high-speed rail, Japan is track-testing its new high-speed magnetic levitation (maglev) train, which is propelled by powerful magnets, and floats above its track, thereby avoiding the friction that limits the speeds of conventional trains. Designed to travel at 300 mph (500 km/h), the first maglev train is planned to run from Tokyo to Nagoya starting in 2027.[71]

By the end of 2009, Europe had 3,862 miles (6,214 km) of high-speed rail on which trains could run at speeds in excess of 155 mph (250 km/h). The European Union was working on a pan-European HSR network, which would integrate the rail networks of its various countries, improve rail safety, and allow trains to cross borders within the European Union without having to stop.[72]

Since Europe's first high-speed rail, from Paris to Lyon, was initiated in 1981, the entire continent has made enormous strides toward fulfilling this intra-continental vision. When the Paris-to-Brussels link first opened, covering 194 miles (312 kilometers) in 85 minutes, the share of those traveling by train between the two cities rose from 24 to 50 percent, and carbon-dioxide-intensive plane travel has now virtually disappeared.[73] Short-haul air service has similarly been replaced by HSR in Germany, between Cologne and Frankfurt.[74] And it is a true pleasure to travel in two and a quarter hours via the Eurostar HSR from Paris through the Chunnel to London.

France's high-speed rail network now extends some 1,240 miles (2,000 km) across the country. With a history of 30 years of successful HSR operation, the French have expressed great interest in building a similar network in Australia, linking the major cities of Sydney, Melbourne, Brisbane, and Canberra. That country should be highly suitable for high-speed rail because of its vast expanses of flat land.[75]

In Spain, the 375-mile (600-km) trip on high-speed rail between Madrid and Barcelona takes only 2 hours and 38 minutes, and, at only $60 for a round trip, has lured away nearly 50 percent of air travelers on that route. The trains (figure 3.7) maintain a 99 percent on-time record, and passengers are offered a full cash refund if the train is more than five minutes late. The high-speed rail system, AVE (Alta Velocidad Española), which also happens to spell "bird" in Spanish, is comprised of four major routes, and there are plans to build another 6,213 miles (9,940 km) of high-speed track before 2020.[76] Spain's HSR system is expected to become one of the world's most comprehensive, with 90 percent of the country's population living within 31 miles (50 km) of a station by 2020. Rider enthusiasm and economic development have followed wherever it has been built.[77]

In China, with the massive job layoffs that had occurred with the 2008 global economic downturn, construction of high-speed rail was used as a highly effective stimulus project. Some 110,000 laborers were swiftly mobilized to build the 820-mile (1,319-km) route between Beijing and Shanghai. This opened in June 2011, with trains running at nearly 200 mph (320 km/h), cutting travel time between the two cities from twelve to five hours. Huge high-speed rail stations were built in industrial districts on the outskirts of the cities, which passengers can reach from the city centers by subway or bus.[78]

Included in China's HSR network are two new bullet trains between Beijing and the cities of Chengdu and Chongqing in southwestern China. These lines are seen as an integral part of bringing moderate prosperity to the west China regions that are home to much of the country's poor population. Tickets for second-class soft seats on these trains were reported to have been sold out within several hours of the lines' openings.[79]

China has now resumed its rapid construction of one of the world's most ambitious high-speed rail projects—a network that will span the country, consisting of four north/south routes and four east/west routes. Work commenced in December 2012 on one of these routes, from Beijing to Guangzhou, roughly 1,200 miles (1,930 km), which will be traversed by HSR in only eight hours.[80] The target is for China to have established, by 2015, a high-speed rail network that will cover almost all of that nation's cities with a population of more than half a million. It is also intended that much of China's passenger rail travel be moved onto high-speed rail by 2020, in order to free existing passenger tracks for freight. But speed in construction has taken a toll. A tragic crash of

Figure 3.7
Velaro high-speed rail—vehicles that run at 230 mph (368 km/h) between Madrid and Barcelona on the intra-continental European network.
Source: Siemens Transportation Systems.

two Chinese bullet trains occurred in July 2011 in the eastern city of Wenzhou, killing 50 people and injuring 191, when the signaling system was struck by lightning, sending one high-speed train smashing into the rear end of another on a viaduct.[81] This evoked a flood of criticism and some a serious reassessment of the speed of Chinese high-speed rail development and operations, in particular, the reliability of their signaling systems, which had already been sold to more than twenty countries, including Pakistan, North Korea, Iran, and Zambia.[82] Additionally, both Chinese and foreign engineers have questioned the long-term strength of the concrete that was used in Chinese HSR bridges and viaducts under contracts that were awarded through a subsequently-dismissed rail minister. There was also anger expressed among the Chinese public over the high fares on the high-speed rail lines. Under a remedial plan, the Railway Ministry consequently lowered top speeds on many routes from 217 to 186 mph (350 to 300 km/h), to address safety concerns, while saving on electricity costs and allowing some reductions in fares.[83]

Even the oil-rich nation of Saudi Arabia has been constructing high-speed rail. The first phase of a 276-mile (444-km) long Haramain line connecting Mecca and Madinah with Jeddah was started in 2009, with a consortium of Chinese and Saudi companies. The track will be furnished with trains capable of running at 224 mph (360 km/h).[84] Work on the second phase, to be built by a consortium of Spanish and Saudi companies, was expected to continue throughout 2014. Travel time between Mecca and Madinah is projected to be cut to two hours.[85] These rail lines will, in three or four years, be part of what is being planned as one of the most extensive rail networks in the world, consisting of 4,351 miles (7,000 km), and rivaling grids in such advanced countries as Spain, France, and Germany.[86]

In Mexico, the federal government and officials from the central state of Queretaro have signed an agreement to build a 124-mile (200 km)-long high-speed rail line between Mexico City and Queretaro, which will operate at speeds up to 112 mph (180 km/h). The project is expected to cost between $1.95 and $2.5 billion, and to be funded by federal and state governments.[87] And in Turkey, the government is initiating a high-speed rail line between Ankara and the Asian side of Istanbul, eventually to link to Europe.[88]

High-speed rail progress in the US

The United States currently has just one "high-speed" train: Acela Express, which connects Boston, New York, Philadelphia, and Washington, DC. The Acela vehicles operate much more slowly than their maximum speed on most of the Northeast Corridor, because of the limitations of tracks and tunnels. Therefore, neither its speed, averaging only a sluggish 70 mph (112 km/h)—half that of the Paris-to-Lyon HSR—nor its reliability come even close to those of high-speed rail systems in Europe or the Far East. Nevertheless, Acela is currently running at a 60 percent profit—that is, it is making 160 percent of its operating costs.[89]

Moreover, high-speed rail has the *potential* to ultimately replace at least one-third of all US air travel. Eleven multi-city regions in the US have been designated by the Federal Railroad Administration as suitable for the building of high-speed rail corridors, shown in figure 3.7. These potential corridors represent a tremendous market; already, nearly three-quarters of the US population now lives in these "mega-regions," and the great majority of the anticipated 130 million people who will be added to the population by 2050 will live in these areas. The mega-regions range in diameter between 200 and 600 miles (322 and 965 km), sizes that make them uniquely well-suited to high-speed rail infrastructure, which can serve to knit the mega-regions together.[90]

An 84-mile (135 km) route in Florida linking Tampa and Orlando was selected for the nation's first HSR line because of its relative simplicity and projected speed of construction. However, the funds that had been allocated to it were turned down in 2011 by the state's newly elected governor, and the HSR funds and attention have since been shifted to the Northeast Corridor and California.

The US Northeast Corridor, which encompasses Boston, New York, Philadelphia, Baltimore, and Washington, DC, is an obvious candidate for high-speed rail. This "Bos-Wash" megaregion is home to more than fifty million people and generates more than two trillion dollars in economic activity. The corridor possesses well-developed, albeit, underfunded, local networks of rail transportation, and these networks, together with existing bus networks, could well serve to convey passengers to higher-speed rail. Amtrak's Northeast Corridor line already accounts for more than a third of total Amtrak ridership and is virtually the only

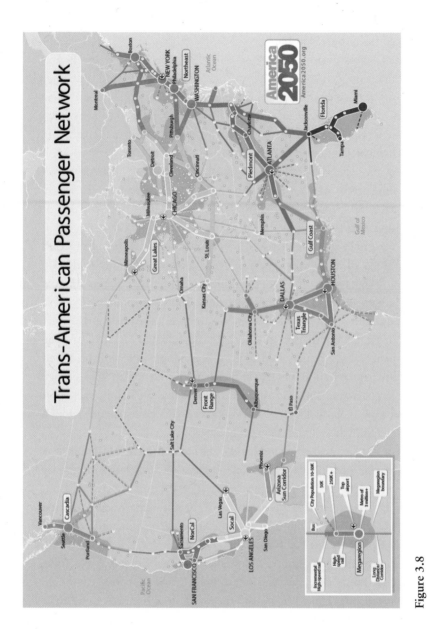

Figure 3.8
Eleven urban corridors in the United States that have been designated as potential candidates for high-speed rail. Already, nearly three-quarters of the US population lives in these "megaregions."
Source: Regional Plan Association.

portion of Amtrak's system that makes a profit.[91] Plans are for the Northeast Corridor to be incrementally converted to higher-speed rail.

There is in any case a pressing need for high-speed rail in the Northeast Corridor because of increasing congestion at its airports. In particular, the three airports serving New York City have a record of creating the country's worst flight delays. Because New York is a central travel hub, these delays ripple out all around the nation. A similar case exists in Chicago, also a major travel hub. High-s[eed rail could greatly alleviate these conditions.

The most ambitious of the US high-speed rail proposals is for a 790-mile (1,271-kilometer) route in California, for which speeds of 220 mph (354 km/h) are envisioned, comparable to those of the European, Japanese, and Chinese HSR lines. The California line will connect Sacramento, San Francisco, Los Angeles, and San Diego, and is said to have by far the largest market potential of all the US high-speed rail proposals. In the summer 2012, the California legislature approved the release of the first installment of funding for the HSR, and ground breaking for the first 30-mile (48-km) segment between Fresno and Madera was scheduled for 2013. While the investment will be very large, it will be cheaper than accommodating California's projected growth in travel demand with more air service and highways, which are already near saturation. While the state's population was around thirty-four million in 2000, it is forecast to swell to some fifty million by 2032, and to nearly sixty million by 2050.[92]

Another ambitious plan for high-speed rail that was proposed back in 1991 in Texas would have linked Houston, Dallas–Fort Worth, and San Antonio; however, it was defeated three years later by opposition from the competing airlines.[93] Now a new entity, the Texas Central High-Speed Railway, hopes to run a bullet train between Dallas and Houston, and to do this with private funding and no subsidies. The area is largely rural and flat, and therefore favorable from a geographical standpoint. But because it lacks an extensive *local* public transit system, passengers' *access* to the HSR stations could be a real problem. The company was, in March 2014, still in the early process of securing funding, engineering analysis, and environmental studies.[94]

Unfortunately, construction of high-speed rail in the US is likely to be far slower than hoped for, unless there is a much more serious and reliable financial commitment than there is at present. While wish lists for federal HSR grants in 2009 totaled some $102 billion, this was more than twelve times the $8 billion that was made available in that year's stimulus package. California's high-speed corridor alone is projected to cost $52 billion, and it was estimated by the Passenger Rail Working Group, a coalition of state transportation and railroad officials, that a national system, encompassing only ten of the eleven designated regional corridors, would cost some $357 billion in 2007 dollars.[95]

In any country, land acquisition is the most difficult part of building high-speed rail lines, because the tracks need to be as straight as possible. In addition, in order for high-speed rail in the US to reach the European standard of 220 mph (354 km/h), it will need to meet at least six challenging requirements:

• Completely new double-track corridors, with crossties made of concrete, rather than timber,

• Wider ROWs, with protected track running in trenches or on embankments,

• Long straightaways with limited curves,

• Grade-separated bridges to replace road crossings,

• Overhead electrical wires to power new, lighter locomotives—lighter than the Federal Railroad Administration currently allows, and

• Positive Train Control—wireless communications systems to automatically slow or stop trains.[96]

There is no shortage of international expertise for the US to call upon for assistance in meeting these requirements. China, whose Ministry of Railways has committed to spending about $300 billion in constructing that country's transportation systems through 2020, has been offering to not only build high-speed rail in California, but also to help finance its construction.[97] The Chinese have also expressed their willingness to comply with all US laws and regulations. And other countries have expressed interest in selling high-speed rail equipment to the US: they include Germany, Japan, France, Spain, Italy, and South Korea.[98]

Yet the US commitment to the completion of these ambitious projects is subject to the shifting US political tides. Immediately after the November 2010 elections, successful candidates who opposed high-speed rail threatened to deprive the California project of funds; three years later, they continued, as a block, to prevail.[99] And support for HSR projects in Wisconsin and Ohio, as well as in Florida, evaporated when the governorships of those states changed political parties. (Subsequently, at least two-dozen other states applied to receive the rejected funds for their own high-speed rail projects, and twenty-eight states have continued with their HSR plans.)

Federal funding for US high-speed rail has proven particularly controversial for lawmakers coming from those areas lacking urban corridors that are already high-density and economically active. Building on a review of international experience, a group of transportation experts at the Mineta Transportation Institute at San José State University has recommended that the funding of high-speed rail be skewed heavily toward state bonds that would be guaranteed by the federal government. By ensuring that the states that benefit directly from the HSR projects pay most of these costs, this plan could make it more palatable to the dominantly rural and suburban states. Detailed negotiations would of course be required for projects that span multiple states.[100]

While the concept of high-speed rail has captured the imaginations of much of the public and the popular press, it should not be forgotten that, in order for sufficient numbers of passengers to easily access the HSR stations, these trains will need to be matched with transit-oriented and transit joint development, as well as with local and intra-regional transit systems that are appreciably upgraded and far better patronized than they are at present in the United States. Otherwise, the use of HSR will depend on access to its stations by private car and by a vast surround of car parking facilities, rather than urban development. This would be a waste of the economic potential of this remarkable mode.

As observed by Cervero, "If land use is simply an afterthought ... the added infrastructure will be a force toward more decentralized growth ... which in America equates to sprawl. Such infrastructure simply adds a new layer of accessibility to far-flung places, which, absent regulatory controls, unleashes new layers of sprawl."[101] Again, the transportation choices circle back to public preferences regarding the character of land use, since land use follows transportation access like the night the day.

Automation in transit of various types

There is a general consensus among planners that transit service frequencies of a minimum of ten minutes are needed to support a transit-oriented community lifestyle.[102] In fact, frequent service is commonly more important to transit riders than the actual speed of the vehicle. And the headways between vehicles can be dramatically reduced through automation. Once a system is automated and driverless, its trains can be broken up into smaller, much more frequently available units, supplying the same passenger capacity and greatly improving service without a corresponding increase in operating costs.[103] Thus, while driverless systems are relatively capital-intensive, their operating costs can be appreciably reduced, which can allow very short headways between vehicles, and around-the-clock service.

The invention of individually programmed automated guideway transit (AGT) systems commenced in the early 1960s, having sprung from the ongoing evolution of computer technology. Electronic intelligence is fundamental to the control of the speed and spacing between vehicles, their scheduling and dispatching, and their distribution onto alternate routes and spur lines, where these exist, techniques that have been found to be truly transformative. Automatic train control has been very successfully incorporated in many metro lines worldwide, including those in Paris, New York, São Paulo, Barcelona, Guangzhou, Budapest, Nürnberg, and Algiers.

The VAL system in Lille, France, was the world's first primarily *elevated* AGT metro (figures 3.9–3.10). It began passenger service in 1983 and has undergone several expansions. It connects sixty stations today and reaches from Lille north toward the Belgian border. Because of its complete automation, it has run at a profit since 1989.[104]

Several existing automated rail lines on elevated guideways consist primarily of light rail elements, while having fully separated rights-of-way. While their vehicles are basically of the light rail type, they take advantage of many features of rapid transit (metros), including full signalization, level boarding, and high maximum running speeds. This "mini–rapid transit" mode is used where high performance is required, but where passenger volumes are insufficiently high to justify long trains and large stations. These lines are defined as Light Rail Rapid Transit

Figure 3.9
The VAL system in Lille, France, was the world's first automated guideway transit (AGT) metro. It began passenger service in 1983, and has undergone several expansions. Today it connects sixty stations, and reaches from Lille north toward the Belgian border. The system has been significantly enhanced for both urban and airport applications and to adapt to new green environmental standards. It has run at a profit since 1989.
Source: Siemens SAS.

(LRRT)—examples are the Vancouver Skytrain (figure 3.11), the Copenhagen mini-metro, the London Docklands line, the JFK Airport Line in New York, the Norristown line in Philadelphia, Line 8 in Gothenburg, the Kuala Lumpur Metro, and the Manila Metro.[105]

Automated people movers (APMs) and AGTs serve two basically different roles. A third type, the downtown people mover (DPM), was built in the 1970s in three US cities.

• APMs are used on short lines as shuttles or loops, often likened to "horizontal elevators" (figure 3.12). They far outnumber AGTs in their application, and have established a solid niche at airports, where they have been found to meet the critical on-time demands for interflight connections. They are also operating successfully at fairgrounds, university campuses, gambling casinos, and major urban activity centers. Their vehicle capacities range up to one hundred passengers, and the vehicles operate either as single units or entrained, at speeds up to 30 mph (48

Figure 3.10
The ultimate in safety: the stations of the VAL system have platform-edge glass walls and automatically opening sliding glass doors that are synchronized with the operation of the train doors.
Source: Roxanne Warren.

km/h), and at headways between 15 seconds and 1 minute. They can be either self-propelled or, for distances up to 4,000 feet (1,220 m), more simply cable-drawn. The first APM installation at a major US airport was at Tampa International Airport in 1971; today there are close to fifty APMs operating at airports around the world.[106]

• AGTs are used on regular transit lines in cities as "driverless metros." Examples, as noted above, are the Lille VAL system (figures 3.9–3.10), systems in Taipei, Copenhagen, São Paulo, Toulouse, Rennes, Turin, Kuala Lumpur, Osaka, Yokohama, the Kobe New Transit system, and systems in other Japanese cities. A similar system of 20 miles (32 km) and twenty-one stations has been planned for downtown Honolulu.

• DPMs, which were built in Miami, Detroit (figure 3.13), and Jacksonville, Florida, in response to a 1975 federal initiative, represent an overlap between the functions of AGTs and APMs, in that their routes are more elaborate than simple shuttles or loops. Their capital costs were unexpectedly high, due to the complexity of installing elevated lines within existing city centers.[107]

Figure 3.11
Light rail rapid transit is exemplified by Vancouver's Skytrain, which began service in 1986. It is fully automated on completely separated ROWs, and is used on routes where high performance is required, but passenger volumes are not high enough to justify long trains and large stations. The Skytrain's automated operation has proven extremely economical. Its three branches cover almost 60 miles (96 km) and connect nearly sixty stations.
Source: Bombardier Transport International.

Most APM, AGT, and DPM systems in passenger service today operate with online stations. Other automated systems have been conceived and realized in pilot form, for more extensive, area-wide networks—dubbed personal rapid transit, or PRT. Proponents of PRT envision that large fleets of small vehicles would carry individuals or groups of up to six seated passengers on non-stop trips from origin to destination over grid-like networks. It is fundamental to the PRT concept that these networks would ultimately be constructed throughout extensive portions of urban areas. Lines perpendicular to each other would be at different elevations, with interconnecting ramps. The stations of such a system would invariably be off-line (allowing other vehicles to bypass those waiting) and sufficiently numerous to offer a kind of personalized convenience that would aim to be truly competitive with the automobile.

Figure 3.12
An automated people mover (APM) designed by Otis Elevator, operated as a kind of horizontal elevator at Duke University Medical Center in North Carolina from 1979 to 2009. Its vehicles were propelled by linear induction motor, suspended on a bed of compressed air, and could move sideways as well as conventionally. *Source*: Roxanne Warren.

A 3.6-mile (5.8-km) automated transit system with medium-size vehicles and relatively low capacities has been serving five stations of a university campus in Morgantown, West Virginia, with no serious accidents since 1975, when it was launched as group rapid transit (GRT). It is frequently claimed by PRT advocates that Morgantown is a PRT system; however, while it operates on similar principles, its vehicles are too large and heavy, with eight seated and thirteen standing passengers, and its stations too few, to meet this definition.

A 2-mile (3.2-km), three-station PRT pilot project opened at London's Heathrow Airport in the summer of 2011, the first such system to go into public operation. The twenty-one Heathrow vehicles can each carry four adults and two children, plus luggage, and are battery operated. The system links one station in Terminal 5 to two remote stations in the

Figure 3.13
Detroit's downtown people mover (DPM) brings passengers directly into the Millender Center. This 2.9-mile (4.7-km) single-track loop has thirteen stations in Detroit's central business district.
Source: Trans 21.

Business car park.[108] That same year, the Swedish Transport Administration was in the process of negotiating with three Swedish candidate cities for co-funding a PRT pilot project. While this pilot has been indefinitely postponed, the governments of these cities have retained a lively interest in the concept and meet monthly to discuss it, as well as the possibilities for using PRT as feeder systems to and from high-speed rail.[109]

In 2013, the government of Uppsala, Sweden, was seriously considering building a 4-mile (6.3-km) single guideway PRT with fourteen stations and sixty vehicles, estimated to cost 445 million krona (US$68.5 million).[110] By 2014, this was still being postponed. In Suncheon, South Korea, a 2.9-mile (4.6-kilometer) PRT had gone into passenger operation in fall 2013.[111] There was also continued interest in PRT in Delhi, India's capital, and in Masdar City, a new development on the outskirts of Abu Dhabi, capital of the United Arab Emirates.[112]

However, whatever the potential of PRT may be as a local connector or feeder system to longer-distance, higher-capacity carriers, this concept as an area-wide system has been deemed operationally and economically unfeasible, since it would provide only very low capacities, while requiring an elaborate and costly infrastructure, with very large off-line stations—all elevated.[113] In attempting to emulate the level of personal service afforded by the private automobile, PRT might in fact be repeating some of its worst *disadvantages*, and at an elevated level, at that.

In a 1975 report—still pertinent—by the congressional Office of Technology Assessment (OTA), basic questions were raised about the long-term desirability of large urban PRT systems, in light of the inefficiencies of small vehicles in the use of energy, raw materials, and space, and in terms of the costs and aesthetic impact of extensive networks of guideways, which, when added to the existing street system, could be seen as constituting a "double set of roadways."[114] It was observed by some of the OTA panel members that there appeared to be no reason why PRT vehicles would be any smaller, lighter, or (with their expected low average loading) any more energy-efficient than small cars and vans, which can, after all, use the already-existing and even finer-grained network of roads at grade, instead of requiring a guideway, stations, and centralized control.[115] In this respect, the PRT concept was described by another critic as "inherently self-contradictory," in that it would combine small vehicles, which are of an optimum size for dispersed travel, with expensive fixed facilities, which are economically viable only along densely traveled corridors.[116] The fact that empty vehicles would need to be shuttled back to stations where they are in highest demand at peak hours also suggests the compounding of energy expenditures.

PRT vehicle designs—small, aerodynamic pods—have a distinct aesthetic appeal that has managed to attract the attention of the public and even some transit authorities from time to time since the early 1970s. However, as commented by Vuchic: "The popular view that the solution to present-day urban transportation problems lies in new technology is for the most part incorrect, because these problems have been created by incorrect policies rather than by inadequate technologies."[117]

PRT has been conceived as an overlay on the existing automobile-based transportation system, an accommodation to prevailing patterns of low-density suburbanization. Whether an overhead network of PRT guideways and stations, even if the guideways are relatively slim, would be welcome in low-density suburbs is another question. PRT has also been based on the unproven premise that people are unwilling to take public transit with strangers. If that were indeed the case, then ordinary elevators would also need to be programmed to carry only one person, or one small, private group at a time. This supposition is out of sync with the realities of a future in which, as inhabitants of a more crowded Planet Earth, we will be needing to learn to *share* our resources and spaces.

A key issue—automated transit's lack of relationship to the urban street
In fact, modern, thoroughly updated incarnations of what worked so beautifully in the early twentieth century could be judiciously inserted into our current urban environment. It is the premise of this book that extensive networks of a variety of forms of passenger rail should be developed to ultimately form ideal multiple spines of public transportation infrastructure for our current and future cities and their surrounds. Walking, cycling, and small, flexible vehicles, as well as local streetcar and bus systems, and even APMs and AGTs, could serve as important feeder modes to the rail stations. Automation is invaluable for the safety and greater frequency of metros and longer-distance rail. Urbanistically, however, as already noted, the clear *disad*vantage with the automated modes as local feeder systems is that they must be either elevated, tunneled, or securely fenced off, and cannot, therefore, be easily physically integrated within the urban street or neighborhood. For this reason, local systems may, in fact, be better socially-oriented for the urban street because of their personal, manual operation.

It is thought provoking that, despite the financial success of the VAL automated transit guideway system, the French have not repeated this experience with most of their subsequent metros but, with an eye toward revitalizing their cities, chose to commit to on-street light rail trams and mini-metros instead—frequently running them in pedestrian-only streets. That is, as a priority, *the French city planners instead chose to return their urban streets to pedestrians and manually operated public transport, and, at the same time, to reduce the role of the car.*

Thus in the cities where light rail has been inserted, private motoring has been diminished. In contrast, in Lille, with the introduction of AGT on elevated guideways, the cars have retained their dominance of the street. This is the case with all of the automated guideway systems described above. And *the choice between these two very different approaches is a critical choice for the transportation planning and urban design of our cities.*

4

Easing Access to Rail

With our already widely dispersed development in the United States, how convenient and even relevant can networks of public transport be made for significant numbers of suburban residents? And can the issues of access to transit stations that were cited in chapters 1 and 2—including the dominance of the space around rail stations by park-and-ride lots—be effectively resolved?

Despite resurgent trends toward urban living and the increased use of transit, it is estimated that there are still only six million US households living near rail transit stations, or about 2 percent of the country's total population.[1] Even if, as some have predicted, this figure rises to 5 percent by 2030, there may still be a large percentage of the population living far enough from transit of any kind that their mobility will remain largely reliant on private motoring. How can transit in general, and rail transportation in particular, be made relevant to more of these people, and thus be recognized as a national priority meriting substantial public funding?

Need for alternatives to car-park-and-ride

Congestion, pollution, and the competition for space around stations
The most obvious means of station access from our currently spread-out and auto-dependent development would seem to be driving, and indeed this is the most common. There are of course the obvious options of feeder buses and minibuses for access to longer-distance transit. However, these are far from ideal, as they may be slow and unpredictable in their timing, and may consume a great deal of space and generate considerable pollution at drop-off and pick-up points close to the transit station. They

are also expensive to operate at frequent levels of service, particularly when they are only lightly patronized, as they are in most US suburbs and cities.

Given the sizable dimensions of most US automobiles, neither are they the most favorable mode for this function. A major deterrent to transit ridership on systems that rely primarily on car-park-and-ride lots is the inconvenience and tension inherent in traffic bottlenecks at the stations, particularly when transit schedules must be met. Studies have found that travelers consider time spent in these access activities at least twice as noxious as time spent in the transit vehicle itself, and that furthermore, if a car is necessary on one end of the trip, and free or affordable parking is available on the other end, they will instead typically decide to drive all the way, even where heavy traffic is anticipated.[2]

Nor are car-park-and-ride facilities very helpful against pollution or climate change. For example, in examining the greater Washington, DC, area, metropolitan Toronto, and the San Francisco Bay area, Cervero, Ferrell, and Murphy found that the automobile accounted for some 60 to 80 percent of access trips to suburban rail stations. They noted that little improvement in air quality was gained from the use of transit when people used their cars to reach the stations. This is because the polluting emissions from cold starts are high—so that the total emissions from a short access trip are nearly as significant as those from a 10-mile (16-kilometer) solo commute. Additionally, they found that, because of pollution, noise levels, and traffic snarls, a decline in residential property values typically occurs within the immediate impact zone—some 800 feet, or 244 meters of a rail station's park-and-ride lot.[3] Pollution, noise, and traffic certainly decrease a station area's desirability for transit-orented development as well.

It is also true that as long as there continue to be high ratios of access by park-and-ride lots, *the practical capacities of transit systems will be effectively limited by the sizes of their parking facilities*. For example, all across the suburbs of New York City, there are long waiting periods for reserved spaces in park-and-ride lots at the train stations. Waiting lists are for more than four years in Darien, Connecticut, and for as many as eight to ten years in Rye, New York.[4] At New Jersey's Princeton Junction, some lots have waiting lists for up to eight years. In Rowayton,

Connecticut, the annual parking permit sale is an epic frenzy, with residents camping out overnight to ensure they get a $325 parking permit. The privileged few will often keep permits within the family, passing them down to their children when they die.[5] Even with the Great Recession of 2008 resulting in job losses among commuters, many were unwilling to give up their parking permits, and were looking instead to rent out their spaces. The unlucky commuters on long waiting lists simply resorted to driving into New York City's awesome traffic.

Reducing the scale, environmental impact, and costs of access to transit
Thus, it seems clear that, to obtain the maximum benefit from costly rail investments—in both increased ridership and acceptance by surrounding communities—*both the scale and environmental impact, as well as the costs of access modes to transit will need to be reduced. Specifically, the possibilities for safe walking and cycling to transit in the United States will need to be expanded.* Not incidentally, while a typical car in the US emits nearly a pound of carbon dioxide per mile driven (282 grams per kilometer), a bicycle of course emits nothing, which makes it an obvious mode for reducing greenhouse gases and other air pollutants.[6] Furthermore, the bicycle is, like the automobile, not only a freedom-enhancing kind of vehicle, but as noted in chapter 3, it is walking and cycling that are the only transportation modes that are financially self-sustaining. It therefore makes *perfect economic, as well as spatial and environmental sense* to encourage both walking and cycling for access to a framework of public transportation infrastructure. Lessons can be drawn from several countries in northern Europe, as well as Japan, where this has been substantially achieved.

It has been emphasized in regard to transit-oriented development that walking to transit should receive the very highest priority of any means of station access, since walking entails the smallest ecological footprint of any travel mode, and involves no need to park or transfer between modes. Additionally—given the bicycle's ability to speedily cover far more territory than walking, and the fact that a bicycle requires less than one-tenth of the parking space needed for a medium-sized car—cycling should also be respected as an important potential mode of access to and from transit stations, and accordingly provided with safe routes to transit stations and secure bike parking facilities there.

Potential for safer walking and cycling networks in the United States

Appropriate distances and pathways

Professor John Pucher and Dr. Lewis Dijkstra have pointed out that this is particularly relevant for the United States. This is because the spread-out land use patterns of our urban areas have led to average trip distances that, for comparison, are approximately twice as long as they typically are in Europe. And while ultimately developing more compact and transit-oriented development is a highly desirable option, it is a long-term approach. In reality, 41 percent of all urban trips in the US already *are* shorter than 2 miles (3.2 kilometers) in length, and 28 percent are shorter than 1 mile (1.6 kilometers).[7] According to the Nationwide Personal Transportation Survey, "50 percent of the working population commutes only 5 miles (8 km) or less to work ... [however] more than 82 percent of trips five miles or less are currently made by personal motor vehicle."[8]

So the potential for access to transit and to other local destinations by cycling, as well as by walking, already exists in the US, and the exceptionally low percentages of trips made by cycling and walking cannot be attributed primarily to longer trip distances. In fact, if this were the case, one would expect more trips by cycling than by walking. But the reverse is true—less than one percent of the nation's trips are made by cycling, while 6 percent are made by walking. Rather, there are two very obvious key reasons for the low figure for cycling in the United States: the current lack of safe cycling routes, and the ease of owning and operating a car. Driving is made almost irresistible by the fact that US gasoline and other auto-related taxes are among the lowest in the developed world, and by the fact that up to 95 percent of all parking in the US is free.

This is a lost opportunity, since cycling can extend the catchment area of a transit station far beyond walking range, and at a much lower cost than cars or feeder buses. Lester Brown of the Earth Policy Institute has observed that:

Few methods of reducing carbon emissions are as effective as substituting a bicycle for a car on short trips. A bicycle is a marvel of engineering efficiency, one where an investment in 22 pounds of metal and rubber boosts the efficiency of individual mobility by a factor of three. On my bike I estimate that I get easily

7 miles per potato. An automobile, which requires at least a ton of material to transport one person, is extraordinarily inefficient by comparison.[9]

Pucher and Dijkstra have emphasized that the major deterrent to pedestrians and cyclists in the US is that our "auto-dependent transportation system and land use patterns ... make walking and cycling dangerous, inconvenient, unpleasant, and in some cases, impossible." They detail how the numbers of fatal accidents contrast among countries:

> ... non-motorist fatality rates in the USA are much higher than in the Netherlands and Germany. Per-km and per-trip walked, American pedestrians are roughly three times more likely to get killed as German pedestrians, and over six times more likely to get killed as Dutch pedestrians. Per-km and per-trip cycled, American bicyclists are twice as likely to get killed as German cyclists and over three times as likely to get killed as Dutch cyclists.[10]

The authors also point out that improving the conditions for walking and cycling in the US would allow millions of Americans—many of whom are dangerously overweight—to obtain healthful exercise as a matter of daily habit. They note that in the year 2000 estimates of obesity based on clinical measurements of height and weight indicated that 30 percent of US adults were obese, and 64 percent were overweight.[11] This has grave implications for the nation's health care and its costs for such ailments as heart disease and diabetes, well into the future.

Similarly, it has been remarked by *Washington Post* columnist and author Neal Peirce that in 1969, 50 percent of US children walked to school, but that by 2004, coincident with the rise of childhood obesity, that figure had declined by 14 percent. Peirce notes that much of the blame lies with local planning that provides "thin if nonexistent sidewalks, dangerous-to-cross highways, and sprawling development."[12]

A daily commute by bicycle can be a simple and highly appropriate contribution to health for a sedentary city-dweller—something like a half-hour of moderate physical activity five days a week to keep fit—exactly the recommendation of public health authorities in several countries.

And not to be dismissed is the fact that the bicycle can provide affordable mobility to low-income individuals; its initial cost and operating costs are minute compared with those of an automobile. Once wildly popular as a pleasure mode before the turn of the twentieth century, there is now the potential for bicycles to re-emerge as a simultaneous solution to many of our current problems.

Safety in numbers

As early as 1949, research by R. J. Smeed on drivers' safety showed that the risk of accidents *per motor vehicle* was lower in countries where drivers were more numerous. Similarly, more recent work in 2003 by public health researcher Peter L. Jacobsen documented how the risks *per cyclist or pedestrian* are substantially lower in cities where a higher percentage of the population cycles or walks on a regular basis. Therefore, concluded Jacobsen, the very best way to improve the safety of cyclists— much more important than mandating the wearing of helmets, which he believes can often actually work as a *deterrent* to cycling—is to encourage more people to regularly travel by bike.[13] Greater safety in numbers for cyclists and pedestrians has, in fact, been occurring in many cities worldwide, as the cycling and pedestrian populations in these cities have increased.

Jacobsen found an inverse relationship between the number of cyclists in a city and the number of crashes with automobiles: the fewer the cyclists, the more crashes, and the more cyclists, the fewer the crashes. The relevant question is why this occurs. Adaptation in the behavior of motorists seems to be the most plausible answer. *When there are many cyclists on the street, drivers become more attentive, slow down, and, sensing that the street has become a more complicated place, adjust their behavior accordingly.*[14] The same can be said about pedestrians.

This is not to underestimate the critical role of developing more appropriate cycling and pedestrian infrastructure in the first place.

Low percentages of cycling in North America

Research by Pucher and Dr. Ralph Buehler, completed in 2011, reviewed trends in cycling levels, safety, and policies over the previous two decades in the US and Canada, focusing on nine large North American cities—Portland (Oregon), Minneapolis, Vancouver, San Francisco, Montréal, Washington, Toronto, Chicago, and New York. They found that, although cycling rates in the US rose by 64 percent between 1990 and 2009, as a share of *total* commuters they rose from only 0.4 to 0.6

percent of total trips by all modes. (In light of the remarkable potential for cycling, this very low cycling share can only be deplored.) Canada has done only marginally better in its portion of cycling commuters: over the decade from 1996 to 2006, the number of cyclists in Canada increased by 42 percent, but as a share of total commuters increased from only 1.1 to 1.3 percent. Low percentages of cyclists have persisted in most of the cities studied, but are growing with the implementation of a wide range of efforts to increase cycling and promote its safety—such as expanded bike lanes and paths, bike parking facilities, traffic calming, bike sharing, bike-transit integration, and bike training programs. The numbers are far lower in cities such as Dallas, Houston, Detroit, and Kansas City, where municipal efforts to promote cycling have not even been undertaken; so they were explicitly excluded from the study.[15]

Pucher and Buehler found that climate does not appear to be a serious obstacle to increasing cycling, as proven by high numbers of cyclists in Portland and Vancouver, with their rainy weather, and in Montréal and Minneapolis, with their very long and cold winters. However, special challenges appear to discourage cycling in very large cities—in particular, high-density traffic, with its dangers and high levels of noise and pollution. More extensive public transit systems in the larger cities also provide a viable alternative to both driving and cycling. Thus, despite major initiatives to promote cycling, the largest cities in this study, New York and Chicago, showed the lowest percentages of cyclists of all the cities studied—only 0.6 and 1.2 percent of total trips, respectively. (Similarly, the two largest cities in Europe—London and Paris—also have relatively low percentages of cyclists of 1.6 and 2.5 percent, respectively.) [16]

All nine cities in the Pucher and Buehler study have concentrated their efforts on expanding their bike lanes and bike paths. The research concluded that even car-dependent US cities can greatly increase cycling by employing an integrated package of infrastructure, programs, and policies. Portland has provided the most dramatic example of this. That city's commuting bike share rose more than fivefold between 1990 and 2009, from 1.1 to 5.8 percent—the highest rate of any large North American city. Cycling rates have risen much faster in the nine case study cities than in their countries as a whole, more than doubling in all of these cities

since 1990. This is not surprising, given the fact that the relative compactness of cities makes for shorter traveling distances, which are therefore
more appropriate for cycling. By the same token, all nine cities show
much higher cycling rates in the cities themselves than in their suburbs
and metropolitan areas, and higher rates in the centers of the cities
than in their outlying districts. Portland's bike mode share in its Inner
Northeast and Inner Southeast districts is actually as high as 13 percent—
which is comparable to some of the cycling mode shares in northern
Europe.[17]

Of the nine cities in this study, New York came out with the very worst
scores in nearly every respect—the highest rates of cyclist fatalities and
injuries, the lowest percentages of cyclists commuting, the lowest number
of bike parking facilities per capita and integration with transit, and the
lowest rate of cycling by women, children, and seniors. However, of the
nine cities examined, New York was also by far the largest, and all of
these comparisons were made *relative to the size of the population*, which
in New York is some 8.4 million. Clearly, the challenges to improving
upon the status quo are far greater in this huge city. (Despite these challenges, and the quadrupling of bike riders since 2001, the number of bike
crashes does not seem to have seriously increased, according to information gathered by the NYC Department of Transportation.)[18] Chicago, the
next city in size, with the next-smallest bike mode share, came in second
in its fatality rate. Not surprisingly, the smallest of the nine cities in the
Pucher/Buehler study, Vancouver, Portland, and Minneapolis, had the
safest cycling.[19]

Nor has the attitude of the New York City police department been
helpful. Pucher and Buehler point to the refusal of New York's police to
protect bike lanes from blockage by motor vehicles, which has compro-
mised the cyclists' safety.[20] Surely this disrespectful attitude is contagious
among the general public and among motorists in particular, for whom
the addition of bicycles to "their" already-crowded streets is undoubtedly
an irritant.

Changing the public's attitude toward cycling

While the Department of Transportation in New York City has taken
major successful initiatives to expand bike lanes and bike parking facilities, the confrontational attitude of the city's police personnel toward

cyclists differs markedly from attitudes found in the eight other major cities investigated by Pucher and Buehler in this report. Some of these cities have made special efforts to educate motorists about the rights of cyclists, and about their legal responsibility to avoid endangering them. "Share the road" campaigns exist in all nine cities, and exams for drivers' licenses in five of these states include questions that highlight the responsibility of drivers to protect non-motorists. Portland hires plainclothes police to catch drivers who are endangering cyclists, and Chicago puts police on bikes to help convey the perspective of cyclists. All of the case study cities have bike training programs for both children and adults; however these programs are generally voluntary in the US, and nowhere near as comprehensive as those that are found in Denmark, Germany, and the Netherlands.[21]

A number of initiatives in the Netherlands, Denmark, Germany, and Belgium give priority to the most vulnerable users of the streets—pedestrians and cyclists—and have been aimed quite successfully at elevating bicycling above the status of "fringe" mode. A non-governmental group based in the Netherlands, Interface for Cycling Expertise, has been active in sharing the Dutch experience with advocacy groups in at least eleven less-developed nations—designing modern transport systems that feature bicycles prominently. As observed by Roelof Wittink, head of that organization, "If you plan only for cars then drivers will feel like King of the Road. This reinforces the attitude that the bicycle is backward and used only by the poor. But if you plan for bicycles it changes the public attitude."[22]

Changing the legal relationships among pedestrians, cyclists and drivers

In the boating world, the smallest and slowest vessels are normally granted priority, so that the motorboater looks out for the sailboater—rather than the other way around. This is simply a mark of courtesy and civilized behavior. But currently on our streets in the US, when a motorist hits a pedestrian or cyclist, there is no presumption of guilt, even for liability purposes. Urbanist/journalist Alex Marshall has reasonably recommended that this should change—that is, if motorists knew that their insurance companies would raise their rates or cancel their policies if they hit a pedestrian or cyclist, they would be much more careful in their driving behavior. Marshall points out that this is quite fair "… when you consider that a contest between soft flesh and hard metal is not one of equals."[23]

Thus, the motorist, as the driver of the far larger, far heavier vehicle, should—by default—be considered at fault in any collision. By the same token, cyclists should pedal with respectful caution around pedestrians, as pedestrians are the more vulnerable co-users of the street. That should mean no more racing, heads-down cycling around pedestrians.

There is some progress in legal defense in favor of cyclists beginning to take hold in the US. In September 2011, a first-of-its-kind-in-the-nation cyclists' anti-harassment law went into effect in Los Angeles, having been passed unanimously by the city council. The law established a threshold minimum level of damages, set at a thousand dollars or three times the value of the actual damages suffered by a cyclist as a result of a motorist's aggression, whichever is greater. For actual physical injuries or damages, the amount is tripled, and the law provides for the recovery of reasonable attorneys' fees for successful litigants.[24] And in Washington, DC, an "Assault of Bicyclists Prevention Act" has been proposed, which should make it easier for cyclists to sue drivers, and offers incentives for lawyers to take up such cases. It aims to serve as a signal to the minority of motorists who are hostile to cyclists that aggressive behavior will no longer be tolerated in the city.[25]

Financial viability of transit linked to easier access to it

Lessons from Europe
Creating safe walking and cycling routes to transit, thereby encouraging its use, has been especially successfully achieved in the Netherlands, Denmark and Germany. Germany is also a prime example of how an increase in the use of public transit has helped to make transit operations quite *economically sustainable*. Average transit operating subsidies in Germany as a whole are only 28 percent of total operating costs, and in the city of Freiburg, only 10 percent. These figures compare with an average of 67 percent transit subsidies in the US.[26]

There are, granted, some additional conditions that underlie the financial success of transit operations in Germany. One is that nation's higher average density of development: it has a population of eighty-two million living in an area of only 138,000 square miles (357,420 km²), an area only slightly smaller than that of Montana. An equally basic factor is that integrated transportation and land use objectives have been coordinated from the outset at the federal level and passed down to the localities. Feedback then filters back up from the local level. It has also been a fundamental tenet of German planning to focus new urban development around transportation infrastructure. This approach contrasts with that in the US where it was not until March 2009 that the federal Department of Transportation and the Department of Housing and Urban Development agreed to work together on joint planning policy.[27]

A number of other specific factors contribute to the greater viability of German transit. These include highly enlightened management techniques, as well as federal policies that strongly discourage solo driving. One of the most basic reasons for German transit's lower operating costs is higher total revenues from passenger fares. German transit vehicles—buses, trams, metros and commuter trains—regularly carry more than twice as many passengers as their US counterparts, thereby requiring fewer drivers per given number of passengers. The greater attraction to transit for riders is in part because transit in Germany has been made highly reliable and convenient to the public, with relatively seamless transfers among modes. But the more widespread use of transit in that country can also be at least partially attributed to the public's far easier and safer access to it via walking and cycling.[28]

Policies abroad that favor pedestrians and cyclists

Several policies and provisions have been very effectively employed in both the Netherlands and Germany that, with decades of successful experience, have made walking and cycling safe and attractive alternatives to driving:

• Safe paths for pedestrians and cyclists and good storage facilities for bikes,

• Design/redesign of streets to accommodate the needs of non-motorists,

• Traffic calming of residential neighborhoods,

• Rigorous traffic education of both motorists and non-motorists, with special attention given to motorists' avoidance of collisions with pedestrians and cyclists,

- Restrictions, including speed restrictions, on motor vehicle use in cities, and

- Strict enforcement of traffic regulations protecting pedestrians and bicyclists, wherein *not stopping for pedestrians at crosswalks is considered a serious offense that can merit a ticket, even if the pedestrians are only waiting at the curb and not actually in the crosswalk.*[29]

Since the early 1970s, virtually all of the German cities have made sweeping improvements in their safety conditions and infrastructure for both pedestrians and cyclists. For safer walking, sidewalk bulges and pedestrian refuge islands have been created to shorten the distances for crossing wide streets. There are pedestrian-activated crossing lights, zebra striped, and in some cases raised street-crossing paths, as well as wide, well-lit sidewalks on both sides of every street. Improvements include not only traffic-calmed residential neighborhoods, where cars are slowed by obstacles such as landscaping and circuitous routing—but also auto-free zones that cover large areas of the centers of many cities. Cycling paths are safely separated from other traffic, and street designs send the signal that it is pedestrians and cyclists, not motorists, that have priority. These improvements have been financed through local funds, often supplemented by state and federal funds. The benefits for cyclists have been remarkable—*there was a nearly 80 percent decrease in cyclist fatalities between 1970 and 2005*, despite a biking boom between the mid-1970s and mid-1990s in which cycling had doubled or tripled in most German cities.[30]

Throughout Europe, private motoring has been effectively discouraged, and public transit has been supported, through relatively high automobile and gasoline taxes. At the same time, in those countries where extensive curbed bike paths safely connect residential and commercial areas, large numbers of the public regularly cycle to work and other activities—30 percent in the Netherlands, 20 percent in Denmark, 12 percent in Germany, and 10 percent each in Switzerland and Sweden—despite weather that includes plenty of rain and snow.[31] This compares with the previously cited 0.6 percent in the United States and 1.3 percent in Canada—a dramatic gulf. So cycling has been thriving in precisely those countries where policies have been adopted that make it safer, faster, and more convenient.

The Netherlands is an unquestioned leader among advanced countries in encouraging cycling, and happens to contain more bicycles than people. Amsterdam is the planet's premier city for cycling, and contains more bicycles than cars. The city's traffic improvements for bicycles include extensive protected cycling paths and bike rental facilities, as well as outside racks and underground sheds that hold thousands of bicycles under guard. In many Dutch cities, spaces that had been consigned to auto parking have now been converted to bicycle parking.[32] Not only have the Dutch created cycling lanes and trails in all of their cities, but their traffic regulations give bikers the advantage over motorists in rights-of-way and at traffic lights.[33]

In Belgium, the "Code de la rue" was inaugurated in 2004, which gives priority to the most vulnerable travelers—pedestrians and cyclists. Similarly, in Copenhagen, cycling is given priority in city planning, and adult tricycles equipped for carrying children, groceries, and other heavy loads are a common sight. No cars are allowed in the city center, and very high car and gasoline taxes discourage private motoring in general. Some of Copenhagen's cycling paths are raised to a level a few inches higher than the street, but a few inches lower than the sidewalk. Others are at the same level as the street, but protected by low barriers. Bright blue bicycle lanes and crossing paths boldly alert motorists to the fact that cyclists have the right-of-way.

A full 37 percent of Copenhagen's people were commuting to work and school by bike by June 2010, and the city's leadership was looking to increase this to 50 percent by 2015. Also in planning was the expansion of Copenhagen's network of 220 miles (350 km) of physically separated bikeways. The most impressive aspect of this scene is the normalcy of it all. Large numbers of families with small children are cycling; so are the elderly; so are well-dressed professionals; and even Nobel Laureates and the Crown Prince ride bicycles for transportation. This has been occurring despite the fact that car ownership increased by 50 percent between 1995 and 2010.[34]

In the Netherlands, Germany, and Denmark, bicycles are used by all social classes, and politicians as well as royalty ride bikes. Cycling is so popular in Copenhagen that its many bike paths can become congested. Because the roads are jammed with cars, many of them driven in from the suburbs, the city has begun converting some of its extensive cycling network into a system of thoughtfully designed "Cycle Super Highways" to facilitate cycling for longer distances from the suburbs, providing fast, direct routes of up to 14 miles (22 km). The goal is to ultimately encourage a 30 percent increase in cycling among the city's commuters, as part of Copenhagen's efforts to become carbon neutral by 2025. A total of twenty-eight routes, comprising 308 miles (495 km) are planned. By the spring of 2013, two of these Cycle Super Highways, connecting the city with western and northwestern suburbs, had been built, and nine more routes were under construction and due for completion by 2015. They include green uninterrupted traffic lights that are programmed to prioritize bicycles over cars. They also include "conversation lanes" where two or three cyclists can ride abreast. As more of these Cycle Super Highways are built, it will become difficult to squeeze them into the existing traffic system in the city center; this may be resolved by giving the cyclists exclusive use of some streets at particular times of day.[35]

Safe and convenient parking facilities are as important for cyclists as they are for motorists, and providing them is an essential part of encouraging cycling. For new multi-family housing developments in Münster, Germany, regulations now require one bike storage space for each 323 sf (30m²) of housing area.[36] In Freiburg, as in most other German cities, a large bicycle parking garage is provided at the city's main train station. Local building codes also require varying amounts of bike parking facilities for residences, schools, universities, businesses and stores. With these measures, cycling has been made not only convenient and practical, but has achieved a firm status of respectability.[37] In both the Netherlands and Japan, concerted efforts have been made to integrate bicycles and rail transit by providing enormous bike parking facilities at the rail stations. The use of bicycles for access to trains has reached a point in Japan where some rail stations have built multi-level bike parking garages to accommodate the overflow.[38]

Integration of cycling and transit in eight major North American cities
In 2009, Pucher and Buehler studied progress on the integration of bicycles and transit stations in six major US cities—San Francisco, Portland (Oregon), Minneapolis, Chicago, Washington, and New York—and two

major Canadian cities—Vancouver and Toronto. They found that each of these cities had undertaken a range of measures to promote the practice of bike-and-ride, and that a considerable amount of progress had been made over the previous decade in coordinating cycling with transit. They noted that the US federal government had provided funding for a wide range of projects that had been implemented at the state and local government levels, granting as much as 95 percent of the funds for some categories of bike-transit integration projects. Yet the demand for bike-and-ride facilities still far exceeds the supply.[39]

In North America, cyclists have often preferred to take their bikes right onboard the transit vehicle, where allowed, so that they will have them available at both ends of the trip. However, this tends to cause overcrowding on transit vehicles at rush hours, so it is prohibited at those hours in many cities. The northern European approach has instead favored the provision of secure and sheltered bike parking at transit stops. Pucher and Buehler favor this latter approach, and point out that, although bike-and-ride facilities cost money, they are far cheaper than car-park-and-ride facilities for motorists.[40]

By way of comparison, car parking garages cost Washington, DC's Metro system some $30,000 per space to build, while a secure bike cage costs only $1,000 per space and bike racks cost much less.[41] Certainly a major additional advantage in this feasibility is that bike parking is also much more economical of *space*.

Achieving change in America

Regulatory hurdles

Significant improvements for both pedestrians and cyclists in the US should entail only modest investments for big gains. But these have to date been meager relative to the need. Although pedestrians account for some 6 percent of total trips in the US and comprise 11.8 percent of all traffic deaths, less than 1.5 percent of the funds authorized under the 2009 federal transportation law were dedicated toward improving pedestrian safety.[42] As for cycling, a survey by Rodale Press in 2009 found that in the US, 40 percent of the public would actually choose to commute by bicycle instead of driving—if only safe pathways were available.[43]

Figure 4.1
Electronic bike lockers at the North Berkeley BART station in California.
Source: Bay Area Rapid Transit.

Figure 4.2
Easy access for bikes on the SkyTrain in Vancouver.
Source: Translink.

The redesign of streets to accommodate safe cycling is more complex in the US than it may sound. One of the rulebooks that currently govern US street designs is the Federal Highway Administration's *Manual on Uniform Traffic Control Devices (MUTCD)*, of the Federal Highway Administration (FHA). That document specifically governs traffic control devices, rather than street design, and is oriented toward the conventional, auto-oriented priorities of most state highway officials. It includes only one provision for bikes—roadway markings indicating that motorists must share a lane with cyclists. Alternately, cities may use either local street manuals, guidelines that have been published by the Institute of Transportation Engineers (ITE), or the more flexible standards in the *Green Book* of the American Association of State Highway and Transportation Officials (AASHTO). The *AASHTO Green Book* actually encourages design flexibility within certain parameters, such as traffic lane widths of only 10 feet (3.048 meters), which will allow more space for bicycle lanes. While cities may use road designs that are not listed as approved by one of these guidebooks, few cities are willing to do so, since this may require applying to the FHA with a special "request to

experiment." The project is then subject to laborious federal oversight.[44]
In our litigious society, many cities are understandably concerned about
liability issues related to the use of street designs that have not yet received formal approval.

"Complete Streets"
The cars-only model of streets without sidewalks or cycling lanes—extensively built in the US in the 1960s through the 1980s—is now under
challenge by the National Complete Streets Coalition, a powerful assemblage of citizens' groups that includes the Natural Resources Defense
Council and the American Association of Retired Persons. This coalition
is responding to a "perfect storm" of issues that have come to a head—air
pollution, climate change and an urgent need to cut carbon emissions,
volatile gasoline prices and the economic turndown, mobility constraints
on an increasingly aging population, and the nation's obesity epidemic.
Thus, in December 2009, the state of New Jersey approved a policy that
called for highway engineers and planners of all state-operated roads to
give as much consideration to all road users—including pedestrians, cyclists and wheelchair users—as they have traditionally given to motorists.[45] By the summer of 2011, twenty-four states, Puerto Rico, and
Washington, DC, had already passed some type of Complete Streets
legislation.[46] And in January 2013, Memphis, Tennessee, became the
500th city in the US to adopt a Complete Streets policy. Although each
state and city writes the laws somewhat differently, broadly speaking,
each of the laws calls for future road design and construction to factor
in the needs of pedestrians, cyclists, and other non-car users.

These non-motorists comprise, after all, more than one-third of the
US population, since they include, but are not limited to, those who are
either too young or too old to drive.

There are some problems with the limited scope and execution of the
state-based Complete Streets laws, which will need to be amended. The
new laws cover only state-owned roads, which are a minority of streets.
The laws also exempt the most common type of roadwork—repaving—
although this is an ideal phase for incorporating such low-cost solutions
as narrowing traffic lanes and painting in bike lanes. Also exempted from
the laws are any improvements for which there may be concerns about
safety or cost overruns—and this constitutes a gaping loophole.[47] For

Figure 4.3
Ninth Avenue in Manhattan after street improvements. This Complete Street design gives equal weight to all street users. The pedestrians have sidewalks, and a bike lane is protected by a lane of parked cars, while the street continues to accommodate buses and cars.
Source: NYC Department of Transportation.

these reasons, efforts have been ongoing since 2009 to pass a *national* Complete Streets bill in the US Congress.[48]

Specific US initiatives promoting cycling

In much of the United States, cities and towns both large and small are finding the biking movement infectious. High-profile protests notwithstanding, the widespread acceptance of bike lanes in cities throughout the nation comes as much from an interest in making the street a more civilized place as it does from concern with making cycling safe and more viable.

As noted above, between 1990 and 2009, the number of US commuters cycling to work increased by 64 percent, with Portland, Oregon, showing by far the biggest gain. After twenty years of transportation planning with bicycles in mind, that city had, by the end of 2010, achieved the highest share of cycling commuters in the nation. Portland is adopting Copenhagen's tactic of painting cycling paths a bright blue to command the attention of motorists. And in 2010, Portland's city council unanimously approved a 2030 Bicycle Master Plan that aims to furnish the city with three times the bike lanes it had in 2010. Metro, a regional governing body elected by Portland's entire metropolitan area, has set a goal for 40 percent of all city and suburban trips of under three miles to be made by bicycle by 2040, and for the number of cyclists to be tripled by that year. The city is now focused on answering the needs of the 60 percent of its citizens who have indicated in surveys an interest in biking, but concern about doing it in traffic.[49]

Portland has been installing "bike corrals"—converting one or two on-street parking spaces into parking for bikes, each corral having a capacity of ten to twenty bikes. By 2010 the city had more than sixty-one of these corrals; they were attracting customers for local businesses, which wasprompting requests for even more corrals.[50]

San Francisco, second only to New York among US cities in its density, is second only to Portland in its portion of commuters traveling by bike.[51] San Francisco now has 79 miles (127 kilometers) of bike lanes throughout the city, which are regularly used for commuting by 40,000 cyclists. [52] Many driving lanes throughout San Francisco are being converted to bike lanes, and all public transit vehicles in that city are equipped to carry bikes. As in Portland, bike "corrals" are going up all around San Francisco.[53]

Minneapolis is beginning to rival Portland as a cyclist's haven. In addition to a very popular 5.5-mile (nearly 9-km) Midtown Greenway that was opened in 2000, the city has many dedicated bike lanes buffered from traffic and plenty of bike parking. The city has also adopted "bicycle boulevards" with speed humps and "diverters" that block cars but allow bikes to pass safely through. On some roads the number of car lanes has been reduced in order to widen cycling lanes. As a result of all these measures, the commuter biking rate in Minneapolis has increased to 3.8 percent.[54]

Even in Los Angeles, cycling is beginning to benefit from a network of bicycle lanes. With its largely flat topography and a genial climate, that city could become a kind of cycling paradise. Periodically, the city closes some of its streets to cars for an event known as CicLAvia, for which in April 2012, the streets were flooded with nearly 100,000 cyclists of all ages—remarkable for this city of cars.[55] In Philadelphia, efforts by city government and local biking advocates have resulted in the creation of an east–west cycling corridor on two central streets, Spruce and Pine, which, because of its heavy use, has been made permanent. In September 2011, the city launched another pilot project for a north–south pair of cycling streets, 10th and 13th Streets. Philadelphia has roughly 380 miles (610 km) of bike lanes, having created many of them in the decades of the 1990s and 2000s. The city has a robust program of providing bike racks on its buses, and bikes are allowed on trains except at peak hours. Philadelphia is also in the process of converting many car parking spaces to bike parking.[56]

A number of smaller US cities have made big strides in developing cycling and pedestrian paths. Notable are programs in Davis and Long Beach (California), Boulder (Colorado), Seattle (Washington), and Madison (Wisconsin). In Boulder, 21 percent of the population now commutes by bicycle, and one of the city's schools has reported that 75 percent of its students now walk or cycle to school—a 620 percent increase since before Boulder's Safe Routes to School pilot program.[57]

There are, in fact, 6,489 schools in all fifty states have been participating in the Safe Routes to School program, which supports infrastructure projects (such as sidewalks, bike paths and improved signage), education, and law enforcement—all aimed at making conditions safer for children walking and cycling to school. Unfortunately, because the program is voluntary, it has been reaching fewer than 7 percent of the nation's primary and secondary schools.[58]

Although the Washington, DC region has some of the worst car traffic in the nation, it also has the sixth-highest rate in the US of a commuting by bike (2.2 percent).[59] The District of Columbia also spends more per capita to promote cycling and walking than any other city in the US. While most states spend an average of $2.17 per capita on improvements for cycling and walking, the District actually spends some $9.82.[60]

In 2010 the Washington Metro completed a study of pedestrian and bicycle access to Metrorail stations. Its strong resolutions included a goal of tripling the number of riders who arrive at the stations by bicycle by

2020, and of quintupling this number by 2030. For while the Metro's ridership is growing, adding more capacity for car parking would be both extremely expensive and completely unfeasible spatially. One solution being considered is to add modular bike parking—basically, covered bike parking rooms or enclosed bike stations that can be easily inserted into a parking area.[61]

As part of a citywide strategy to make the District of Columbia more bicycle-friendly, a large new $4 million bike storage and rental facility has been built at Union Station—an ideal location for transfers to the Metro. Its iconic, tapered design serves as a dignified complement to its Beaux Arts surroundings. This center, the first of its kind on the east coast of the US was 80 percent federally funded. It has 150 enclosed bike racks and 20 outdoor racks, as well as changing rooms, personal lockers, a bike repair shop, and a retail store selling drinks and bike accessories. It now helps to serve the estimated 87,500 people in the Washington area who currently use bikes as their primary means of transportation. Washington already has 40 miles (64 km) of cycling lanes in streets and more

Figure 4.4
A new bike station, inaugurated in 2009 at Washington, DC's Union Station, is convenient to both Amtrak and the city's Metro system.
Source: Roxanne Warren.

than 100 miles (161 km) of cycling trails through parks, and is planning a trail that will link the Capitol Hill area with the Maryland suburbs.[62]

In New York City, almost half the city's workforce lives within 5 miles (8 km) of its place of work. And given New York's high densities of development, it is not surprising that 60 percent of its trips are under 3 miles (4.8 km)—an ideal length of trip for cycling.[63] Starting in 2007, Transportation Commissioner Janette Sadik-Khan took bold initiatives—in this most challenging of cities for innovative projects—to convert many driving lanes to bike lanes, while converting numerous barren asphalt strips into landscaped pedestrian plazas and "pedestrian priority zones"—areas that are designed for pedestrians, but allow limited access to buses and cars. Her successful experiments with pedestrian plazas in Times Square and Herald Square are discussed in chapter 6. (While these bicycle and pedestrian improvements have been featured prominently in the local press, they have accounted for only a very small portion of New York City's transportation budget, the vast bulk of which is still spent on road and bridge repaving and reconstruction.)

New York nearly tripled the length of its bike lanes and paths between 2000 and 2010, from 170 miles (274 km) to 416 miles (670 km). Because of the city's very large population (exceeding 8.3 million), it still had the smallest number of bike lanes and paths *per capita* of the nine cities in Pucher and Buehler's 2011 study.[64] Yet the cyclists' response to these provisions had been dramatic: by the spring of 2010, there were an estimated 201,000 daily cycling commuters on New York's streets, or an increase of 20 percent over the previous year's estimate.[65] By July 2011, there was yet another 14 percent increase in New York City cyclists from the spring of 2010.[66] And, true to Peter Jacobsen's projections, there had been an increase in safety with the increase in numbers: cycling accidents in New York have declined steadily as the biking population has risen. As noted by Noah Budnick, senior policy advisor to the bicycling/walking/transit advocacy group, Transportation Alternatives, "... the more cyclists there are on the street, the more drivers are aware of them and are looking out for them."[67]

A major deterrent to cycling is the concern that one's bike will be stolen or vandalized; therefore, efforts to create safe bike parking have been made in all nine cities studied by Pucher and Buehler.[68] Bike parking space in New York (by extreme comparison with Portland) is severely limited. However, bikes in New York can now be stored for free in twenty municipal shelters and on more than 6,000 bike racks. Additionally, a law was passed in 2009 requiring the owner of any multi-family residential building, commercial building, or public parking garage to provide specified amounts of secure parking areas for bikes.[69] The Portland concept of bike corrals has also begun to take hold in New York.

Bike rental/bikesharing systems

By the summer of 2010, there were already 125 cities worldwide that were operating public bike rental, or bike-sharing programs, up from only 60 cities two years earlier.[70] More than 100 of these were in European cities.[71] Bertrand Delanoë, who was elected Mayor of Paris in 2001, had initiated in mid-July 2007 an innovative city bicycle rental program, dubbed Vélib', which has been immensely popular and has served as an inspiration for bikesharing plans in other cities around the world, including London and New York. The Paris system now includes 20,600 bikes that are available at 1,450 docking stations throughout Paris. The bikes do not need to be returned to the same station from which they were rented, which makes them highly convenient as a means to reach transit stations (but makes management of the fleet appreciably more complex). Much of the revenue from the system comes from tourists. Access to the bikes is by credit card, and there is a choice of daily, weekly, or annual rentals for very nominal fees, while for the first 30 minutes, the ride is free. Parisians report that bike sharing has changed the city's atmosphere to a much more sociable and friendly one.[72]

Paris's Vélib' has unfortunately experienced serious vandalism and theft of its bikes, much of which has been attributed to social unrest in the city's troubled suburbs. Nevertheless, both the city of Paris and JC Decaux, the outdoor advertising company that is the major financer and organizer of the project, are pressing on, with a heavy maintenance and repair program and an educational advertising campaign aimed at youthful offenders.[73]

London's bike-share system, launched in July 2010, and dubbed "Boris Bikes," for Mayor Boris Johnson, who inaugurated it, has an extremely enthusiastic public. An animated archive, searchable on Google under "Boris Bikes animation," charts the movements of the bikes, showing each as a colored dot of light sweeping across a map of London. Dozens of websites and smartphone apps help users find and return bikes, plan their routes and track their account balances. London's fleet of 6,000 grew to 8,000 by the spring of 2012, and has served as a model for a similar system in New York City.[74]

An organization called the International Council for Local Environmental Initiatives (ICLEI) was founded in 1990, with the purpose of providing consultation on a variety of tools for urban environmental sustainability, including guidance on cycling and bike-sharing systems. Based in Bonn, its members include more than 1,200 cities, towns, and counties from more than 70 countries worldwide, with 605 member cities in the United States, including New York. Another member city, Denver, began a large-scale bike-sharing program in the spring of 2010, dubbed B-Cycle, and is one of several cities in the US to have done so. B-Cycle ludicrously became the target of an anti-bike political campaign in Denver that claimed it was a specifically left-wing strategy "dictated to us by this United Nations program that mayors have signed on to"—a reference to Denver's membership in the ICLEI (whose only actual connection with the United Nations is that its inaugural conference was located there).[75]

The low costs of owning and operating bikes have led many colleges and universities to turn to bike rentals for their students. Typically, the demand has come from students themselves. Nearly ninety universities in the US now offer some sort of free or low-cost campus bike program, including New York University, Chicago's Saint Xavier University, Atlanta's Emory University, Stevens Institute of Technology in Hoboken (New Jersey), North Carolina State University, Ripon College in Wisconsin, and the University of Alaska in Anchorage. Some of the bike programs require membership, others are free, and some charge a modest rental fee. Faced with a car parking crisis, the University of New England in Maine has actually *given* bikes to incoming students on the condition that they agree to leave their cars at home. This has not only decreased traffic congestion and air pollution; it has also fostered a sense of community.[76]

Montréal has a bicycle rental system named Bixi (= bike plus taxi), whose docking stations are solar-powered, and which by 2009 was already comprised of 5,000 bikes and 400 stations. The largest bike stations are at subway stops, since the bikes are typically used for the first and last mile of transit trips. The bike stations can be moved around by season or event, so that they serve beach-going trips in summer, the university in fall and spring, and football events and concerts year around. In winter the bike paths are cleared of snow and ice even before the sidewalks are. The system is very popular, and the citizenry has petitioned to expand it.[77]

By 2011, at least nine US cities had active bike-sharing programs, and seven more cities were planning to start them. Washington, DC, opened its system in 2010, and has more than 1,200 bikes operating from 165 stations. In fact, it was found to be too popular; that is, the number of bikes was inadequate for the demand, so the city planned to expand it, with 30 to 50 new stations and hundreds of new bikes. Capital Bikeshare's territory now includes Arlington County, Virginia, and Montgomery County, Maryland.[78] It has been moving forward with a corporate sponsorship plan, including sign advertising and visual branding of the bikes.[79] At the same time, bike-share's shortcomings have led many of its users to buy bikes of their own. Not only are the bikes a bit heavy and slow, but on busy days, there can be a scarcity of bikes at nearby docks, or no open docks where a bike can be conveniently returned. Between cyclists renting bikes and people purchasing their own, cycling has now reached a "critical mass" in Washington, so that motorists have to be courteous and accommodate them, even where there are no bike lanes.[80]

San Francisco, having experienced a 70 percent growth in biking in the previous four years, prepared in 2012 to pilot bike-sharing.[81] Chicago and New York both launched bike-share systems in the spring of 2013. Chicago's system, dubbed "Divvy" to reflect the dividing-and-sharing nature of bikeshare, included more than 4,000 bikes in its first week of operation. More than 1,700 Chicagoans had already signed up for annual membership.[82] And even Fort Worth, Texas, opened a bike-share system in April 2013, with 300 bikes and 30 docking stations located throughout the downtown, Near Southside, and cultural districts.[83]

New York's bikeshare system is the largest in the nation and the largest worldwide outside of Paris, with 10,000 bikes and 600 stations. Run by Alta Bicycle Share, which operates the systems in Chicago, Washington, DC, Boston, and Melbourne, New York's bike-share docking stations are solar-powered, which avoids the need for expensive underground cable installations. It is the first bike-share share system to be run without government subsidies, and shares any revenue it earns with the city.[84]

New York's system is used primarily for short-range trips to extend the reach of the city's already-extensive transit offerings. One of its major advantages is its affordability, as it costs the rider an average of only $90 per year. Surveys have indicated that 72 percent of the public supports the program—support that was confirmed when the Department of Transportation invited the public to suggest locations for the system's 600 stations, and received over 7,000 suggestions. At the initial planning of New York's bike-share system, many business owners said that they didn't want bike-share stations in front of their stores, but six months prior to the launch of the system, the same store owners were already pleading for them.

For New York's bike-share system there are apps available for determining how many bikes are available, and at which stations. There is also interest in extrapolating what the health benefits from future increases in biking may be, using data on miles ridden.

With the initiation of each bike-share system, there is a question of whether the primary funding will be public or private, and whether some public funding will be available. While most of the European bike rental systems are based on municipal support, those in the US are typically initiated privately. The system in Denver and one in Minneapolis are operated by non-profits, and one in Miami Beach is based on a concessionaire model, with ad revenue supporting the system.[85] It cost the city of Washington just over $6 million to start up its bike-share program, with federal highway money paying 80 percent of the cost.[86]

Some backlash against cycling
Not surprisingly, with the surge in cycling in New York, there have been a number of hotly waged disputes over street space between motorists and cyclists. These have taken on the aspect of cultural conflicts between the adversaries' contrasting notions of urban transportation. Business owners have also legitimately complained about bike lanes eliminating curbside delivery access to their stores. The Complete Street designs are having to be more finely tuned, since the space to be shared is very limited, while the cycling population has become more substantial and assertive about its rights.[87]

The backlash against cyclists in New York has been exacerbated by some overly aggressive, highly sportive, heads-down, racing-style cyclists, who can, in fact, present a hazard to pedestrians, particularly where they fail to obey traffic rules. These aggressive cyclists have, much to their own surprise, become a target of the police department, many of whose members, as noted above, already had a confrontational attitude toward cyclists.[88] In contrast, there are the "upright" bikers, who cycle to work, to errands, and to entertainment in their normal attire, obey the rules of the road, and pose a threat to no one, but rather symbolize urbanity and style, much as they did when the first bicycling craze hit the nation in the 1880s.[89]

Other mini-modes for access

Electric bicycles and scooters

As the rising attraction to cycling coincides with the aging of the population, interest is growing in electric bikes, whose extra boost can be especially helpful in wind and on steep slopes. Electric bicycles are powered by two sources—muscle and battery power. They can be recharged by pedaling, and in contrast to plug-in hybrid cars, do not directly use fossil fuel.

In the US a relatively modest market for electric bicycles has developed—approximately 200,000 were sold in 2009, and the popularity of this mode is increasing. However, the use of electric bikes on bike lanes can constitute a hazard to riders of conventional bikes; their speeds and power therefore need to be regulated. In New York, for example, while electric bikes are not yet officially permitted on city streets (which precludes the purchase of accident insurance), a bill is in the State legislature that would permit bikes with less than 1,000 watts of power and top speeds of 20 mph (32 km/h). The limit on power output in several other US states is 750 watts.[90]

In China, where the industry began, there are already an estimated 120 million electric bicycles on the roads, and their use has been spreading to India and Europe, as well as to the US. In the Netherlands, approximately a third of the money spent on bicycles in 2009 went to the purchase of electric models. Two types of electric bikes are emerging—the most popular type in the US and Europe is similar to a standard bike but has an electric motor. In China, bigger, more powerful electric bikes have become common, and these do indeed become an obvious hazard if they are traveling in bike lanes. They resemble Vespa scooters and can travel up to 30 mph (48 km/h). Globally, transportation planners are considering banning them from bike lanes, while permitting them on streets, mixed with car traffic.[91] Dutch law, on the other hand, places *low-speed* scooters in the same category as bicycles; these can therefore not be legally excluded from using bike paths. So to improve safety for cyclists, some Dutch cities construct speed bumps on their bike paths, designed specifically to slow motorized scooters.[92]

Mini-cars and the provision of slower, safer roadway networks for them
Walking and cycling are of course not for everyone, and cold, wet weather can serve as a deterrent to cycling. Nor are car-sharing systems, discussed in chapter 2, the only option for weather-protected mobility. The MIT Smart Cities research group has been developing a whole family of lightweight electric vehicles for rental—including low-speed electric bikes, motor scooters, and mini-cars that would be interchangeable—these different types of vehicles could be mixed and matched in a rental system dubbed Mobility on Demand. A radio-frequency reader (RFID), access card, or credit card would release the vehicle to the user. Similar in concept to Paris's Vélib' system, the vehicles would be docked at charging stations throughout a city, and would not need to be returned back to the same station from which they were taken. Therefore, as with Vélib', a very good fleet management system would be required. The mini-cars would be flexibly stackable for more compact parking, as shown in figures 4.6.[93]

This project has advanced from the theoretical to the commercial, with the creation of the Hiriko Driving Mobility Group, a consortium of auto parts suppliers in the Basque region of Spain that has worked together with MIT and the Spanish government. Dubbed the Hiriko Fold, this tiny, two-seat electric vehicle has a hinged body, which can retract its front and rear modules to shrink the 8-foot (2.44-m) car to 5 feet (1.52 m) when parked. It has a front hatch that houses the windshield and doubles as the car's only door. Its four wheels each turn 60 degrees to the left or right, which enables the car to travel sideways or spin on its axis, making parallel parking effortless. The Hiriko Fold was

Figure 4.5
The CityCar.
Sources: Smart Cities, MIT Media Lab, and William Lark Jr.

scheduled for test drives in mid-2014, and is expected to go on sale for around $16,000. There are plans to sell the car to municipalities such as Barcelona, Berlin, and San Francisco. There have also been inquiries about its use for car-sharing systems in Hong Kong, Florianopolis in Brazil, the Spanish island of Ibiza, and the Basque biosphere reserve of Urdaibai.[94]

An issue that immediately arises is that of safe roadway networks for mini-vehicles. As observed in chapter 1, small, light cars are ill-suited to long highway trips at high speeds, particularly in competition with far heavier vehicles. The same can be said for travel on urban streets with even moderately high speed limits. This issue has been carefully explored by the Oregon Transportation Research and Education Consortium (OTREC). Their concern is that, while there are increasing numbers of low-speed electric vehicles in use on public streets, these vehicles have been designed for use only in protected environments and on roads with posted maximum speeds of 25 mph (40 km/h). As such, the design of

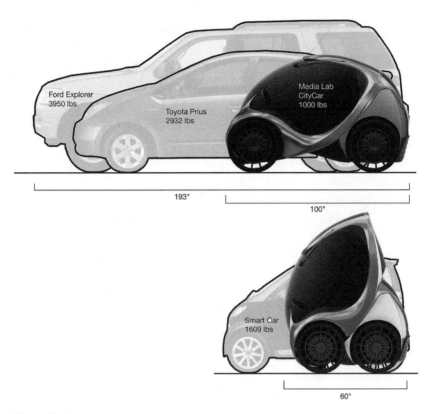

Figure 4.6
The CityCar, weight-length comparison, deployed and stacked.
Sources: Smart Cities, MIT Media Lab, William Lark Jr. and Ryan C. C. Chin.

these vehicles has not been subject to the same requirements for occupant protection as those for passenger cars. And certainly their small sizes and light weights would be a severe handicap in any crashes with standard passenger cars. The consortium therefore recommends the following:

• That low-speed vehicles be limited to public streets with maximum allowable speeds of 25 mph, and be restricted to crossing high-speed streets at four-way stops or traffic-controlled intersections.

• That local transportation authorities should work with users of low-speed vehicles and representatives of the bicycling community to develop parallel or secondary low-speed transportation networks that connect residential neighborhoods with major activity centers that include education, employment, retail, medical, and recreational facilities.

• That users of low-speed vehicles need to be educated about the safety risks of these vehicles, particularly of those that have a "car-like" appearance, and about the safety risks of modifying their speed regulators.[95]

There is also a question of whether even tiny mini-vehicles, with their power and speed strictly limited, should be allowed to travel on bikeways—in which case, existing bikeways would need to be significantly widened, at the sacrifice of considerable space for standard automobiles. With urban space at a premium, such sensitive questions would need to be weighed and carefully negotiated.

Another alternative, described in chapter 5, may be found in a movement—"20's Plenty for Us"—that is gathering momentum in England, Ireland, and the US toward establishing 20 mph (32 km/h) zones in residential neighborhoods and urban centers. This concept has already been in popular practice for several decades in many Dutch, Danish, and German towns and cities, in the form of traffic-calmed 18.6 mph (30 km/hr) streets. Vancouver has also been a leader in providing traffic-calmed residential streets, in lieu of building extensive bikeway networks.[96] Such zones could be established relatively simply, easily, and inexpensively in certain settings, such as older suburbs characterized by narrow roads that lead to transit stations. These could comprise the "secondary" roadway network that is needed to safely accommodate mini-vehicles, as well as bicycles and pedestrians.

Mini-modes and the size-based pricing of parking

To date, the ultimate in tiny vehicles under development, which can fit nicely within one-fifth of the parking space required for a "full-sized" US car, is the P.U.M.A. (Personal Urban Mobility and Accessibility) prototype. This is a two-seat, two-wheeled, 700-pound vehicle based on the Segway, the product of a collaboration between Segway and General Motors, with torque steering that allows zero-radius turning. This vehicle is not very complex—it is basically a bunch of batteries with electric motors in the wheels.[97]

And there are other appealing options to full-sized automobiles. If acceptable on enlarged bike paths, or driven in 20 mph zones, they could be ideal for access trips to and from transit stations, as well as for other, relatively short neighborhood trips. They are variously known as "station cars," and by such names as "Smart Car," "Wheego Whip," "Smart for

Two," and "Think City EV." A variety of similarly tiny vehicles are coming to market—some of them with rechargeable electric batteries, others powered by the sun.

At transit stations, the fee for renting a parking space could then be based proportionately on the size of the vehicle. With such a price incentive, one can envision the gradual downsizing of vehicles used for station access. Parking facilities at the stations will be commensurately smaller, more discreet, and less expensive to construct. The traffic generated by smaller vehicles will also be less imposing, and access to the station via foot, bike, or mini-vehicle less environmentally noxious to any adjacent development, whether conventional or built as transit-oriented.

There's a nice logic to this size-based pricing. As the mode with the very least environmental impact, walking of course incurs no parking charge at all. As the next most compact and environmentally benign mode, cycling incurs only a modest fee for secure parking. And the parking fees for mini-cars will be one-third or less of those for standard cars.

5

Different Speeds for Different Settings

Speeding for a high

In March 2007, a motorist from Connecticut was arrested for driving along Interstate 684 at a speed of 142 mph (229 km/h), his car tires smoking as he slammed on the brakes. On the same road in 2006 and 2007, three other drivers were stopped for speeding at more than 130 mph (209 km/h). Seven more motorists were recorded reaching speeds of more than 130 mph during that period in nearby Westchester, Rockland, and Putnam counties. These incidents were extreme enough to have been reported in the local newspapers; however, less flagrant, but nonetheless potentially deadly examples are commonplace along this highway. And there has been a consistent increase in the number of speeding tickets from year to year. So the state troopers along Interstate 684 routinely ignore speeders going at only 75 mph (121 km/h)—wryly remarking, "We can't write everybody up."[1]

It should not be surprising that there are more than six million car crashes each year in the United States, resulting in typical years in the deaths of some 33,000 people and about two million permanent injuries.[2] As of 2009, motor vehicle crashes continued to be the leading cause of deaths among the younger age groups.[3] The habit of speeding on highways carries over directly into our urban environments: between 1994 and 2009, more than 76,000 were killed by automobiles in the US while crossing or walking along streets within their communities.[4] This is roughly the equivalent of a jumbo jet crashing every month; yet it receives nothing like the attention that would be provoked by such a disaster. The experience of extreme speeding apparently fulfills drivers' fantasies of omnipotence that are so effectively cultivated in the car commercials.

Which may, in part answer the question of why this kind of behavior is even tolerated by society.

In US road design, there is an insufficient distinction drawn between this kind of highway speeding and everyday driving in and around our urban areas. A survey of the most hazardous areas in the nation for walking was completed in 2011 by the organization Transportation for America. It ranked a number of metropolitan areas in the South and Southeast as the most dangerous locales in the US to be a pedestrian—four areas in Florida, in particular.[5] These are all places that were built up quickly in the era of auto-centric design, and they contain many wide arterials and superblocks. In these areas, crosswalks are few, and are disliked and dishonored by motorists, who typically and naturally regard them simply as pesky impediments to the high speeds that these roads were designed for. Children and the elderly, in particular, are put at considerable risk.

Historical perspective on auto speeding

It wasn't always like this. As described by Peter D. Norton, assistant professor at the University of Virginia, across the country, and well into the 1920s, drivers were held criminally responsible when they killed or injured people with their motor vehicles. The automobile was seen as an intruder in the cities and a menace, since the streets were typically filled with a multitude of users and uses. If someone, particularly a child, was struck and killed by a car, it drew enormous attention and was treated as a serious public loss. Even in the case of a child darting out into traffic, the responsibility for crashes always lay with the driver. Mayors dedicated monuments to the victims of these traffic crimes, attended by marching bands and children dressed in white, carrying flowers.[6]

The automobile manufacturers and auto clubs increasingly realized that they had an image problem, and moved aggressively and effectively to change the way Americans thought about streets, cars, and traffic. Turning first to the younger generation, they financed safety education programs in the public schools which taught children that the streets are for cars, not for children, and that *they* had to stop for traffic—not the other way around.

According to Norton, one key turning point in shifting public attitudes about cars came in 1923 in Cincinnati. Citizens' anger over pedestrian deaths had given rise to a referendum drive in support of a rule that would have required all vehicles in the city to be equipped with governors limiting their speed to 25 mph. Some 7,000 signatures were gathered in support of this rule, whereupon auto clubs, dealers, and manufacturers became alarmed, realizing that cars would be much harder to sell if a curb were placed on their speed. They mounted a highly successful campaign against this initiative, sending out letters to every car owner in the city, warning that such a rule would condemn the US to the same fate as China, which they depicted as the most backward nation in the world. And they hired pretty women to urge men to come to the polls and vote against the referendum. So the referendum failed. This was followed by vigorous lobbying efforts that promoted the adoption of traffic statutes designed to restrict pedestrian use of the streets and give primacy to cars.[7]

The turnaround of public opinion in favor of cars over pedestrians and cyclists was dramatic. Today, as revealed in a survey by the Governors' Highway Safety Association, the public's perception of speeding and aggressive driving is quite apathetic. Few advocates exist for speed reduction, and for many drivers, speeding is a routine behavior. While speed enforcement tools such as radar and speed detection devices are commonly used in many US states, a large majority of these states also allow motorists to use technology to *avoid* speeding tickets.[8]

The "traffic world" of the highway, contrasted with the "social world"

Since the mid-twentieth century, it has been customary among traffic engineers in the US to take design standards that were intended for highway safety, such as 14-foot (4.27-m) wide lanes, and apply them to urban and suburban streets. This not only results in the replacement of large swaths of sidewalk and landscaping with asphalt; it also directly encourages faster motoring. As confessed by "recovering" traffic engineer Charles Marohn:

When people would tell me that they did not want a wider street, I would tell them that they had to have it for safety reasons.

When they answered that a wider street would make people drive faster and that would seem to be less safe, especially in front of their house where their kids were playing, I would confidently tell them that the wider road was more safe, especially when combined with the other safety enhancements the standards called for.

When people objected to those other "enhancements," like removing all of the trees near the road, I told them that for safety reasons we needed to improve the sight distances and ensure that the recovery zone was free of obstacles.[9]

The late, great Dutch street designer and engineer Hans Monderman envisioned a dual universe of human circulation. There is the "traffic world" of the highway—standardized, homogeneous, made legible by simple instructions to be read at high speed. On the other hand, there is the "social world," appropriate to situations such as dense urban settings, where traffic moves at a slow-to-moderate pace, where human interaction is both expected and desired, and social rules govern. According to Monderman, there is often no need for a third party to regulate traffic in a well-designed urban space. In fact, over-regulation by signs, barriers, signals, or other mechanical devices meant to corral behavior should be discouraged, because these can tame and frustrate the very diversity of function that is the city's reason for being. In the "social world" that typifies dense cities, it is human interaction that matters the most, is expected and desired, and allows for the efficient and pleasurable use of urban space. On a busy urban street, pedestrians are good at adjusting their paths so as not to collide with each other; similarly, people will hold the door an extra beat for the person following behind, and will stand on the right side of an escalator, allowing others to pass.

The other approach, the "traffic world," is appropriate only in high-speed situations, such as highways and airport runways, where regulation and uniformity are absolutely essential for avoiding disaster. As Monderman pointed out, *our major planning mistake has been to routinely apply the rules of the "traffic world" to human-centric urban situations.*

Monderman pioneered the concept of the "naked street," or "shared space" in a number of Dutch towns, removing all of the traffic regulatory features that were supposed to make it safer for pedestrians, such as traffic lights, curbs, railings and road markings, to create a completely open and level surface on which pedestrians and motorists "negotiated" with each other by eye contact. To the surprise of many skeptics, this resulted in fewer collisions, since drivers, being unsure of what space belonged to them, became more accommodating.[10] Whether this approach in its pure form would be workable in the US, with our generally more ungovernable public—and accustomed as we are to more privileged private motoring—is another question.

Ideally, city streets ought not to be places dismissed as single-use pass-throughs, but appreciated as *destinations*. The lower-speed movement of pedestrians, cyclists, local transit vehicles, and (limited-speed) cars can allow ample opportunity to share the urban space; the streets can serve many diverse functions simultaneously and democratically. Urbanists Norman W. Garrick and James G. Hanley have cited the Homme de Fer area of downtown Strasbourg as a premier example of the application of this principle of shared space. There, pedestrians, cyclists, beautiful light rail trams—designed with large windows and therefore a maximum of transparency—and the occasional car or bus successfully flow in continuous and vibrant interplay, with a minimum of traffic signaling.[11]

Given the relative compactness of cities, they ought to be ideal venues for cyclists and pedestrians, including children and the elderly. For these and other considerations, urban roads should be designed for significantly lower traffic speeds than highways. Certainly children and the elderly are at the most risk from speeding drivers. Children can be endangered by their own unpredictable behavior, by their difficulty in judging the speed of oncoming cars, and by the fact that they are often too small to be seen by motorists. The elderly frequently cross streets too slowly for typical traffic light settings. They are a segment of the population that is expected to more than double in the US by 2050,[12] and they are increasingly drawn to living in cities, where walking and the use of transit can allow them continued mobility even as their driving skills decline. So speeding traffic in cities is an overriding concern, especially relative to the safety of these non-motorists.

Addressing fast, aggressive driving is a key part of the mission of the New York City–based Transportation Alternatives (TA). The organization points out that "Speeding motorists have less time to react to avoid collisions, tend not to yield the right-of-way ... [and that] there is a direct relationship between a motorist's speed and the odds that the driver will kill pedestrians or bicyclists that he or she strikes."[13] TA refers to Federal Highway Administration data on the relationship between motor vehicle speed and the likelihood of pedestrian deaths in accidents:

- At 20 mph (32 km/h) the odds of pedestrian death are 5 percent;
- At 30 mph (48 km/h) the odds of pedestrian death are 45 percent; and
- At 40 mph (64 km/h) the odds of pedestrian death are 85 percent.[14]

New York City has a posted speed limit of 30 mph (48 km/h), but it is widely ignored—most drivers are, in fact, unaware of it. And while driving 10 mph (16 km/h) above the speed limit occurs regularly in New York, only 2 percent of moving violations for which the police issue tickets are for speeding, as it is very difficult to enforce speed limits in this crowded city. Transportation Alternatives has observed that "*Speeding is often viewed as a victimless crime, almost a driver's right, rather than the extremely dangerous and anti-social behavior it is, especially on city streets.*" TA notes that Federal Highway Administration research suggests that fully two-thirds of traffic deaths in New York City involve speeding. This compares with fewer than 9 percent of traffic deaths in the city that are caused by drunken driving, which receives far more attention.[15]

An awareness of this reality, whether conscious or unconscious, is commonly manifested in peoples' reactions to the dangers of heavy and speeding traffic in their neighborhoods. Urban designer Donald Appleyard in his seminal 1981 book, *Livable Streets*, demonstrated explicitly how the social and recreational functions of streets are severely impaired by heavy car traffic. It serves as a barrier to people cultivating friends and acquaintances among their neighbors, and to walking in their neighborhoods, shopping locally, and playing outside. On streets with heavy traffic, Appleyard found that people kept very much to themselves, and had very little relationship to their community.[16] Similarly, a 2006 study by Transportation Alternatives on the impact of vehicular traffic on social life in sample neighborhoods in Manhattan, Brooklyn, Queens, and the Bronx found that residents living on streets with high volumes of traffic had fewer relationships with their neighbors, spent less time walking, shopping, and playing with their children, and were more likely to restrict their children's outdoor play than were their counterparts living on streets with low traffic volumes.[17] It is not only children's lives that are affected by their inability to play freely in urban streets without fear of cars. Parents feel compelled to supervise play, which deprives them of their own preferred or necessary activities. Thus, car-dominance of the streets creates pressures on the whole family.

20 mph zones and "blanket" zones in England, and similar US and Irish experiments

There is a highly successful campaign for slower speeds in England, spearheaded by founder Rod King, who was inspired by a visit to the German town of Hilden, near Dusseldorf. Because Hilden was famous for its large population of cyclists, King was surprised to see that the town's cycling infrastructure was not particularly well-developed. Instead, in the early 1990s, the town had simply reduced the speed limit on all of its residential roads to 18.6 mph (30 km/h). King started a similar movement in the UK, "20's Plenty for Us," which has swept rapidly across the country in a relatively short time, despite political opposition that has often been initially intense. A broad swath of British cities and towns that had been accustomed to speed limits of 30 mph (48 km/h) have now welcomed the safety, and particularly the quality of life allowed by slower streets.[18]

Between 2001 and 2009, London established more than four hundred 20 miles per hour zones in residential neighborhoods, near schools, and in other areas of high pedestrian activity. By 2009, the zones covered 11 percent of the total street length of the city. The safety benefits have been enormous for pedestrians, cyclists and motorists alike. Serious traffic injuries and fatalities within London's 20 mph zones have fallen by 46 percent, according to the prestigious *British Medical Journal*, and those sustained by children have dropped 50 percent. Consequently, in 2004, the World Health Organization endorsed 20 mph zones as a strategy essential for saving lives. More recently, Transport for London has recommended 880 more sites for this traffic-slowing treatment, and envisions that by 2020, motorists could be limited to 20 mph on streets within the M25 highway that encircles London, that is, on all but a few major arteries leading into the capital.[19] Portsmouth has, meanwhile, become the first British city where *every* residential street is limited to 20 mph, and there are nine other cities that have committed to doing the same.[20] Additionally, in September 2011, the full European Union parliament called for 18.6 mph (30 km/h) to be adopted as the default speed for all residential and urban roads.[21]

London's 20 mph zones include many traffic-calming devices to make the speed limit self-enforcing—such as road humps, raised crosswalks and junctions, chicanes, and speed cameras. But it actually costs much less, by as much as a factor of 50, to change an *entire* city or district to 20 mph speed limits, instead of confining the limits to discreet neighborhoods. In the UK, some of the fiercest opposition to 20 mph streets has come from those who would fail to benefit from them personally; that is, they would still live on fast-moving streets, while having to drive through adjacent streets at 20 mph. The alternative—a "blanket" uniform speed limit over a wider area—reduces confusion and helps people buy into the concept of driving slowly. Thus, by the spring of 2010, eight of London's 32 boroughs were moving toward blanket 20 mph speed limits.[22] And in June 2013, the mayor's transport advisor was envisioning that nearly all of London's residential streets would have 20 mph limits by 2020. (Exceptions to this limit would, as noted above, be made for major arterials.)[23]

These zones have proven extremely popular. In January 2013, the London Assembly, acting in direct response to requests from borough councils, schools, pedestrian groups and cycling organizations, called on the mayor to introduce more 20mph limits on the city's roads. It also called on Transport for London *to publish the rationale for retaining the 30 mph limit* wherever it chose to decline a request from a local council to reduce it to 20 mph.[24]

If any big US city is ready to follow suit, it should be New York, where the city's extensive, twenty-four-hour rapid transit system makes it even easier to live without a car than in London, and where more people do live without cars than in London. And, in fact, the idea of Slow Zones has already been spreading rapidly in New York. A 2010 groundbreaking study on pedestrians by the NYC Department of Transportation had recommended a pilot program of 20 mph zones in at least 75 residential neighborhoods, in addition to the re-engineering of 60 miles (96 km) of dangerous corridors and 20 dangerous intersections.[25]

The first 20 mph zone in New York City was launched in November 2011 in the Claremont neighborhood of the Bronx.[26] Less than eight months later, more than one hundred neighborhoods had applied for the program.[27] Requests for the Slow Zones have been especially numerous from the Bronx, Brooklyn, and Queens, where motorists come speeding off of peripheral highways and fail to slow down as they enter neighborhoods. Guidelines are posted on the NYC Department of Transportation website; applications for the zones may be submitted by local community boards, civic associations, business improvement districts, or elected officials. The website stipulates that: "Neighborhood Slow Zones are established in small, self-contained areas that consist primarily of local streets. Signs and gateways announce the presence of a Slow Zone. The Zone itself is a self-enforcing, reduced-speed area with speed bumps, markings and other traffic calming treatments."[28]

It is specified on the website that the locations should be primarily residential, and approximately a quarter square mile in area (0.65 km²). Wide, major streets and industrial and commercial areas should not be included within the zone. Criteria for approving the zones include the presence of schools, day care centers, senior centers, and small parks, as well as an analysis of traffic crashes within the zone, using official crash data records.[29]

The Inwood neighborhood in northern Manhattan had been habitually used by northbound drivers as a shortcut to avoid tolls and traffic lights. But in the summer of 2012, with the unanimous approval of its community board, this neighborhood became Manhattan's first Slow Zone.[30] The city also designated an additional dozen Slow Zones in New York to be implemented by the end of 2013.[31] And the chair of transportation for the New York City Council was pushing to establish these zones throughout the city.[32]

Because the size of the city's police force has been shrunken under an austerity policy, enforcement of Slow Zones will probably need to be with cameras. The city has requested permission from the state of New York to use them, but has long been stymied by a reluctant state legislature.[33] This has been a source of frustration, as speed cameras have been found to be very effective in Washington, DC, where, since their introduction in 2001, traffic fatalities have fallen by 56 percent, according to the Washington police.[34] Another approach to constraining speeds, which has been adopted by cities around the world, is the strategic timing of traffic lights; this method might well be helpful in enforcing new 20 mph zones in New York City.

Slow Zones are also catching on in Ireland. In the interests of encouraging safer walking and cycling, the National Transport Authority (NTA) of Ireland is planning to introduce an across-the-board speed limit of 18.6 mph (30 km/h) in city and village centers and residential neighborhoods throughout the Greater Dublin Area (GDA). The NTA has, additionally, proposed congestion charges and the closing of certain roads to private cars at peak hours, warning that, without these measures, traffic in the GDA could grind to a halt by 2020.[35]

Establishing 20 mph zones could, in effect, be accomplishing simultaneously the creation of slow-speed networks of streets appropriate for bicycles and mini-vehicles, the need for which was cited at the end of chapter 4. As noted in that chapter, a number of the mini-cars coming to market are specifically low-speed vehicles, most of which are designed to be driven only on streets with speed limits of 25 mph (40 km/h) or lower. They are highly appropriate for local driving, for access to transit, and for newly licensed teenaged drivers, who are in any case better discouraged from traveling at 55-plus mph (88-plus km/h) on highways. Roads in 20 mph zones can be ideally suited for these mini-cars as well as for walking and cycling.

Designing cities for the most vulnerable among us—the example of Bogotá

In the three years that Enrique Peñalosa served as mayor of Bogotá, Colombia, he managed to totally transform the quality of life in that city. When he took office in 1998, he was determined to make life more pleasant for the 70 percent of the citizens who did *not* own cars. Peñalosa contends that a city that is designed to make children and the elderly happy and safe will in turn work well for everyone. Under his leadership, the parking of cars on sidewalks was banned in Bogotá, 1,200 parks were either renovated or created anew, 100,000 trees were planted, and hundreds of kilometers of pedestrian streets and bicycle paths were built. A bus rapid transit system (described in chapter 3) was introduced, which was highly successful and resulted in the reduction of rush hour traffic by 40 percent. The involvement of local citizens in the improvement of their neighborhoods was actively encouraged, and this created a sense of civic pride. As a result of all of these measures, the streets of Bogotá in that strife-torn country became safer than those in Washington, DC.[36]

Peñalosa has observed that "The first need of a sustainable city is an environment that is most propitious for human happiness ... A good city is like a good party, in that people simply do not want to leave."[37] He remarks that we must choose between a city that is friendlier to cars or to people, and notes the irony that parks are considered a luxury in most city budgets, whereas they are very important to a democratic society, and deserving of far more generous resources than they normally receive, since they are the only place where people of all ages and incomes meet as equals.

6

Urban Design for Pedestrian- and Transit-Oriented Cities

With growing populations throughout the world being increasingly drawn to the cities, both the scale and the pace of city streets need to be more thoughtfully designed, since they are the most plentiful part of the urban commons. It is worth examining some fundamental features that have distinguished the very best of European city planning and design: (1) the basically democratic principle of designing city streets for pedestrians and cyclists, as the most vulnerable users of the streets, and (2) the favoring of walking and cycling as the most environmentally sustainable modes of travel. This latter orientation has only been strengthened by concerns about the role of the automobile in exacerbating climate change, and was affirmed by the adoption in 2011 by the European Parliament of an 18.6 mph (30 km/h) speed limit for all residential and urban roads. It has also stood in distinct contrast to prevailing US urban street design, which, until very recently, has favored cars over pedestrians, cyclists, and public transport, but is beginning to change.

As remarked by noted American landscape architect Laurie Olin:

Around the world, cities are growing everywhere. We like to be together. We need to be together. So learning how to make cities rich and fecund and great places to be so we're comfortable and healthy and happy is the biggest problem we face. The only way we'll not go crazy is to build beautiful, rich, life-enhancing cities. It's challenging to convince developers and officials that building those spaces that are not buildings are equally important if not more important for cities.

It's what we have in common. The majority of open spaces in cities are streets. That means the street system is too important to leave to transportation engineers. They're way too important to leave to just moving traffic. So I'm interested in cities because they are the design problem for a habitable planet.[1]

The centers of European cities have, in any case, long been appreciated as focal points of culture and as preferred residential locations, and transportation policies have been formed in response to this choice. A key strategy has been to strictly limit car parking in the densest parts of cities, with the explicit purpose of discouraging vehicular traffic from even entering the city center. Thus, driving in cities is deliberately made both frustrating and impractical. In Zürich, traffic lights are synchronized for pedestrians, while cars have shorter-period green lights and closely spaced, longer-period red lights. Stockholm, London, and Milan have adopted a policy that was first instituted in Singapore in 1975, wherein motorists pay high congestion charges just to enter the city center, and this has cut down significantly on traffic in these cities, while yielding the important benefit of collecting income for public transport. And both large and small European cities have entirely closed large swaths of their downtown streets to cars.

Traffic calming

Origins in Europe
One of the most effective ways to solve the problem of vehicular speed enforcement is through traffic calming, employing the techniques described in chapter 5 in reference to London's 20 mph zones—narrowing and reconfiguring streets so that the street design itself helps enforce the speed limit. The street networks themselves can also be restructured to exclude through-traffic from neighborhoods, with culs-de-sac and median strips. All types of vehicles are welcome in the neighborhood, as long as they don't exceed 18.6 mph (30 km/h); but it is the pedestrian who has priority, while cars enter only as "guests." There are varying degrees and methods of traffic calming in many towns across Europe, two of which are illustrated in figures 6.1–6.2. These are the very simplest forms of traffic restraint, and can be applied to a very wide range of densities, including the low densities that characterize most of our existing residential neighborhoods. Traffic calming projects can be achieved with relatively limited resources and tend to be strongly supported by local residents.

These and similar innovations originated with a basically unplanned citizens' initiative in Delft, Holland, in 1968, under the guidance of Hans Monderman.[2] Known as *Woonerven* (living streets), they had, by the 1980s, been constructed in one-third of Dutch towns, and the practice was being disseminated throughout Germany, Denmark, England, Japan,

Figure 6.1
Traffic calming in Dortmund, Germany, includes a tree planted at the entrance to the 18.6 mph (30 km/h) main street.
Source: Michael King.

Figure 6.2
A traffic-calmed cul-de-sac in a neighborhood of Heidelberg, Germany.
Source: Michael King.

and, to a minor extent, North America.[3] In the German cities of Esslingen and Buxtehude, traffic calming measures have been implemented which cover the entire town. While traffic calming has become especially comprehensive in small-sized towns, there is no large city in the former West Germany that does not have a substantial area where these principles have been applied.[4]

Freiburg is a city of about 220,000 inhabitants, located in sunny southwestern Germany at the gateway to the Black Forest. Freiburg's economy is based on tourism, university teaching and research, government and church administration, and on a broad range of services that it provides to its surrounding region. Up until the late 1960s, Freiburg had been encouraging greenfield development, abandoning its trolley lines, widening its streets, and building parking lots. But four decades ago, with the city sprawling, and air pollution, traffic fatalities and congestion all rising, public opinion shifted decisively away from automobile-centered growth and toward a more sustainable transport system that emphasizes walking, cycling and the use of transit.[5]

Freiburg now contains Germany's most comprehensive plan of car restraints, with a very large pedestrian network in the center of the city, extended by traffic calming and local area pedestrianization over most of the city.[6] In Freiburg, *all* of the residential streets are traffic calmed, with speed limits of 18.6 mph (30 km/h) or less. The city has also designated 177 "home zones," where cars are required to travel no faster than a walking speed of 4.35 mph (7 km/h).[7] This has made the streets utterly safe for cyclists and for children at play.

With its strong trend away from private motoring, Freiburg has earned a reputation as the environmental capital of Germany. And the city's focus on sustainability has been good for tourism and the economy in general. Although per capita income in Freiburg was 29 percent higher in 2005 than it was for Germany as a whole, by 2006 the city had 23 percent fewer cars per capita than the German average. This represented a stunning decrease from the 1950–1970 period, when Freiburg's citizens had owned more than twice as many cars per capita as West Germany as a whole. At the same time, the city's public transit system has become extraordinarily successful—as noted in chapter 4—requiring only 10 percent of its operating funds to be subsidized by the government, as compared with 28 percent for Germany as a whole.[8]

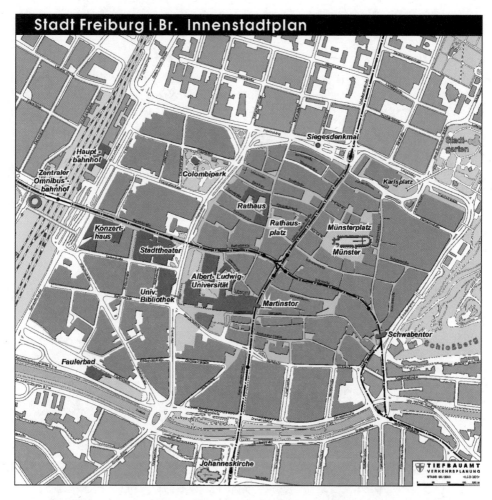

Figure 6.3
Map of Freiburg, Germany. Its pedestrian and traffic-calmed areas (shown in yellow) are the most extensive in Europe, relative to city size. Light rail lines cross in the center of this medieval city core.
Source: City of Freiburg.

Figure 6.4
Klarastrasse in Freiburg in the 1960s—a street designed for cars, not for people.
Source: City of Freiburg.

Figure 6.5
Klarastrasse after traffic calming.
Source: City of Freiburg.

Figure 6.6
Traffic calming in a typical neighborhood "home zone" in Freiburg, where car speeds are limited to a maximum of 4.35 mph (7 km/h).
Source: City of Freiburg.

"Eco-communities"—Rieselfeld, Vauban, Hammarby Sjöstad, and others

On the outskirts of Freiburg near the French and Swiss borders, the suburb has been reinvented as a high-density, mixed-use place where cars are seldom used, and children and low-consumption living can thrive—in effect, a child-oriented transit-oriented development. Two "eco-communities" have been constructed there on a large scale. Their popularity offers empirical evidence of a demand for housing that is pedestrian-, bicycle- and transit-oriented, and less reliant on the automobile. These two towns are located at the ends of branches of Freiburg's light rail network about 2 miles (3 km/h) from the city center. Rieselfeld was built on 193 acres (78 ha) that had formerly contained a French military base. With a population projected in 2009 to include 10–11,000 residents, there was no change made to the parking codes of the state of Baden-Württemberg, which require one parking space per dwelling unit. Vauban, on the other hand, was founded by its future residents, who formed a cooperative in order to self-finance the project, and pressured the authorities to allow lower parking provisions.[9]

Vauban was built on 84 acres (34 ha) of another former French military base, and houses a population of 5,500. Its streets are basically car-free, except for a few streets on one edge of the community. A light rail tram to downtown Freiburg runs on Vauban's main street, which is easily accessible by foot from all residences because of the town's long and relatively narrow site plan (figure 6.7). Car ownership can be accommodated, but car parking is largely limited to two large garages on the edge of town, where a car-owning household can buy a space. Seventy percent of Vauban's residents do not own private cars, and 57 percent of them sold a car before moving there. For occasions when a car is needed, most residents either buy a car together with another family, or rent one from the town's car-sharing club. Development of Vauban began in the mid-1990s and was completed in 2006 as part of a budding movement in Europe to decouple suburban life from auto use. Residents of the town have expressed pleasure and relief over the opportunity to raise their children on streets free of traffic.[10]

Households in both Rieselfeld and Vauban have high percentages of children, who comprise about one-third of the residents, and the safety and independent mobility of children are top concerns. There is no single-family detached housing, but there are extensive shared green spaces and large nature reserves on the edges of these districts. An arrangement of low- or no-traffic areas between buildings reduces exposure to cars and provides ample cycling and play areas. Both communities are designed to limit internal car circulation and to prevent cut-through traffic. The founders of Vauban, however, felt that Rieselfeld's transportation plan had not gone far enough in its effort to reduce car ownership and fuel consumption, so they developed a new street typology for their town:

Figure 6.7
Site plan of the eco-community of Vauban, south of Freiburg. The long blue line intersecting the site indicates the light rail tram that leads to Freiburg, and is easily accessible by foot from all areas of Vauban. Car-free residential buildings are shown in orange; residential building with parking (built early in the project) are depicted in brown.
Source: Institute for Transportation and Development Policy.

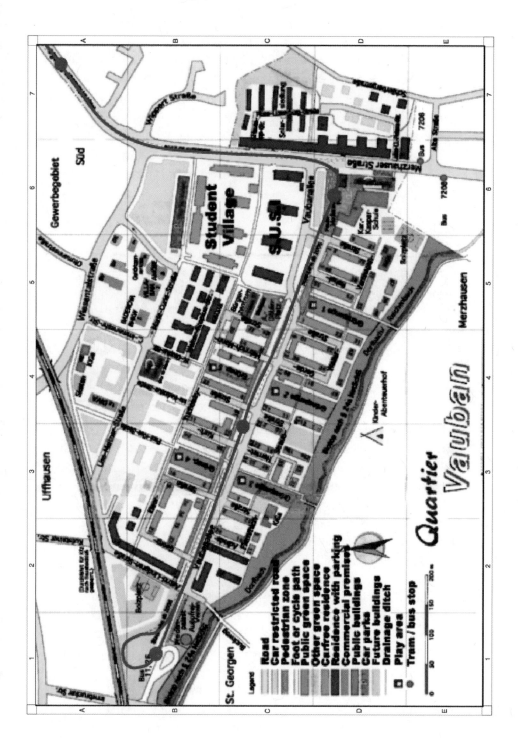

- Car-related costs should be made transparent to residents; therefore these should be unbundled from the costs of the housing itself. Parking spots should only be provided to those willing to pay garage construction cost.

- Driving should be the least convenient travel option. Toward this goal, residents should be able to reach their bicycle within a 2-minute walk from home, to reach transit within a 5-minute walk, and to reach their car within a 10-minute walk. [This technique is known as "filtered permeability."]

- To make cycling the most convenient option, sheltered bike parking should be provided directly in front of the entrance to each residential building.

- In order that walking and cycling should provide greater accessibility than driving, a network of off-street foot and cycling paths should provide access to every destination within Vauban, and a direct route to the city center. Cars should have only limited access to enter Vauban, and very limited circulation within it at low speeds.

- Housing should front onto narrow streets that are used only for loading purposes, and not for general circulation. These streets should have a 3 mph (5 km/h) speed limit, with no parking permitted, except for brief loading/unloading.[11]

Because potential investors in the Vauban project declined to embrace the car-free housing model, the town's founders had to struggle with the Freiburg city leadership and the state of Baden Württemberg to achieve their vision. The city felt that *future* residents of the suburb might prefer to have cars, so a creative compromise was negotiated that banked land for possible future parking needs. The fact that parking costs were unbundled from housing costs allowed the garages to be financed and sold separately, and interested households could purchase garage spots for the construction cost of about 17,000 euros (approximately US$24,000) per spot. Car-free households are *theoretically* required to buy a parking spot in a plot of land reserved on the edge of Vauban, but they in fact only need to pay 3,700 euros (about US$5,200), which is the land value of an *unbuilt* parking spot. In 2009, the site set aside for a new parking garage was being used instead for community barbecues and soccer games. In reality, residential parking is oversupplied in both Vauban and Rieselfeld. Although in Rieselfeld 3,300 parking spots have been provided (one for

Figure 6.8
In Vauban, driving is deliberately made the least convenient option. Toward this end, bicycle shelters are located two minutes from the residents' front doors, access to transit is a five-minute walk away, and a ten-minute walk is required to reach car parking at the edge of the district. This technique is known as "filtered permeability."
Source: Andrea Broaddus.

every dwelling unit), there are only about 2,400 vehicles registered. In Vauban, there are an estimated 1,200 parking spots, but only about 800 personal vehicles are actually registered.[12]

Vauban's environmental orientation is not confined to transportation. Many of its buildings have solar collectors and/or photovoltaic panels, and produce a positive balance of energy. The solar energy surplus is then sold back to the city's utility grid for a profit on each home.

Vauban's site plan shows how the street layout specifically discourages through-traffic and speeding, with its characteristic U-shaped residential streets. These streets connect to a main thoroughfare and the tramway that leads to Freiburg's downtown. No long-term parking is allowed on these U-shaped streets—only brief stopping for loading and unloading—and driving on them is constrained to walking speed to reserve space where children can safely play. The driving speed on all other streets in Vauban is limited to 18.6 mph (30 km/h), and the Monderman principle of "naked junctions" applies, which obliges drivers to negotiate intersections at low speed.

The entire town of Vauban is permeated with public green space. Its residential buildings are of four or five stories, and its net density, including green and other open space, is approximately 38 units/acre (95 units/ha). A majority of the town's residents prefer doing their daily grocery shopping within the district itself, a reflection of the excellent planning provisions for local facilities. Along the main spine of the development are located a supermarket, a neighborhood grocery store, two cafés, a pub-restaurant, a fast food take-away, a bakery, offices, doctor's surgery, pharmacy, and primary school. Additional stores are located along another main street. There is a public square in front of the pub that is used for a weekly farmers' market and community events.

Some of Vauban's buildings (shown in brown on the site plan) do contain bundled underground parking; these were built as part of the first construction phase. The community's ratio of less than 0.5 parking spaces per dwelling unit is nevertheless extremely low: there are only 160 cars per 1,000 residents, and, significantly, only 16 percent of travel by the town's residents is by car.[13]

The Institute for Transportation and Development Policy (ITDP) published in the summer of 2011 a report on eight new low-car/low carbon communities in Europe, including Vauban. Located in Germany, Sweden, Switzerland, England, and the Netherlands, they vary greatly in size. All but one are built on brownfields, the exception being by far the largest—Houton, built in the province of Utrecht in the Netherlands, an entire cycling city for a population of 45,000. All eight communities are located in or near cities that are established job centers, and all are either directly served by, or convenient to rail transit lines.[14]

The most successful of these districts had well-organized grassroots support from the outset for the concept of car-free living. Typically, they provide direct and safe walking and cycling routes and the "filtered permeability"—described above in the case of Vauban—that gives walking and cycling a competitive advantage over driving by making travel by foot or bike more direct than by car, and by locating bike parking closer to homes than car parking.

Of the eight communities reviewed by the ITDP, it was found that their residents generate less than 771.62 lb (350 kg) of car-related carbon dioxide per capita per annum, equivalent to a savings of around two-thirds compared with their surrounding areas.[15] As such, *these communities effectively demonstrate hopeful new templates for urban development in our warming world.*

Figure 6.9 shows the site plan of another of these communities, Hammarby Sjöstad ("Sea City"), a 395-acre (160-ha) district built on a formerly run-down industrial and harbor brownfield site, 1.86 miles (3 km) south of Stockholm's city center on the south side of Hammarby Lake, and just outside of that city's congestion zone. Hammarby Sjöstad is located in one of the world's most progressive cities with respect to sustainability. Its planning originated with Stockholm's bid to host the 2004 Olympics, for which it was envisioned as part of an ecological Olympic Village. Although Stockholm did not win the bid, planning for the town went forward, and its construction began in 1999. By 2011, 325 of its 400 acres had been developed (130 of its total 160 ha), with 8,000 residential units housing 17,000 people. Completion of the development is expected by 2017, with 11,000 housing units and 24,000 residents.

One of Hammarby Sjöstad's goals was that, by 2010, 80 percent of travel by its residents and workers should be by foot, bike, or public transport. By 2007, that goal had been nearly met, with only 21 percent of trips by the town's residents being made by car. (The town has an overall parking ratio of just 0.65 parking spaces per household.) An extension of the Tvärbanen tram line now runs through Hammarby Sjöstad, with four stops in the community. It serves a full one-third of all trips made by residents, and it interchanges with a metro station that lies just outside the town's border, providing direct service into central Stockholm. A ferry service was also introduced, which welcomes bicycles aboard, and transports passengers between Hammarby Sjöstad and Stockholm's city center, as well as to an island in between. Studies suggest that some 24 percent of travelers use the ferry for a portion of all their trips.[16]

The transportation spine of Hammarby Sjöstad is a 123-ft (37.5-m) wide boulevard and transit corridor that creates a natural focus for activity and commerce, while connecting key transit nodes and public focal points. The district is divided into twelve sub-neighborhoods; these are

NORR

HAMMARBY SJÖSTAD
ÖVERSIKTSPLAN APRIL-MAJ 2005

FRAMSTÄLLD AV STOCKHOLMS STADSBYGGNADSKONTOR

being developed in phases with different architects. As with Vauban, the general building layout is one of blocks built around green inner court-yards. The entire community of Hammarby Sjöstad is high-density, the average height of its buildings being six stories, with higher densities concentrated along the transit corridor, where buildings are seven to eight stories. A variety of ground floor uses, front doors and front balconies all enhance the safety of the streets. The architecture is based upon prin-cipals of contemporary design, utilizing environmentally sustainable tech-nologies, while maximizing the use of daylight and views of green spaces and water. One of the town's design principles is to provide 161.46 sf (15 m^2) of private courtyard space per apartment.

As with Vauban, the planners of Hammarby Sjöstad recognized the importance of providing a good mix of shops and other uses to ensure that residents would have access by foot and cycling to a full array of goods and services from the start. Toward this end, the town offered a two-year rent-free subsidy to commercial and service providers, which was instrumental in attracting them during the early phases of develop-ment. Today the town includes nearly 100 shops and restaurants, in addition to office space and light industry, employing more than 5,000 people. No one lives more than 0.62 miles (1 km) from a grocery store. Hammarby Sjöstad contains twelve pre-schools (for ages one–five), three primary schools (for ages six–sixteen), two high schools, a library, a cultural center, child care facilities, a health center, an environmental center, and a chapel.[17]

Similar communities are being developed across northern Europe. On the grounds of yet another former French military base in Germany, on the southern outskirts of the old university town of Tübingen, a new eco-community is rising on 148 acres (60 ha). By 2010 this development,

◀ **Figure 6.9**
Site plan of the eco-suburb of Hammarby Sjöstad, south of Stockholm. An exten-sion of the Tvärbanen tram line from Stockholm now runs through Hammarby Sjöstad, creating a natural focus for activity and commerce. The district is divided into twelve sub-neighborhoods, being developed in phases with different archi-tects. As with Vauban, the general building layout is one of residential blocks built around green inner courtyards. The entire community is high-density, the average height of its buildings being six stories, with higher densities concentrated along the transit corridor.
Source: Institute for Transportation and Development Policy.

which incorporates many of the car-reducing principles described above, had been partly realized, and its construction was still in progress.[18]

Closer to home—an American example

Traffic-calming projects worldwide over the past four decades have demonstrated a substantial benefit that appears to pertain to *all* types of traffic restraint: that the simple act of detouring through-traffic can result in dramatic improvements not only to the environment but also to the social solidarity of communities and the reduction of crime.

The community of Five Oaks, located a few miles from the center of Dayton, Ohio, is a case in point. This once-stable suburb, averaging 6.25 units per acre (15.4 units per ha), had by 1990 become eroded by the through-traffic of motorists commuting to and from Dayton, which had made it an increasingly undesirable place to live. Over a period of three decades most of the home-owning population had departed for more distant suburbs, having sold their houses to absentee landlords, who had subdivided and neglected them. Disinvestment, deterioration, and serious crime had followed in quick succession, and by 1992 the community was in critical distress and caught in a downward spiral.

Planner Oscar Newman, well-known for his design methods for "defensible space," was invited to work on these problems with local residents. The community was divided into ten "mini-neighborhoods," each comprised of only three or four streets, protected by speed humps, neckdowns, and gates, over which the residents were subsequently able to exert considerable surveillance and control. Most internal streets were converted into culs-de-sac, a measure that not only greatly reduced traffic and its speed but also made the streets unappealing for criminals, who prefer open escape routes.

The planning and most of the construction were accomplished with exceptional speed, within about a year, at an average cost of less than $10,000 per street. Because of the social and economic decline in this case, the physical plan was accompanied by two vital economic programs—assistance in the form of low-cost loans to help people purchase their homes, and both financial aid and technical education in rehabilitating them. But the results were striking: just eleven months after the project's completion, traffic volumes were down by 67 percent, and car crashes had decreased by 40 percent; crime overall had dropped 26 percent, and violent crime by 50 percent. Significantly, no displacement of either traffic or crime to nearby neighborhoods had occurred. There were dramatic improvements to the condition of the housing, and disinvestment in real estate had virtually halted. Two years later, by 1994, property values had actually *increased* by 15 percent. Newman has implemented similar projects in Saint Louis, Miami, and Fort Lauderdale, with similar positive results.[19]

Efforts toward creating an eco-community in California

A Vauban-like community named Bayview Village is being planned by the Hayward Area Planning Association on the outskirts of Oakland, California, accessible by shuttle bus to the Bay Area Rapid Transit system and the campus of the California State University in Hayward. The site, with 23.5 buildable acres (9.5 ha), is owned by the California Department of Transportation. Plans are for 1,024 three- and four-story condominiums and townhouses for a population of 2,200 to 2,300. Unlike most US developers, who typically aim at a more affluent market, the association is planning this community for middle-income residents. The parking is to be unbundled from the housing, both financially and physically. In addition to a long-term parking ratio of one space to ten residential units, plans are for 100 carports on existing roads, 22 spaces for car-sharing and car rental, and 18 short-term parking spaces, using the SFPark system that was described in chapter 2. The streets are to be designed to favor walking, rather than cars, and made just wide enough for fire truck access. The City is supporting these efforts with the needed zoning changes, but the planning association is having difficulty attracting equity, since investors remain reluctant to buck the standard US zoning that requires at least two parking spaces per residential unit.[20]

Additional cases of substantial traffic calming in the US

In 2006, Reid Ewing and Steven J. Brown surveyed ten jurisdictions in the US that had adopted traffic-calming programs, and found that, while none of them had made a complete transition to European standards, five had made substantial progress. These were in Bellevue (Washington), Charlotte (North Carolina), Eugene (Oregon), Sacramento (California), and Austin (Texas). The primary problem that was addressed by all of these cities was speeding, followed by cut-through traffic in residential neighborhoods. Bellevue has raised its crosswalks around a number of elementary schools, in coordination with a walk-to-school program. Austin and Sacramento have similar walk-to-school programs, and both cities have built traffic-slowing speed lumps with wheel cutouts to accommodate safer bicycling. For residential neighborhoods, the aim has also been to keep the paved street as narrow as possible. And although most of the traffic-calming strategies in these cities are being applied to the local neighborhoods, some are beginning to be applied on busier streets. In Charlotte, some arterials are being put on a "road diet," whereby the number of driving lanes has been dropped from four to three, which include a center lane for left turns, interrupted by pedestrian refuge islands. The freed-up space is given to bicycle lanes. As in Europe, street crossings have been reconfigured to shorten crossing distances, with such devices as flared corners, which compel motorists to slow down, and which make waiting pedestrians more visible to motorists.[21]

Suburban Montgomery County draws a "car-free" plan for growth

The county council of Montgomery County, Maryland, a suburban jurisdiction directly north of, and larger in area than Washington, DC, voted unanimously in November 2009 for a plan that would build new "car-free" development over the next twenty years. The plan calls for incentives for developers to create high-density projects around transit hubs, as long as they build pedestrian and cycling paths, shops, and other amenities, and use environmentally sustainable construction methods. Although the plan is actually not precisely car free, it differs radically from most suburban growth plans and zoning regulations in the US which typically discourage building in congested areas, including those near public transit, on the theory that new development should be directed instead to areas where traffic is still tolerable.

The Montgomery County council has also endorsed a plan to use development fees to improve the area's transit system, which is increasingly inadequate for commuters. The Planning Board is adamant that improving nearby transit be an ironclad condition of new development, since 200,000 more people are predicted to move into the county over the next twenty years, bringing the population to over one million. The first leg of a light rail line between Bethesda and Silver Spring has been proposed; it would run along an abandoned rail right-of-way.[22] In July

2012, Maryland's governor, county officials, and private sector partners broke ground on White Flint, the first of these TOD projects, employing a "Fast Track" program that will make it possible for selected projects to obtain necessary permits and approval in an expedited manner.[23]

For the downtowns—pedestrian streets

Where pedestrian densities are high, the case for restraints on cars and their replacement to the greatest extent possible with public transportation becomes correspondingly more compelling. This second type of traffic restraint is basically car-free at most hours; examples are found in cities all over the world today.

Pressures for auto-free zones in downtowns gained appreciable momentum after World War II, as the proliferation of cars inspired something of a citizens' insurrection against the effects of motor traffic on cities. Europe has been at the epicenter of this movement, and contains some of the most beautiful and best functioning examples. Now scores of cities worldwide have declared car-free areas, including Rome, Paris, London, New York, Boston, Tokyo, Beijing, Shanghai, Hong Kong, Toronto, Stockholm, Copenhagen, Vienna, Florence, Athens, and Prague—to name only a few.

One clear benefit of pedestrianization is a radical drop in the local air pollution that normally occurs, even when traffic continues on nearby streets. These districts also provide the security and interest of increased pedestrian activity, and relief from the tension inherent in the noise and presence of moving traffic, while allowing vehicles for public transport and emergency services to move more freely than before.

When pedestrian zones are initially proposed, they often evoke reactions of wariness and even staunch opposition from local merchants because of fears that restrictions on cars could hurt their trade. Such reservations have been especially strong in the United States, with our relatively weak city centers and the extensive suburbanization and addiction to driving of our citizenry. Numerous experiments have nevertheless gone forward in relatively small towns and cities, even in the face of considerable opposition. Many pedestrian zones, most notably in Europe, have proven unexpectedly popular with respect to expressed public reactions and to the very practical gauges of increased retail sales and property values.[24] It seems that a good physical environment creates a good economic environment where people will actually want to spend their time and money.

Pre-auto age precedents

The idea of pedestrian streets is hardly new. The problems of pre-auto age cities were only of a different scale and nature than those that we encounter today. In the first century before Christ, traffic in Rome was heavy enough to move Julius Caesar to declare a ban on carts and chariots between sunrise and sunset. In Pompeii the City Forum was reserved for pedestrians only, and the streets which led to it were terminated as culs-de-sac. Throughout the city, large stones were set in the middles of streets, both as stepping stones and as impediments to speeding vehicles. Similarly, on the Via Appia, when traffic became totally congested, which occurred frequently, it was banned altogether. And in fifteenth-century Milan, Leonardo da Vinci proposed the multi-level separation of pedestrian and vehicular traffic, with special routes reserved for hauling the heaviest goods.[25]

In nineteenth-century London, as the population grew and congestion increased in the center of town, the transport of merchandise was prohibited on selected streets during most daylight hours. In the early decades of the twentieth century it was not uncommon to find at least the partial closing of streets to traffic in the centers of a number of US, French, and German cities. Examples included some of the most prestigious streets in downtown Buenos Aires, the main boulevards of Chicago, and key streets in New York City's financial district.[26]

Ingredients for the success of contemporary pedestrian streets

In our era of the automobile, at least three primary ingredients have been essential to the success of pedestrian streets: (1) a sufficient number of pedestrians to populate the street; (2) readily available and environmentally compatible public transportation to serve the street; and (3) a high quality of design and maintenance of the public areas. While a number of pedestrian streets in the US have been commercially successful, the failure of others has been attributed to the lack of one or more of these components.[27] A basic shortcoming of many of the US experiments has been our very low public transit ridership, and the consequent absence of adequate numbers of pedestrians in the cities to begin with—certainly integral to the nation's dominant suburbanization.

But where downtown car-free streets have incorporated these three elements, their success has typically been striking. Commercial real estate on the auto-free streets of Cologne, Essen, Bremen, and Nürnberg was considered prime property after pedestrianization, and was virtually unattainable for purchase.[28] The city of Florence banned automobiles from a forty-block area in its center known as the "blue zone." This proved to be so successful for retail trade that merchants who had originally opposed the plan subsequently favored it, and those who were located just outside the zone were pressing to have it enlarged to include them.[29] The British research group TEST performed a comprehensive review and documentation of pedestrian zones in Europe and North America, completed in 1988. The group found that in most of the cases they studied, migratory movements out of the cities by residents and businesses that were occurring prior to introduction of the zones had been checked, and most of these cities were showing increases in population.[30]

European pedestrian zones

In many of the cities of Europe where pedestrian zones have been established, the central medieval cores have either survived over the centuries largely intact, or were painstakingly restored after the devastating bombings of World War II. These districts were originally built at a scale that has been utterly inappropriate for the automobile, but is intimate and ideal for the person on foot. They also contain a rich architectural heritage, which one really needs to be on foot to appreciate, including many fine-textured and carefully preserved landmarks. Public buildings, churches, and traditional marketplaces have been incorporated wherever possible into the zones, as well as frequent restaurants and cafés, with outdoor seating provided in pleasant weather. To this inherited cultural wealth are often added fountains, special paving, and street furnishings—lamps, flower gardens, benches, and kiosks—which have enhanced the streets' commercial success.

Copenhagen is home to Europe's longest pedestrian street, the Strøget. Its conversion was initiated in 1962 despite the initial protests of merchants; originally it was comprised of only 4 acres (1.58 ha) . As its popularity grew, it was gradually expanded in four subsequent stages to encompass some 25 acres (10 ha). Copenhagen established a policy of, each year, converting 2 to 3 percent of the parking in the city center to civic or pedestrian space.[31] This incremental approach to change has been key to the success of the pedestrian street, in that it has allowed time for people to make the transition from habits of driving and parking to habits of cycling and using public transit.[32] At the height of the summer tourist season, the Strøget is now used by some 250,000 people daily, and even in winter by nearly half as many. Danish architect and urban quality consultant Jan Gehl and his firm have been instrumental in the Strøget's creation and expansion, and many other European cities have followed the Copenhagen example.

In Freiburg, Paris, Vienna, Zürich, Cologne, Rouen, Leeds, and Amsterdam, as well as in Copenhagen, the pedestrian zones are comprised of one or more principal shopping streets, and in some cases, adjacent

Figure 6.10
The Strøget in Copenhagen, Europe's longest pedestrian street, initiated in 1962. *Source*: Gehl Architects.

Figure 6.11
Bicyclists, upon entering the pedestrianized Strøget, dismount from their bikes.
Source: Gehl Architects.

side streets. In Bern, Besançon, Norwich, Essen, Munich, and Oldenburg, they include extensive lengths of the original medieval street networks. Additional European cities that have pedestrianized their downtown streets and plazas include Berlin, Stuttgart, Hannover, Hamburg, Bremen, Lyons, Colmar, Florence, Strasbourg, Montpellier, Aix-en-Provence, Lisbon, Bologna, Athens, Norwich, London (Carnaby Street), Linz, Stockholm, Gothenburg and Gronignen. Dusseldorf alone has more than 17 miles (27 km) of auto-free streets.[33]

While nearly every country in Europe has developed pedestrian zones, the unquestioned leader in their creation has been Germany. Hundreds of that country's cities, including nearly every city in the former West Germany with a population of 100,000 or more have permanently eliminated traffic from at least some of their major shopping streets.[34] Although the impetus in initiating the zones has typically come from city administrators, the pressures for their expansion have come from people owning businesses in adjacent areas who wished to be included in the

Figure 6.12
Neuhauserstrasse in Munich is part of that city's highly popular pedestrian network.
Source: Roxanne Warren.

prosperity that the zones have induced.[35] In many of the German pedestrian zones, there had, by 1991, been a decrease in store vacancies to approximately zero.[36]

The city of Paris has for centuries held a special status as a paradise for walking. But as the car population multiplied, underground garages were built all over the city, so that at least the stored vehicles would remain out of sight. Unfortunately, because this, in effect, made it easier to own cars in Paris, the streets became thoroughly saturated with traffic, and the air with pollution. So in 1997, the city's mayor created a number of traffic-calmed areas from which standard cars were banned.[37] They included stretches of quais along the Seine on Sundays. On days when air pollution is assessed at dangerous levels, driving is now prohibited in the center of Paris; for this reason the city began planning in 2009 to make much of its central area traffic-free.[38]

London has established a number of pedestrian zones in its neighborhoods on weekends, and the cities of Italy instituted similar practices during the Romano Prodi coalition government. Car-free days were decreed in *all* the major cities of Italy, with scheduling posted in the media. A major goal, besides the general well-being of the population, has been to protect the country's wealth of historic landmarks, which were being corroded by car emissions. A similar preservation program is in effect in Athens, where, since the early 1980s, the Plaka area that surrounds the city's major monuments, including the Acropolis, has been declared car-free.

Vienna's ambitious "Environmental Oasis"
The city of Vienna embarked in the early 1970s on a very ambitious plan of pedestrianization, one to convert the entire historic core of the central city, an area of about 0.8 miles (1.3 km) in diameter, into an auto-free 'Environmental Oasis.' The plan, by architect Victor Gruen, was to route all traffic except for emergency vehicles around the core on Vienna's Ring Road, a boulevard built where the old medieval wall had once encircled the city. Peripheral parking was to be located outside of this road. In the original plan, the main means of access to the Oasis for pedestrians, for the delivery of goods, and for the disposal of waste were to be by subway, which was to have underground depots for goods and waste adjoining the stations. "Accessory" modes would be available within the core for the auxiliary transportation of both people and goods. These could be minibuses or small vans powered electrically or by liquid gas, or any other vehicles that are devoid, or nearly devoid of toxic fumes, and which conform to specified restrictions on speed, noise and weight. Construction began in 1971 on the subway, and a step-by-step approach was planned toward the construction of the pedestrian areas.[39]

Although the fruition of Vienna's plan has fallen far short of these goals, there were, by 1983, nearly 9 acres (3.6 ha) of pedestrian streets within central Vienna and nearly 24 acres (9.61 ha) in the city at large. In the pedestrian zone of central Vienna a 70 percent drop in air pollution had been achieved.[40] Increases in retail sales in that zone ranged between 25 and 50 percent during the first week of the ban on cars. An analysis of retailing turnover between 1970 and 1986 showed that, within the inner city, it was only the pedestrianized streets that had not experienced a fall in retail trade in those years, bucking a general area-wide trend toward decentralization.[41]

Figure 6.13
Graben, in the large, pedestrianized center of Vienna, was named as offering the highest quality of living among 221 cities by the 2010 international Mercer surveys.
Source: Roxanne Warren.

Pedestrian zones for residence

Together with their appeal for shopping, pedestrian zones, particularly in Europe, have been credited with the increased attraction of many city centers as places of residence; pressures for more housing in the zones attest to their desirability for this use. Cities such as Lyons, Hanover, Bologna, and Gothenburg have therefore coupled their creation of auto-free districts with new housing construction, which has in turn further enhanced the climate for retail.[42]

In fact, one of the only drawbacks of the European zones has been that their extreme popularity has elevated rents and real estate values to an extent that has driven some restaurants and low-volume commercial amenities out of the main stream onto side streets. Similarly, in the United States, Boston's pedestrianized Quincy Market at the reconstructed Faneuil Hall has attracted a large share of affluent suburbanites, and has become about twice as profitable as its private developer had predicted. In the process, it has priced out of the market most of the original tenants

Figure 6.14
One of Lisbon's many downtown pedestrian streets, furnished with its famous Portuguese paving. Antique street-car lines run perpendicular to the pedestrian streets.
Source: Roxanne Warren.

Box 6.1
A Brazilian pedestrian street quickly realized

The city of Curitiba, Brazil, offers a fine example of a conversion to a pedestrian street, and one that was quickly accomplished—taking only seventy-two hours for the first phase of construction. Rua XV de Novembro (15th of November Street) is an important artery running through downtown Curitiba. In 1972, under the direction of architect and then-mayor Jaime Lerner, the street was transformed into the first major pedestrian street in Brazil. Although it was initially unpopular, Rua XV de Novembro has now become a central meeting spot. Fifteen blocks long, it is beautifully embellished with landscaping and special Portuguese paving, and has become the epicenter of local business in the heart of the city.[a]

Note

a. Elizabeth Press, "Jaime Lerner on Making Curitiba's First Pedestrian Street," Streetsblog, July 7, 2009, http://www.streetfilms.org/archives/jaime-lerner-on-making-curitibas-first-pedestrian-street.

who gave the district its authentic flavor.[43] Such disadvantages should not, of course, be construed as an argument against pedestrian zones; they rather substantiate their appeal to a broad cross-section of people.

Current status of pedestrianization in the United States, and its experimental return

Some 200 pedestrian streets, or "malls" were created in the United States in the 1970s, backed by grants from the US Department of Housing and Urban Development. It seemed at the time that they might prove to be "just the ticket" to save the dying downtowns, which were suffering badly from the migration of population and businesses to the suburbs. But while much hope was invested in the malls, they were incapable of counteracting the underlying problem—the lack of a pedestrian market, in the form of city residents, office workers, and retail activity. In too many cases, few pedestrians and vacant storefronts made for lonely, desolate streets. Although the malls themselves were not the basic reason for the decline of the downtowns, they were given the blame by public space "experts," who advised local planners to remove them as a step toward urban revitalization.[44] Gradually, towns began to reopen their pedestrian streets to traffic: by the early 1990s at least one-half of the approximately

Box 6.2
Polar opposite conditions for pedestrians in two hemispheres

As populations burgeon worldwide, and large numbers of people migrate from rural to urban environs, extreme overcrowding is occurring in many of the world's cities. In China, large throngs of people have therefore benefited from newly created car-free shopping streets, filled with exciting lights and shops, in all of the country's major cities, including Shanghai, Beijing, Guangzhou, and Hong Kong.[a]

In Mumbai, the commercial capital of India, the streets around train stations are so packed with cars, motorcycles, and vendors that they have become very difficult to navigate on foot. A partial solution has been found in the construction of skywalks, which sprout from the stations and snake across the city over traffic. While these are popular with pedestrians, retailers on the streets below complain that the skywalks are causing them to lose business. Local residents are equally unhappy with the skywalks, because they block views, while allowing passersby to peek into private homes. The residents also claim that the skywalks are as likely as the sidewalks to be taken over by homeless families and shopless vendors, and must therefore be closely monitored.[b] It is regrettable in a city where close to 60 percent of travel is by foot that the pedestrians have difficulty circulating at the street level, where it would be most convenient for them to enjoy the city and to patronize small retailers. Indeed, these streets might well be considered candidates for at least partial pedestrianization, if only their vehicular traffic could be rationalized.

At the polar opposite have been conditions in much of the United States, where, from the mid-twentieth century until the turn of the twenty-first century, we were experiencing an exodus of population from most of our cities—an exodus that has worked directly against the prosperity of many of our pedestrian streets.

Notes

a. Colin Rowan, "The Pedestrian Way: Streets to People in China and the United States," August 23, 2012, http://psuchina.wordpress.com/2012/08/23/pedestrian-streets-streets-for-people-in-china-and-the-united-states.

b. "Packed Streets Have a City of Walkers Looking Skyward for Answers," *Wall Street Journal*, January 19, 2010, http://online.wsj.com/article/SB100014240527487 03837004575013193075912272.html.

200 US malls had done so, and by 2008, only some 15 of the original malls remained. So at the end of the twentieth century, there were no major pedestrian streets in the downtowns of the largest US cities—New York, Chicago, Los Angeles, or San Francisco.[45]

Yet, several quasi-pedestrian streets had been initiated as bus transit malls in the US—including Nicollet Mall in Minneapolis in 1968, the Fifth and Sixth Avenue Malls in Portland (Oregon) in 1976, and the 16th Street Mall in Denver in 1982—and these have all survived and prospered. The presence of surface public transit has been a vital component in the success of all of these streets. As noted in chapter 3, a number of pedestrian streets have recently been combined with, or reinforced by light rail lines in the downtowns of Portland, Denver, Houston, Dallas, San Diego, and Sacramento. Nicollet Mall in Minneapolis, the city's auto-free office and retail spine, is now also served by a station of the Hiawatha light rail line at 5th Street. This has helped to spur an unprecedented amount of redevelopment on the mall, including the headquarters of six major corporations. Unlike many other US cities, Minneapolis had managed to retain its retail core, including some major stores and art galleries. Additionally, the light rail service has expanded opportunities for new job and residential development near the downtown.[46]

Plans to revitalize Nicollet Mall by James Corner Field operations and Minneapolis architect Julie Snow include a transparent stairway that will cascade down from the skyway to the street in front of the IDS Center. Snow's purpose in this design was "to give people a reason to come down from the skyway to Nicollet Mall."[47]

In the twenty-first century, the resurgent back-to-the-city movement in the US has also opened excellent potential for experimentation with auto-free streets, mini-parks, and plazas. In San Francisco, Seattle, and New York, inexpensive pedestrian plazas have been emerging in the downtowns, which are proving highly popular. Flexibility in their planning and implementation has been key. In many cases, the plazas have been begun on a trial basis, as simple, temporary installations, often with recycled components. Their provisional nature has helped to diffuse the opposition that typically arises when auto-free space is first proposed. At the same time, it has been increasingly appreciated by the planners initiating these projects that having a local partner, such as a business improvement district or community organization, is essential to their success.

Figure 6.15
Nicollet Mall, initiated in 1968 as an office and retail spine for Minneapolis. A single bus line and taxis are the only vehicles allowed.
Source: City of Minneapolis.

Management and maintenance of the space is thereby shared between the city and the community partner.[48]

Author Mike Lydon has dubbed this method "tactical urbanism"—public space reclamation that, using very temporary materials, can be built virtually overnight, and can become a place holder for a more permanent installation.[49]

Taking this approach, the New York City Department of Transportation, in cooperation with businesses and the community, had, by the end of 2010, created nine temporary, very inexpensive plazas in four of the city's five boroughs. Denmark's Jan Gehl was engaged by New York City for consultation on these projects, the most notable of which are large pedestrian plazas in Times Square and Herald Square—the "Broadway Boulevard" experiment. The popularity of the closing of Broadway to cars between 42nd and 47th Streets has been reflected in remarkable safety and economic gains—a 63 percent reduction in pedestrian injuries and a 71 percent increase in retail rents in the pedestrian area. Five high-end retailers subsequently announced plans to open new "flagship" stores

Figure 6.16
Denver's Sixteenth Street Mall, started in 1982.
Source: Downtown Denver Partnership.

in Times Square.[50] After a highly successful trial period, the Times Square plaza was scheduled to be refashioned with more permanent materials. An important side benefit of the plaza has been significantly reduced concentrations of nitrogen oxide and dioxide in its air.[51]

Emulating New York's experience, planners in Los Angeles have designed a remake of that city's Broadway into a more pedestrian-friendly street, in which six lanes of car traffic are to be reduced to three, and sidewalks are to be broadened and beautified. The first phase of this project is a temporary and cost-effective ($1.8 million) conversion, whose funding was approved by the City Council in the summer of 2013, with a target date for completion within a year.[52]

New York's Department of Transportation has also carved numerous small parks out of previously excessively paved (and challenging-for-pedestrians-to-cross) intersections and parking lots, adding welcome greenery, while serving pedestrians as refuges from traffic. These small parks are in addition to the expansion of bike paths described in chapter

4. As a result, the safety of New York's streets has improved dramatically for pedestrians, as well as for cyclists, and traffic fatalities are at an all-time low. Benches have been thoughtfully installed in areas frequented by seniors. *There is a great hunger for these spaces; when they are created, they fill up immediately with people of all ages.* And to help ensure that these improvements will survive the electoral turnover of the city's administration, a *Street Design Manual* was compiled, with the coordinated efforts of many city departments, to set high standards for pedestrian-oriented and Complete Streets, years into the future.[53]

San Francisco's "parklet" program has become a national model for cities looking to infuse new life into their streets. It began in 2005 with a relatively modest gesture, when Rebar, an art and design studio, converted a single metered parking space in the city into an impromptu public park. It has evolved into an occasion in which one, two, or three parking spaces at a time are occupied by people who move in for a day with sod, potted trees or shrubs, and benches. From these beginnings, PARK(ing) Day has become an annual event that encourages citizens around the world in more than 150 cities on six continents to temporarily transform parking spots into whatever is needed in the neighborhood—be it park space, a health clinic, a bike repair shop, or an art display.[54]

San Francisco now has a Pavement to Parks program, officially sanctioned in 2009 as an interdepartmental effort; it includes an innovative permitting system that has been imitated by other US cities. The program allows neighborhood or business sponsors to convert parking spaces into temporary parklets of their own design and at their own expense, provided that they meet a basic set of parameters and are approved by a review board; this has allowed for an experimental and playful approach to design. Parklets typically cost between $7,000 and $20,000, and have included such imaginative features as a bocce ball court, and a bike-rack-with-garden-trellis. The city requires that the parklet space remain public and enforces this rule with plainclothes inspectors.

By 2011, there were twenty-three fully sanctioned parklets in San Francisco, and at least as many in the pipeline. They involve no modifications to the curbs, drainage, or street design, and so preclude the permanent loss of parking spaces. Permits are reviewed annually, and can be revoked for blight or lack of maintenance. By 2012, San Francisco had launched a new website, cosponsored by the city's Municipal

Transportation Agency, Planning Department, Department of Public Works, and Public Utility Commission, to help residents take advantage of city resources and programs for creating neighborhood-scale improvements—such as parklets, bike parking, green infrastructure, and permits for car-free events.[55] Similar parklets to those in San Francisco are now emerging in Vancouver, Philadelphia, and Chicago.[56]

Inspired by San Francisco, even the famously car-oriented city of Los Angeles has been experimenting with car-free pedestrian plazas. In the city's Silver Lake neighborhood, a small, popular triangular park has been created within a busy commercial area. Spearheaded by the city's departments of planning, transportation, and public works, partnering with the county's public health department, the area was converted into a plaza with the simple application of glowing neon green paint; it includes bike racks and planters around the edges and seating in the middle.[57]

Small, seasonal parklets based on the San Francisco model have also been appearing in the fair season on New York City's narrowest streets—dubbed "pop-up cafés." While sidewalk cafés have long been a popular feature of New York, many of the city's downtown sidewalks are too

Figure 6.17
Pop-up café on New York City's Sullivan Street in Soho.
Source: Roxanne Warren.

narrow to accommodate them. Starting from the premise that the highest and best use of limited and valuable street space is not necessarily the storage of cars, the city's Department of Transportation, the Department of Consumer Affairs, and New York's Downtown Alliance have sanctioned the installation of a number of 84-ft-long by 6-ft-wide (25.5-m-long by 1.83-m-wide) wooden platforms, with railings, planters, café tables, and chairs, in the space typically allotted to four parked cars. Each pop-up café is sponsored and maintained by the shops adjoining it, but is freely available for use by the public; these shops are thereby receiving tangible benefits of up to 14 percent increases in their business. The platforms, planters, and furniture are stored over the winter, when the parking spots are returned to their former use.[58]

Even in Dallas, "Build a Better Block" was started as a weekend event, which put a three-lane, one-way street on a "road diet," adding chicanes and a bike lane. The participants created a mock-up of a neighborhood setting that the community was asking for. The result was widely reported on the Internet and produced actual change in the city of Dallas itself.[59]

And in New York City, the highly popular Summer Streets program, initiated by the Department of Transportation, temporarily closes to cars a series of avenues between Central Park and the Brooklyn Bridge, and opens them to pedestrians and cyclists.

Coordinating pedestrian streets with transit

The feasibility of restrictions on cars in the US

How realistic is it to assume that, in a country so closely wedded to the automobile, motorists might be willing to consider effective curbs, other than temporary, on this machine that currently plays so prominent a role in our lives? As emphasized by professors Ralph Buehler of Virginia Tech and John Pucher of Rutgers University:

It is politically difficult and potentially inequitable to restrict car use and make it more expensive unless there are feasible alternatives to car use that provide acceptable levels of mobility. Thus, car-restrictive policies must be accompanied by the provision of high-quality public transport services as well as safe and convenient walking and cycling facilities.[60]

It should not be surprising that two of the countries that have been at the forefront of pedestrianizing their downtowns—Germany and the

Netherlands—are those very same countries that have invested the most per capita in their public transportation systems.

First making transit more economically viable—as accomplished elsewhere

Fiscal conservatives in the US have long criticized public transit for not being self-sufficient (while overlooking the very generous public subsidies that have been conferred on our competing automobile/highway system). In fact, the relatively poor levels of performance of many of the public transit systems in our nation need not be accepted as the norm. As noted in chapter 4, average transit operating subsidies average only 28 percent in Germany, where extensive improvements in walking and cycling routes to transit and in transit-related bike parking facilities have enormously encouraged transit ridership. Buehler and Pucher have detailed how this contributes to major improvements in the economic viability of public transportation in Germany, and how, despite a rapid growth in per capita income and car ownership, the use of public transport in that country has continued to grow, accounting for five times as high a share of trips per capita as in the US.[61]

A key component of lower transit operating costs in Germany—its rising ridership with consequent rising transit revenues—has stemmed not only from improved pedestrian and cycling access to it, but from the high priority given by government to running a first-class system of public transport. The use of generally quite new vehicles has increased reliability and avoided high maintenance costs. Other cost-saving measures include the use of part-time drivers to handle the extra service needed at peak hours, signal prioritization that favors transit at intersections, and the wider spacing of bus and tram stops to preclude frequent stopping. An especially attractive feature of German transit is the multi-modal integration of services, schedules, fares and transfers—which has created a virtually seamless travel experience for passengers. Deep discounts on weekly, monthly, annual, and school semester tickets have also made public transport more economical and convenient to ride.[62]

A carrot-and-stick approach

These improvements have been made concurrently with policies to curb the automobile. As noted by Buehler and Pucher, the fact that public transport in Germany functions so well has made it much more politically palatable to initiate and maintain substantial policies of traffic restraint. One component of the German strategy of deterring private motoring would be considered especially onerous and has to date proven politically impossible in the US—the deliberate raising of the costs of owning and operating a car. For a similar car, these costs are some 50 percent higher in Germany than in the US, due primarily to much higher taxes and fees on car ownership and use.[63] In particular, there is a very large difference between the two countries in the taxes on gasoline. In 2012 in Germany, the tax alone on gasoline was substantially higher than the total average price of gasoline in the US—$4.88 as compared with $4.10, respectively—the result of an explicit policy in Germany favoring environmental sustainability.[64]

Even without an increase in the gasoline tax, substantial rises in the price of gasoline in the US may occur anyway, concurrent with the worldwide competition for petroleum; to date, this has already had some effect on curtailing motoring. Other, more deliberate deterrents to driving may be more acceptable to the US public and more feasible to implement quickly. These include the elimination of free car parking and the conversion of zoning from minimum parking requirements to maximum, as discussed in chapter 2. Such constraints on driving could be paired simultaneously with the "carrots" of not only major improvements in the functioning of public transport, but also some relief from the dominance of cars—in the forms of 20 mph and traffic-calmed zones in residential neighborhoods, and/or some auto-free downtown streets, initiated in conjunction with higher-quality public transport. Freiburg and the eco-communities described above have provided premier examples of this "carrot-and-sick" approach.

Light rail/streetcars/trams in downtown pedestrian streets
As was noted in chapter 3, light rail operates as streetcars, or trams, at limited speeds either within or perpendicular to many of the world's pedestrian streets, with simple, inexpensive, and easily accessed stations that are well integrated with the streets' shopping functions. To serve expanding populations in smaller cities throughout Europe and North America, many tram lines have also been upgraded to light rail to create regional mini-metro systems. While located at grade in the city center (or,

at considerably higher cost, underground), their rights-of-way in outlying areas are normally separated from other forms of traffic by fencing or grade separation, to allow higher speeds for the longer-distance, suburb-to-city portion of the trip. Construction costs for the at-grade portions of light rail in cities have typically been about one-tenth as high per mile as subway construction for the same city.

As also noted in chapter 3, the old tram networks in North America were never entirely abandoned in a number of cities—in North America these include networks in Philadelphia, Pittsburgh, Toronto, Boston, San Francisco, New Orleans, Newark, and Cleveland—and many of these systems have recently been expanded. And in Portland (Oregon), San Diego, Sacramento, Dallas, Houston, and Minneapolis, a downtown pedestrian street has in each case been made an integral part of light rail plans. Typically, these new and expanded light rail lines have prompted a surge of commercial and residential development. In Portland alone, there had by 1996 been over $1.3 billion worth of new development, exceeding 10 million sf (929,000 m^2) that were stimulated immediately adjacent to the light rail stations. When plans were announced for an additional $440 million worth of improvements, the enthusiastic citizenry voted themselves a tax increase to pay for the expansion of the light rail network.[65]

Streetcars in a number of European cities—including Amsterdam, Strasbourg, Freiburg, Lisbon, Zürich, Bremen, Linz, Gothenburg, Heidelberg, and Kassel—have remained in the pedestrian street, and this has provided a relatively inexpensive, efficient, and reliable means of circulation for the city center portions of area-wide light rail networks. The street thereby becomes a tramway, as well as a shopping street. Yet because the vehicles are non-pollutant, quiet, and dependably confined to their tracks, with high carrying capacities for the space that they occupy, the system is thoroughly compatible with Gruen's concept of the "Environmental Oasis." As shown in figures 6.18–6.20, the transit vehicles do not violate the relaxed atmosphere. Their at-grade stations are also the utmost in simplicity and economy, requiring only a concrete platform and some signage.

Zürich's Bahnhofstrasse has functioned over the past four decades as a high-end, car-free shopping boulevard, with light rail running at grade for its entire length, linking travelers with both regional rail and ferries.

Figure 6.18
Pedestrians and streetcars mix well on a main boulevard in Istanbul.
Source: Tina Lund.

Figure 6.19
Freiburg's car-free center, where the lines of the city's extensive light rail transit network converge. The center of Freiburg is essentially limited to trams, pedestrians, and bicycles.
Source: John Pucher.

Figure 6.20
Zürich's Bahnhofstrasse—a high-end, car-free shopping boulevard, served by a light rail line that links the main regional rail station with the city's ferries—is a model for a proposal for Manhattan's 42nd Street.
Source: Roxanne Warren.

The commercial vitality of this street is reflected in its land values, which are the highest in the city, all located along the pedestrian/light rail street. To spread the prosperity, Zürich's citizens in the spring of 2000 voted overwhelmingly, with 99 percent in favor, to apply the same treatment to another of the city's major shopping streets, which borders the Limmat River.[66] Limmatquai is now a pleasant riverside pedestrian street lined with cafés and served by light rail.

With its commercial success and well-though coordination with regional rail and ferries, Zürich's Bahnhofstrasse has served as a model for a proposal—dubbed vision42—that was initiated in 2000 by the nonprofit Institute for Rational Urban Mobility, Inc., to convert Manhattan's 42nd Street into a river-to-river, car-free light rail boulevard, complete with special paving, landscaping, outdoor restaurants, and cafés.

The vision42/Midtown Loop proposal for Manhattan—model for a crowded city

As emphasized above, it is especially desirable for the more fluid functioning of high-density urban centers that motor vehicles be restrained and supplanted to the greatest extent possible with high-quality surface public transit. Manhattan's 42nd Street, with its very high percentage of public transit riders, its confluence of half a million pedestrians every weekday at the street's major transit hubs, and its rich offering of cultural, civic, commercial and entertainment facilities, is in a unique position among US cities for a demonstration of this principle. Today's notoriously slow crosstown bus service on 42nd Street could be replaced with a river-to-river, modern, low-floor light rail tram. This could, furthermore, be the first phase of a continuous two-way 42nd/34th Street Midtown light rail loop.

In large cities such as New York that already have subways and/or commuter rail, light rail can serve simply as a highly effective and pedestrian-friendly local distributor, or streetcar/tram. Running in a pedestrian street, vehicle speeds would be limited to 15 mph (24 km/h) for pedestrian safety, and would therefore not need to possess the power that is required for mini-metro light rail systems.

The light rail tram would double the speed and efficiency of today's buses, which currently crawl on 42nd Street at an average of 3.6 mph

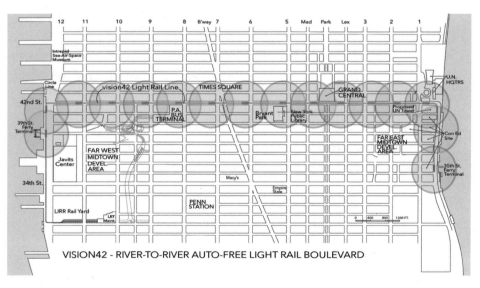

VISION42 - RIVER-TO-RIVER AUTO-FREE LIGHT RAIL BOULEVARD

Figure 6.21
Map of the vision42 proposal—an auto-free light rail boulevard for Manhattan's 42nd Street, linking major transit terminals and the ferries at both rivers.
Source: Roxanne Warren.

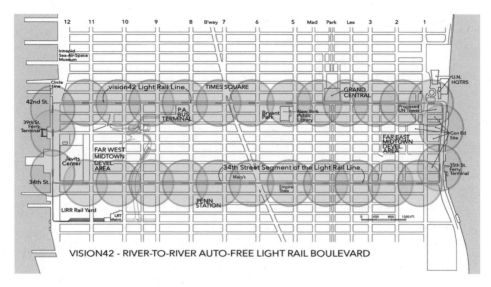

VISION42 - RIVER-TO-RIVER AUTO-FREE LIGHT RAIL BOULEVARD

Figure 6.22
Map of the extension of light rail to 34th Street, to create a continuous two-way
Midtown Manhattan Loop, linking with Penn Station, the hub of the entire re-
gion's transit systems.
Source: Roxanne Warren.

(5.8 km/h)—having been honored in 2010 with the "Pokey" award as
the slowest in the city.[67] Light rail is seen as a more appropriate choice
than bus rapid transit or select bus service for 42nd Street, despite its
much higher initial cost, for several reasons: (1) Light rail provides a
smoother, much more appealing ride, and is therefore highly likely to
attract more of the public out of private cars and taxis. While pos-
sessing the advantages of permanence and smooth ride that characterize rail systems of all kinds, the fact that it operates at ground level
allows for the enjoyment of the cityscape (especially important for
tourists, but appreciated by all manner of citizenry). (2) Light rail
vehicles have three times the capacity of buses, so three times as many
buses as light rail vehicles would be needed for the same capacity. With
stops at every avenue, this would create bus bunching because of the
short distances between stops. (3) Speedy, "limited-stop" bus service
would also be impractical on this crosstown route, because each avenue it crosses is an important transfer point with the north/south
subways and buses—nor would higher speeds even be acceptable in

a pedestrian street. (4) Light rail not only has the permanence that reinforces new development, but its rails discourage motorists from driving on them, and thereby help to create a self-enforcing exclusive path.

On Manhattan's 42nd Street, there could be practical as well as aesthetic objections to overhead catenary wires (because of interference with parades and overhead bridges, for example). But as noted in chapter 3, the power for light rail can be delivered by any one of a number of catenary-free systems, which can also significantly simplify and economize on the construction, operation, and maintenance of the light rail system. One option would likely be long-lasting lithium-ion battery packs, mounted directly on the vehicles. Some batteries that have been developed by major light rail vehicle manufacturers are quite adequate for a system of 5 miles (8 km), which would be the length of a continuous 42nd/34th Street light rail loop. Alternately, an in-ground option for catenary-free light rail, which has been developed by at least three major manufacturers, and has been in successful operation in Bordeaux, France, since 2004, entails the embedding of prefabricated power strip segments between the tracks. The safety of pedestrians, cyclists, and other vehicles is assured, because it is only those lengths of power strip that are directly under the light rail vehicle that are energized as it passes over them. These systems are not impacted by snow, ice, sand or salt on the rails.[68]

As for the auto-free aspect of the proposal, it should be underscored that, to begin with, only 23 percent of the households in Manhattan even *own* a car. The argument that banning cars on a major street in Midtown Manhattan would hurt retail trade is refuted by a 2006 study by Schaller Consulting that found that only 6 percent of shopping trips in this district involve the use of a car. The study also discovered that much of the traffic in Midtown has no business interests there, but is using the central business district simply as a through-route to other destinations. Thirty percent of the drivers who enter the district via the Lincoln and Holland tunnels, and 39 percent who enter by the East River bridges have destinations outside of Midtown.[69] Clearly, all of this excess private motoring is impeding the movement of people and goods in this dense district, sapping its economic efficiency, and adding to pollution.

Box 6.3
The experience of traffic shrinkage

A big concern to drivers is what happens to traffic when streets are closed to cars. However, experience has shown that traffic demand is elastic and can shrink. In most cases, when a street has been pedestrianized, the impact on traffic and travel times has not been as dire as many have predicted. Just as new cars are attracted when a new road is built, the reverse is similarly true. With the road closed to cars, much of the traffic typically "evaporates," finding other routes and other modes, such as walking or taking public transit.[a] Such shrinkage of traffic was demonstrated dramatically in New York City in 1973, when portions of the West Side Highway collapsed, and in San Francisco, when the Embarcadero Freeway was partially destroyed by the 1989 earthquake, and then totally demolished.

Note

a. Sally Cairns, Carmen Hass-Klau, and Phil Goodwin, *Traffic Impact of Highway Capacity Reductions: Assessment of the Evidence* (London: Landor Publishing and London Transport, March 1998). This book details forty-seven cases of street closings around the world where the predicted congestion on adjacent streets failed to materialize. More often than not, the extra traffic simply disappeared. And this was passive shrinkage of traffic, not shrinkage due to congestion pricing, which has been so effective in the heart of London, where traffic volumes are down by 17 percent, and motor vehicle delays are down by 30 percent.

The vision42 proposal would build on the success of the above-mentioned Broadway Boulevard experiment, conducted by the city beginning in the summer of 2009, which banned autos from Broadway in Times Square and Herald Square to create pedestrian plazas. This experiment achieved permanent status in 2010, after an independent online survey had indicated that, of those surveyed, 76 percent of New Yorkers, 75 percent of suburban residents, and 68 percent of retail managers said they would like the plazas to remain permanent.[70] While that project has actually improved the flow of traffic on Seventh Avenue (since it no longer has to cross Broadway at an acute angle), the benefits to people have been even greater. Injuries to motorists decreased by 63 percent, injuries to pedestrians fell by 35 percent, and 80 percent fewer pedestrians have complained about having to walk in the street for lack of space.[71]

Of the daily peak hour commuters into Midtown Manhattan, some 80 percent come there by transit, and since most of the public is already traveling by foot and transit, the argument is very strong for turning major streets like 42nd Street over entirely to the combination of pedestrians and transit. There are at least five times as many pedestrians as motorists on 42nd Street; yet 60 percent of the street space is dedicated to motorists. And the crowds of pedestrians have been swelling, as numerous new office and residential towers have become occupied (and more are planned). As a result, the sidewalks are often filled to, and beyond capacity, causing pedestrians to spill over into the street. Without closing the street to traffic, particularly in its most crowded middle portion between Third and Ninth Avenues, 42nd Street is virtually guaranteed to become inundated with pedestrians—not a desirable alternative to the street's formerly derelict status.

Conversely, the successful fruition of the vision42 proposal could serve as a prominent showcase of urban livability for the nation, demonstrating how even large cities can be humane and enriching places to live and work, and helping to counter many anti-urban inclinations in the United States.

In an ideal world, a cue might be taken from the incremental development of Copenhagen's Strøget, whereby the banning of cars might commence in stages, beginning with the most crowded section of 42nd Street, between Third and Ninth Avenues. However, this approach could be less workable in New York City, because of the lack of continuity in the city's administration, with a new mayoral election every four years.

An earlier 42nd Street light rail proposal, initiated in 1978, would not have closed the street to traffic, but would have retained westbound traffic in the northern half of the street, locating two-way light rail on the south side. The light rail was to have been privately financed, designed, built, and operated by a "super turnkey" consortium of firms. It was expected to allow not only the smoother flow of crosstown transit but relief from the high operating costs of bus services along this major artery.[72] The project was approved by the City Council in 1994 by a vote of 49 to 2 . However, when the city administration changed hands in the following election, the project was shelved.

The major *disadvantage* of this plan was that it would have failed to create more and better-quality space for pedestrians. In fact, it would have placed large crowds of westbound passengers on mid-street

Figure 6.23
Computer image of vision42 light rail connecting with the Hudson River ferry
service, making ferry travel more attractive and ferry operations more efficient.
Source: Mathieu Delorme.

platforms waiting for the light rail, directly adjacent to heavy westbound
car traffic. Meanwhile, pressures for more pedestrian space have grown
enormously.

The first phase of the current proposal, with two-way light rail in the
center of the street, where trolleys originally ran for decades, would
stretch between ferry terminals on the East and Hudson rivers, serving
the United Nations Headquarters and a major new, residential/office
development that is planned along the East River, and the Javits Convention Center, Circle Line, and Intrepid Museum, all located along the
Hudson. It would link these facilities and developments with numerous
existing high-capacity interborough, region-wide, and long-distance transit interchanges along 42nd Street—five four-track subways, commuter
rail at Grand Central Terminal, express buses at the Port Authority Bus
Terminal, and various ferry services at the rivers. At the far eastern end
of 42nd Street, the light rail boulevard would allow, and could encourage
a more fittingly ceremonial public approach to the United Nations. (At

Figure 6.24
Computer image highlighting that an appropriate public approach to the head-quarters of the United Nations could be one of the many benefits of vision42.
Source: Mathieu Delorme.

the same time, some accommodations would need to be made for secure private car access for "VIP" individuals arriving at and departing from the United Nations.)

A second phase of the plan would create a continuous two-way Mid-town Loop, circling around on 34th Street, thereby linking Penn Station, which is the main transit hub of the entire New York region, with the ferry terminals and Grand Central Terminal. With some revisions to traffic on nearby cross streets, 34th Street might ultimately also be made auto-free in the most appropriate blocks, where pedestrian volumes are tremendous, between Fifth and Eighth Avenues, including Penn Station and Macy's department store.

By the spring of 2014, 390 presentations of this proposal had been made to a wide range of community groups, elected and appointed officials, civic and professional organizations, and real estate developers, and had elicited considerable support. An advisory committee had been

Figure 6.25
Computer image of the vision42 light rail crossing pedestrianized Times Square.
Source: Mathieu Delorme.

Figure 6.26
Computer image of vision42 at Theater Row on far West 42nd Street.
Source: Mathieu Delorme.

Figure 6.27
Computer image depicting how the second phase of the light rail would circle around on 34th Street, connecting with Penn Station, the main transit hub of the entire New York region.
Source: Mathieu Delorme.

formed, with more than forty distinguished New Yorkers, including real estate developers and professionals in various related fields.

Projected economic benefits of vision42   The initial 42nd Street segment of this proposal has been studied extensively for its likely costs and its economic and fiscal benefits, as well as its traffic and construction phasing impacts. A series of coordinated technical studies by a team of well-regarded consultants concluded that the payback from this project would be impressive and swift.

All construction projects are far more costly in a complex city like New York (at least in part because the city does not maintain complete and updated records of the locations of underground utilities, which can lead to unpleasant surprises). Nevertheless, the vision42 technical studies confirmed the rule-of-thumb previously noted, which has proven true throughout the world—that at-grade light rail costs approximately one-tenth as much per mile as subway construction for the same city.

Thus, while subway construction in New York City was costing around $2 billion per mile in 2007 ($1.243 billion per km) the 2.5-mile (approximately 4-km) vision42 project was projected that same year to cost one-tenth as much, or some $200 million per mile ($124.3 million per km). Including a very generous allowance for high-quality landscaping, estimates for vision42 ranged from $411.25 million to $582.31 million in 2007 dollars, depending upon the extent of utility replacements, and whether the vehicles would be powered by an overhead wire or, less expensively, self-propelled. Utility replacements, with a large contingency allowance, accounted for the lion's share of these amounts, more than 52 to 64 percent of the total.[73]

However, against these estimates, the combined economic and fiscal *benefits* of the project were projected in 2006 to be $880.3 million *annually* This suggests that the payback for the capital costs of the project could occur within as few as eight months, even using the higher cost estimate. In 2006, under healthy economic conditions, there were 126 active retail establishments on 42nd Street itself, as well as 2 large movie complexes, 67 legitimate theaters, and 61 hotels within a designated 10-block-wide corridor stretching from 37th to 47th Streets, river to river. Improved access via light rail, the large increase in pedestrian space, and the enhancement of its amenities were expected to bring 35 percent more foot traffic to the street, and consequently a 34 percent gain in retail business, generating more than 1,000 new jobs.[74]

These calculations were made prior to the deep economic recession that commenced in December 2007, and the costs and benefits cannot be counted on to have declined in a similar relationship to each other. Nevertheless, the project still seems likely to have a dramatic stimulative effect on the economy.

Financing of vision42 could be accomplished by one of at least two likely methods. One would be tax increment financing (TIF), in which the city would be taking responsibility for paying the debt service on the project from its anticipated annual tax proceeds. These are projected to be well in excess of the annual debt service. The other method would be to set up a special transit improvement district (TID), wherein by prior agreement the benefited property owners would agree to pay a special levy to carry the debt service. The substantial and swiftly realized gains for the property owners that are expected from the project would justify this second method.[75]

The type of Select Bus Service (SBS) that has already been installed on Manhattan's First and Second Avenues, described in chapter 3, is certainly vastly cheaper than light rail, and SBS has been suggested by some for this project in lieu of light rail. However, the gains in property values and fiscal revenues that have been projected for vision42 were predicated on an assumption that a rail system would be in place. Buses are an inferior alternative, as they lack the permanence, the reliability, and the smooth ride of light rail, and simply do not have its stimulative attraction.

Furthermore, there is a general consensus that some sort of crosstown rail transit is sorely needed in heavily populated Midtown Manhattan, and there has been a great deal of interest in building a station at Tenth Avenue and 41st Street on the new extension of the 7 subway line. However, that one station has been roughly estimated by Metropolitan Transportation Authority Capital Construction to cost some $750 million, which exceeds by 1.5 times the amount estimated for the entire sixteen-stop light rail line. Nor would the subway be able to carry travelers river-to-river, since on the east side, it descends steeply to pass under the East River, and because on the west side, it turns south under 11th Avenue.

A study was completed in 2012 which compared the travel time savings and resultant property value increases that could be expected from each of these two projects. It was found that the vision42 light rail would realize travel time savings that are more than three times greater than those that could be achieved with the 10th Avenue station. As a result, the light rail plan, with its 16 pairs of stops, can be expected to result in increases of existing commercial property values some three times greater, on average, than those to be realized by building the 10th Avenue subway station.[76] The light rail would have the additional advantage of serving the East River and Hudson River ferries, as well as massive housing developments on the far east and west ends of the street.

The project's construction engineering consultants have estimated that vision42 should take just two years to build, assuming a scheme of minimum utility relocation, with six months of digging per block. During the construction period, buses can continue to serve the street without interruption, since the sidewalks will remain unaffected.[77]

The economic studies included a detailed survey of business owners and managers, who were shown the construction phasing plans. Although they had previously been unfamiliar with the project, they gave it ratings of 3.4 to 4.0 (on a 0.0 to 5.0 scale, with 5.0 being the most positive). Notable for the quality of life on 42nd Street was the fact that 61 percent of the many restaurateurs interviewed said they would consider expanding to new sidewalk cafés.[78] Equally important, the three business improvement districts that cover much of the 42nd Street corridor could handle maintenance and security of the pedestrian street, and have expressed openness to extending their areas of responsibility.

Traffic studies of the project have indicated that, with standard mitigation methods—such as changes in traffic signals, traffic lane allocations, and parking regulations—vision42 should be quite feasible from the standpoint of traffic.[79] A complete inventory was also made of existing delivery truck parking locations, and the "curb-feet minutes" currently occupied by delivery trucks were carefully observed and compared with the curb space that would be available under the new scheme. The traffic engineers found that, with a few changes in car parking regulations, it would be possible to provide sufficient space for delivery trucks by reserving curb space on adjacent avenues. The increased costs of around-the-corner deliveries and of traffic diversions to adjacent cross streets (where the traffic would not move quite as smoothly, but would still be acceptable by New York traffic standards) were factored into the overall cost/benefit analysis.[80]

Light rail extensions in the future—a shift in priorities for the use of street space   On Earth Day 2007, New York's then-mayor, Michael Bloomberg, projected a growth in the city's population of around a million new residents by the year 2030, and he initiated new environmental goals for the city, under the name PlaNYC. Prior to that announcement, the emphasis at the city's Department of Transportation had been on simply facilitating the faster flow of automobile traffic. But in light of the city's anticipated population growth, it became clear that more street space would need to be allocated to pedestrians—hence the Broadway Boulevard pedestrianization projects that followed two years later.

A logical addition to this shift in priorities in favor of pedestrians would be the provision of *higher-quality surface public transit*. The vision42 project—combined with its second phase, a continuous loop with 34th Street—is seen by its advocates as leading with these dual objectives.

From Broadway Boulevard, the auto-free light rail might ultimately be extended to the north, continuing along Broadway, up through the Theater District and all the way to Lincoln Center—thereby encompassing an enormous range of New York's cultural, commercial, entertainment, and educational offerings within a more benign and transit-friendly environment. North/south avenues at the eastern and western extremities of Manhattan, which are currently not served by subways, would also be likely future candidates for surface light rail, as would major thoroughfares in the outer boroughs of the city, where these are too heavily populated to be well served by buses. In each case, however, the light rail line would be taking at least some street space away from cars—always controversial in the US.

Given its prominent location, vision42 and its extensions could become a useful model for increasingly crowded cities. It has proven very difficult, however, to advance the project in a city as complex as New York, despite the fact that the street has large masses of pedestrians, including tourists, who could enormously enjoy an enhanced environment on 42nd Street, and despite excellent citywide and regional transit systems that bring millions of pedestrians every day into Midtown Manhattan, where they need better local transit, such as a light rail tram would provide. The obstacles are primarily political, and are mixed with those of a difficult economic environment. The proponents of the project are nevertheless committed to persisting with its advocacy, whether or not its realization is immediately achievable.

Strength of the city and compatible public transport

It is difficult and perhaps impossible to obtain an unalloyed evaluation of the impact of a pedestrian street on a city's economic vitality, since there is always a host of other variables—such as the state of the region's dominant industries, its general economic health, and demographic trends—which in turn may help determine the success or failure of the pedestrian street itself. It was observed by urban designer Jonathan Barnett in 1977 that, where US pedestrian streets had not prospered—for example, in Greensboro (North Carolina), Media (Pennsylvania), Fargo

(North Dakota), and Louisville (Kentucky)—this was in some cases because they were begun too late in the process of suburbanization. He noted that there may have been a lack of one or more essential elements remaining in the city—either the existence of an adequately strong shopping district, sufficient office employment, and/or residential critical mass to supply a population of shoppers, or a well-integrated system of public transportation.[81] It has more recently been remarked by planner Philip L. Walker that in the US pedestrian streets are typically successful only in downtowns where there is a high residential or employment density, a large number of tourists, or else some unique feature, such as an adjacent university.[82]

One of the most basic shortcomings in the less successful downtown malls in the US has been their lack of *appropriate* public transportation. For example, herds of noisy buses, spewing diesel fumes, destroyed the ambiance of the outdoor cafés on Chicago's State Street Mall. Furthermore, not only is environmental compatibility needed within the downtown but also good connections to the outer urban area are critical. For pedestrian streets in most US metropolitan areas (unlike the case of Manhattan), a strong reliance on public transport has not been a viable option—since even where a downtown pedestrian street connects with regional rail or bus lines, comprehensive access to transit on the suburban end of a trip has typically been lacking. Which circles back to the issues discussed in chapter 4 on easing access to transit from low-density development.

In Europe, pedestrian zones have reinforced what was already an essentially centripetal urban system, with cities that were economically and culturally strong to begin with. While in Europe it is the centers of cities that have long been the preferred places of residence, it is the suburbs that have held an underprivileged reputation as the neighborhoods of the poor. Until very recently, the reverse has been true in the United States.

By the same token, there is typically a firm commitment in Europe at the various levels of government to provide well-integrated systems of public transport for all levels of society, as a rational means of supporting the cities and conserving urban space, fuel, air quality, and open land outside of the cities. In the US transit has, until quite recently, been commonly viewed simply as a social service for those unable to afford cars. But as noted in chapters 1 and 3, these views appear to be undergoing a fundamental process of change, with the renewed attraction to urban living, the acceleration of multi-dwelling-unit, mixed-use construction, and the growing use of public transit that accompanies it.[83] These trends bode well for more lively and prosperous pedestrian streets in America's cities.

Turning gray cities to green

The importance to human happiness of making room for the beauty of greenery within our urban environments cannot be overestimated. Not only are the positive effects of landscaping reflected in higher land and property values; there is another rationale, this time science-based, for auto-free streets and parks within our densely developed downtowns.

In 2008, a research team headed by Marc Berman of the Department of Psychology at the University of Michigan explored the restorative effects of urban greenery on peoples' memory and attention capabilities. Some of the study participants were assigned to walk through downtown Ann Arbor, and others to walk through the university's impressive arboretum. Upon their return, they were tested, and without a doubt, those who had taken the arboretum walk scored significantly better. The researchers called this phenomenon "attention restoration theory." They observed that:

Unlike natural environments, urban environments are filled with stimulation that captures attention *dramatically* and additionally requires directed attention (e.g., to avoid being hit by a car), making them less restorative.... Nature, which is filled with intriguing stimuli, *modestly* grabs attention in a bottom-up fashion, allowing top-down directed-attention abilities a chance to replenish ... [thus] simple and brief interactions with nature can produce marked increases in cognitive control.

In particular, the researchers emphasized that: "to consider the availability of nature as merely an amenity fails to recognize the vital importance of nature in effective cognitive functioning."[84]

Communities that invest in their parks and other green spaces gain not only economically but in their quality of life as well. In the early 1970s, Bryant Park in the center of Midtown Manhattan was a derelict space that was home to drug pushers and the homeless. In 1992, Bryant Park Corporation president Dan Biederman initiated an enormously successful restoration of the park, and continues with his staff to vigilantly

Figure 6.28
Bryant Park in mid-Manhattan has become a true urban oasis, flooded with office
workers and tourists nearly every day—a welcome green easement in this high-
density city.
Source: Roxanne Warren.

maintain and manage it. Redesigned by Laurie Olin, the park contains a
large lawn surrounded by year-round activities that are enjoyed by thousands of visitors every year. It functions as a true urban oasis, and is
flooded daily with office workers and tourists. Its economic rewards are
only a welcome by-product of the park's renovation—commercial values
of the buildings surrounding Bryant Park have increased by 225 percent,
and retail sales in its vicinity have increased by 150 percent since the
park's revitalization.[85]

The greening of cities as a goal is gaining increasing momentum. Just
four and a half years after New York Mayor Bloomberg's 2007 Earth
Day announcement of PlaNYC, the city had invested some five billion
dollars on new and expanded parks, had planted more than half a million
new street trees, and had plans for planting half a million more.[86] In April
2012, Washington, DC's mayor Vincent Gray unveiled a signature initiative of his administration, "Sustainable DC," which aims to make the
district the greenest city in the nation within twenty years. This plan

includes the targets of having 75 percent of all trips made by walking, cycling, or public transit, covering 40 percent of the district with a canopy of trees, and redeveloping the city's Southwest quadrant, including its underutilized waterfront.[87] Twenty years ago, Curitiba had 600,000 inhabitants, and an average green space of only 54 sf (5 m^2) per person. It now has 2.5 million people, and the green space per person has been multiplied ten times.[88]

As perceptively remarked by architect/urban designer Mark L. Hinshaw: "Trees are a vital ingredient in dense urban neighborhoods. Because residents do not have their own land ... trees offer a collective yard that can be enjoyed by everyone."[89] A natural, green environment, as emphasized in chapter 1, is highly valued for residential locations, especially by families with young children—but this can rightly be said for people of all ages. It is without a doubt that the infiltration of nature into the cities adds immeasurably to their livability.

7

A Market to Match Ecological Truths

In the search for immediately profitable sources of energy, driven in large part by a relentless demand for automotive fuel, humanity needs first to decide whether it is willing to further risk the health of the planet, its climate, and its oceans and aquifers. In accommodating economic growth, we must first come to terms with the fact that the earth's geological and biological resources are finite and being rapidly degraded and depleted— and act more decisively to *shrink* the very large footprint that we are placing on the earth.

Climate goals

The urgency of now

Extreme and record-breaking storms, floods, heat, droughts, and related wildfires worldwide are undeniably and dramatically demonstrating the need for meaningful reductions in the generation of the carbon emissions that are augmenting these extremes. But the long-range outlook for achieving the reductions needed to avoid climate catastrophe is not promising—as long as fossil fuels remain the main movers of commerce, and of transportation in particular, and as long as this pattern is being replicated throughout the fast-developing world.

Abundant stores of natural gas in both the US and China have now been made accessible by breakthroughs in seismic imaging, horizontal drilling and hydraulic fracturing. This has opened the opportunity to replace much dirtier coal as our major fuel for the generation of energy, with the proviso that the drilling for gas must be carefully regulated with respect to water contamination, carbon dioxide and methane emissions, and earthquake. Yet natural gas should be considered an *interim* solution only, since it is still a fossil fuel that emits about half as much greenhouse gas as coal. A sustained glut of inexpensive natural gas could actually short-circuit the prospects for new investments in wind and solar power—which have *no* emissions at all—thereby undermining the large-scale development of truly clean energy, as well as efforts toward energy efficiency and conservation.[1]

In its biennial *Energy Technology Perspectives* report released in July 2012, the International Energy Agency (IEA) described three possible, dramatically different trajectories for climate change. The gravest of these is a business-as-usual scenario in which the world will experience a temperature rise of at least 6 degrees Celsius above pre-industrial levels (about 11 degrees Fahrenheit). This is our current trajectory. A second possible scenario would reflect some of the current pledges of governments for stronger climate policies, by which temperatures would still increase by 4 degrees Celsius. But most scientists confirm that, to avoid the worst effects of climate change, it will be necessary to limit the temperature rise to 2 degrees Celsius by no later than 2017. This will require even stronger policies, global coordination, and very major upfront investments—focused on energy efficiency and on much greater research, development, and distribution of completely clean renewable energy. The political obstacles to achieving this are great, because the payoffs may not be seen for many years.[2]

In the years 2010 and 2011, there was a temporary reprieve in the growth of carbon emissions in the world's wealthier countries, attributed to such factors as the Great Recession, to a sharp decline in driving, conservation and energy efficiencies in buildings, and to the replacement of substantial amounts of coal with natural gas. However, these reductions, averaging 0.6 percent in 2011, were overwhelmed by large carbon gains in the developing countries, where emissions grew by an average of 6.1 percent.[3] China was by far the greatest contributor of carbon, with a growth of 9.3 percent. But although total carbon emissions in the United States fell by 7.7 percent between 2006 and 2011, the US is still number one among the big economies in terms of emissions *per capita*, with 18 tons emitted per person.[4] This contrasts with China at 6 tons per person as late as 2010. India at that time was emitting only 1.38 tons per person, but was slated to continue on a steep upward trajectory, due largely to massive purchases of cars and air conditioners by a growing middle class.[5]

Considering the United States alone, a report by the US Department of Energy, published in July 2013, warned that the entire nation's energy system is very vulnerable to the rising seas, more intense storms, higher temperatures and more frequent droughts that accompany climate change. Record-setting droughts are greatly reducing the water available for cooling power plants and for producing hydroelectric power, and rising heat is driving a steep increase in demand for air-conditioning—which demands yet more power—thus creating a vicious cycle. Among the authors' recommendations: that power plants and oil drillers should use *less* water and recycle what they do use. The report notes that, while the costs of climate change today are measured in the billions of dollars, over the coming decades they will be in the trillions.[6]

"Unconventional" sources of energy relative to climate change

There is currently a powerful drive in the Western Hemisphere, notably in the US, Brazil, and Canada, to boost the output of fossil fuels. To meet this challenge, new high-tech methods have been brought to bear, methods that are being used to extract previously identified reservoirs that were long considered inaccessible because they were too far offshore, too far underground, or too solidly encased in rock to be extracted profitably. Termed "unconventional" sources of supply, these include deep offshore and Arctic oil, shale oil, bitumen from tar sands, and liquids obtained from coal and natural gas.[7]

While relatively abundant, these supplies are extracted using technologies that can be extremely costly, and at the same time pose risks to the environment and climate. Development of oil reserves that are buried beneath miles of ocean is accompanied by the risks of oil spills, on the scale, for example, of the April 2010 disaster of British Petroleum/Deepwater Horizon. More drilling in the Arctic will threaten the structural integrity of the polar ice caps and the survival of already-endangered land and sea wildlife. And excavation for heavy oil in Canada's tar sands would release staggering amounts of carbon, while destroying 740,000 acres (300,000 ha) of boreal forest—which is a vital sink for carbon.[8]

Because of its potential for lifting the economy, while at least temporarily slowing the acceleration of climate change, hydraulic fracturing ("fracking") for natural gas is now being vigorously promoted worldwide, while being strongly resisted by many local inhabitants.[9] Fracking for the production of shale gas requires the injection of mammoth quantities of chemically laced water into underground shale formations to shatter the rock and liberate the gas trapped within. The use of toxic chemicals can then threaten the safety of drinking water, as huge volumes of contaminated water must be kept from escaping into aquifers and other water supplies.[10] A pioneer of the fracking process, billionaire George Phydias Mitchell, maintains that, if good techniques are properly followed, fracking can in fact be made safe. Yet because high standards are more costly, even Mitchell insists that, to ensure that these be maintained, strict regulations will be needed on the federal level to tighten up controls, and that a piecemeal, state-by-state approach will be inadequate.[11]

There are several additional challenges of fracking. In drought-stricken areas, there is serious competition for water between farmers and the drillers.[12] The generation of earthquakes has also been linked to the injection of large volumes of wastewater near active faults.[13] Additionally, when gas and oil wells lose their structural integrity, they can leak methane and other contaminants out of their casings and into water wells and the atmosphere. Numerous industry studies show that some 5 percent of all gas and oil wells leak immediately, and that rates of leakage increase over time.[14]

Unfortunately, methane is also a potent greenhouse gas (GHG). In effect, this can counterbalance many of the climate benefits of gas as a cleaner fossil fuel. According to the International Energy Agency, although natural gas can provide significant climate benefits in the short run by taking over coal's dominant role in the energy mix, thereby reducing GHG emissions, it is not a panacea. Because natural gas power plants emit more than 100 grams of GHGs per kilowatt-hour, the IEA advises that they will need to be swapped out for cleaner fuels at some point around 2025 or 2030 to reduce emissions further.[15]

Producing unconventional oil and gas actually requires far more energy than drilling for conventional fossil fuels, and emits a correspondingly greater amount of GHGs, with a correspondingly greater impact on climate change. Yet the "clean" alternative of nuclear energy can carry its own grave risks, as demonstrated by the ongoing 2011 environmental disaster at the Fukushima Daiichi nuclear plant, from which radioactive water continues to pour into the ocean.

Meanwhile, as vigorous exploration for fossil fuels continues unabated in well-known areas throughout the Western world, major new reserves, both onshore and offshore, have been discovered since 2010 in Mozambique, Tanzania, Kenya, Somalia, and Uganda. These represent an economic bonanza for eastern Africa, and unsurprisingly, there is a frenzy to exploit them.[16]

Capacity of completely clean, renewable sources of energy

A logical alternative course should be an aggressive and diligent pursuit of renewable energy sources such as wind and solar power. How rapidly renewables will grow in the future and the share of humanity's energy mix that they will comprise will depend heavily on public priorities and policy. But the *potential* of renewables is impressive.

A comprehensive report was published in June 2012 by the US Department of Energy's National Renewable Energy Laboratory, the *Renewable Electricity Futures Study*. This was an initial investigation into the extent to which clean, renewable energy can meet the electricity demands of the continental United States over the next several decades. The report indicated that renewable power generation can play a *much* more significant role than previously thought. The study explored the challenges of meeting with renewable technologies alone very high levels of electricity generation—from 30 up to 90 percent, and focusing on 80 percent—of all US electricity generation needs by 2050. While challenges are posed by the geographical distribution, the variability, and the uncertainty in output of some renewable sources, the study found that "Renewable electricity generation from technologies that are commercially available today, in combination with a more flexible electrical system, is more than adequate to supply 80 percent of total U.S. electricity generation in 2050 while meeting electricity demand on an hourly basis in every region of the country."[17] This could result in deep reductions in not only electric sector greenhouse gas emissions, but also in water use.

In the US by 2012, some twenty-nine states and the District of Columbia had set "renewable portfolio standards" (RPS) or "alternative energy standards" which require that electric utilities deliver a specified percentage of their electricity from renewable or alternative sources by a given date. The standards vary from modest to ambitious—North and South Dakota each have targets of 10 percent by 2015; Illinois, Oregon and Nevada each have targets of 25 percent by 2025; New York has a target of 30 percent by 2015; and California has a target of 33 percent by 2020. Qualifying energy sources vary from state to state, and some states require that a certain percentage of the portfolio be generated from a specified energy source, such as solar.[18]

Although the first RPS had been established in 1983, most of these standards were passed or strengthened after 2000, while many have not been in effect long enough to have had a substantial impact. Their success will also hinge in large part on federal policies such as the extension of production tax credit (PTC), which have provided a 2.2-cent per kilowatt-hour tax credit for the first ten years of electric wind production from utility-scale turbines.[19] The PTC was first enacted as part of the Energy Policy Act of 1992, and has since been a major driver of renewable energy generation. However, the US Congress has repeatedly vacillated between extending and retiring the PTC, and on three occasions the PTC has been allowed to sunset, contributing to a boom-bust cycle of development that plagues the renewable energy industries.[20]

This compares with the stable environment for investors in renewables that has been created in Germany, where the return on investment is guaranteed for a full twenty years. As a result, renewables have become a good and relatively secure investment for many people in Germany, and 380,000 jobs have been created. Because of its stability, the renewable energy business was one of the drivers of the economy that carried Germany through the 2008 recession.[21] This occurred despite ongoing challenges in the distribution of the clean energy from the locations in the north where it is generated to the population centers in the south where it is needed.

In the US the true worth of the American Recovery and Reinvestment Act of 2009 (ARRA), known colloquially as the "stimulus" act, was poorly understood by the public-at-large, having been confused in many peoples' minds with the "bank bailout," or Troubled Assets Relief Program (TARP) of 2008. There were even members of Congress who confused these two bills, and the political opposition to the ARRA characterized it as a useless cash dump, an assumption that became accepted as conventional wisdom. On the contrary, according to a thorough investigation by award-winning journalist Michael Grunwald, the ARRA was not only successful, but it was well-administered and virtually scandal-free. It included direct spending on infrastructure, education, health, energy, federal tax incentives, the expansion of unemployment benefits, and other social welfare provisions. In particular, it succeeded with cash grants and production tax credits in significantly advancing the solar and wind industries (which had hitherto been nearly moribund), approximately doubling their output in three years. While the political and media discourse around solar power has focused on the failure of one obscure, federally heavily subsidized company, Solyndra, that project was actually started in 2005 and had been nearly completed when the presidential administration changed hands in 2009. Solyndra's failure subsequently became a political football.[22]

As pointed out by *New York Times* journalist Jeff Himmelman, the potential of the sun as a source of power is nearly unlimited, and when we burn coal, oil, or gas, we are simply harvesting an "archived" version of that same energy, which has been stored in animal and plant life and compacted and preserved under the crust of the earth. Himmelman quotes Danny Kennedy, the entrepreneur/owner of Sungevity, a thriving residential solar company in Oakland, California. Sungevity's workforce expanded from 3 to 260 people in the five years between the company's founding in 2007 and 2012, and its revenues had grown by a factor of eight by 2010, and had doubled again in 2011:

Think about it this way. We're killing people in foreign lands in order to extract 200-million-year-old sunlight. Then we burn it ... in order to boil water to create steam to drive a turbine to generate electricity. We frack our own backyards and pollute our rivers, or we blow away our mountaintops just miles from our nation's capital for an hour of electricity, when we could just take what's falling from the sky.[23]

Globally over the past twenty years, the demand for solar electric energy has grown by an average of 30 percent annually, against a backdrop of rapidly declining costs and prices. Among industrialized nations, the German and Japanese governments have led the way in establishing high incentives that have stimulated the development of their domestic solar markets.[24]

The true potential of solar power is evidenced by the enormous investments that have been made by such companies as Google and Bank of
America in residential solar energy.[25] And since home electricity is an
absolute necessity that comes ahead of other priorities for most people,
the inherent market stability of solar energy in residential installations,
as one of the least risky investments that can be made, was noted in a
2012 Bloomberg article, which forecast a large spike in the market for
rooftop solar energy.[26]

Building-integrated photovoltaics include facade and skylight panels,
as well as roof shingles that act as both roofing and solar collectors. And
windows are now another potential target for the power of the sun: the
California NanoSystems Institute has developed a highly transparent
solar cell exclusively for window glazing, the key to this technology being
its focus on infrared, rather than visible, light. Thus, windows will be
able to harvest this infrared light, converting it into electricity.[27] And one
vastly underused and mature technology is solar heating, which is 80 to
85 percent efficient (more than five times as efficient as photovoltaics),
and whose collectors have been functioning reliably since the 1970s.[28]

An innovation that has added great market appeal to the solar industry
has been the selling of solar *power* instead of the panels themselves. This
idea was pioneered in 2003 by Jigar Shah, a mechanical engineer who
started a company, SunEdison, that offers a twenty-year "solar power
purchase agreement" (PPA) to commercial customers. Large companies
such as Staples and Whole Foods have contracted with SunEdison to have
solar panels installed on their buildings at no initial cost. They are then
charged by SunEdison for the amount of energy produced by the panels,
at a fixed rate that is lower than what the companies were already paying
to the utilities. The twenty-year contracts have allowed SunEdison to
raise capital from outside investors like Wells Fargo, Goldman Sachs, and
MetLife. While the banks pay for the solar systems, they reap returns on
their investments through tax credits and a share of the monthly PPA
payments.[29]

This conceptual model has also been brought into the residential market, with national residential installers offering straight leases instead of
PPAs. In 2007, none of the residential market was made up of such third-
party-owned systems, but by the first quarter of 2012, they accounted
for 63 percent of the new solar systems in California and as much as 80

percent of the solar systems in Colorado. Himmelman observes that "The solar lease has been a key driver for the explosive growth in the residential solar market in California, and increasingly, across the country." He notes, "People don't buy gas stations. People don't buy utilities. Why are we having them buy solar equipment?"[30]

In the western US, some of the best land for generating *large-scale* solar power has long been effectively off-limits to private development because it was federally owned, making for a cumbersome permitting process. But in 2012, the Department of the Interior organized a diverse coalition of stakeholders, including solar energy companies, clean energy advocates, conservation groups, and electric utilities, to find solutions that work not only for solar energy but for wildlife and wildlands as well. This coalition devised an approach that minimizes and mitigates the impacts of solar development and reduces the uncertainty and time needed for permitting solar power projects.

The result was a "road map" for large utility-scale solar energy development on lands in Arizona, California, Colorado, Nevada, New Mexico, and Utah, establishing Solar Energy Zones that cover just under 300,000 acres (121,410 ha) in these six states, plus an additional 19 million acres (7,689,300 ha) just outside these zones that were deemed appropriate for solar development.[31] The first of these industrial-scale, 392-megawatt concentrating solar plants began sending electricity to customers in Southern California by 2013. It is comprised of more than 120,000 heliostats—pairs of billboard-sized mirrors tracking the sun's movements to power a central boiler comprised of 13,000 feet (3,962 m) of tubing atop a 450-foot (137-m) tower. This project would *never* have happened without the support of the federal government, as there is no private sector financing available for such a large and cutting-edge technology project.[32]

Wind power is an equally great success story. As the sizes of the turbines have grown, wind has become increasingly economically competitive with other forms of energy. Other than hydropower, wind is now *the* leading renewable source of electricity worldwide, with 238,000 megawatts of capacity installed by January 2012. At that time, less than 2 percent of this power had been installed offshore, and in the US there had not been *any* offshore installations. Across the world, however, offshore wind capacity had been growing quickly, taking advantage of the powerful winds blowing over the oceans and expanding nearly six-fold since 2006.[33] A long-stalled offshore US project, the 130-turbine 468-megawatt Cape Wind, planned for Nantucket Sound, had, by August 2012, finally received all of its required state and federal approvals, and there were plans for the wind farm to enter service by 2015, although it was still being challenged by local opponents on "aesthetic" grounds.[34]

In the United States in 2011, spurred by the federal production tax credit, which was leveraging as much as $20 billion per year in private investment, wind power accounted for 35 percent of all new power capacity, right behind natural gas.[35] Wind energy capacity in the nation had grown in that year by 31 percent. South Dakota was the leader in wind; it accounted for 22.3 percent of that state's total energy in 2011. In Iowa, wind accounted for 18.8 percent of the state's total energy in 2011, while in Texas, it was supplying 15.2 percent of the state's total power demand.[36] In Kansas, where major utilities have a legislative mandate to produce or buy 20 percent of their electricity from renewable sources by 2020, the wind industry has been poised to meet this goal, but its progress has been repeatedly threatened by Congress' reluctance to extend production tax credits.[37]

In fact, recent conditions of extreme drought have forced some US states, such as Texas, to pursue the use of wind and/or photovoltaics over coal and natural gas for energy generation, because they don't require any water at all. While the legislators in some of these states are actually not very favorable toward climate policy, such actions could significantly reduce greenhouse gas emissions.

The *Renewable Electricity Futures Study* that was completed in 2012 by the National Renewable Energy Laboratory considered five different types of renewable energy technologies—solar (including both photovoltaic and concentrated solar power,) wind power, biopower, geothermal power, and hydropower. It found that every state in the US has the space and resources to generate clean energy, and that solar power alone could generate 200,000 gigawatts, with Texas and California having the greatest potential for solar.[38] However, as start-up industries, all of these technologies will need subsidies and production tax credits for several years, in order to be placed on a competitive plane with fossil fuels, and in particular, with natural gas.

Balancing our approach to the use of energy

Subsidies for energy types compared

Opponents of incentives for clean energy often claim that clean renewable energy sources are too expensive if they can't get by without subsidies. In fact, there is currently no such thing as a "free market" in energy. Fossil fuels have benefited from a full century of subsidies and supporting infrastructure, and are still heavily subsidized. The oil industry, in particular, receives generous tax breaks at every stage of the processes of exploration and extraction. Some of these date back to 1913, when they were aimed at encouraging exploration in an era of rudimentary oil extracting technologies. But today, the industry would be highly profitable even without these tax breaks.

A comparison of federal subsidies for different types of energy was highlighted in a 2009 report by the Environmental Law Institute and the Woodrow Wilson International Center for Scholars, "Estimating U.S. Government Subsidies to Energy Sources: 2002–2008." The report made clear that fossil fuels, together with corn ethanol, were receiving the vast bulk of federal energy subsidies during that period—some 88 percent of the total—in both direct spending and tax breaks, and that corn ethanol was receiving far more than traditional renewables:

Table 7.1
US federal subsidies for energy (2002–08)

Fossil fuels	$72.5 billion, including	$70.2 billion for traditional fossil fuels, and $2.3 billion for carbon capture and storage
Renewable energy	$29.0 billion, including	$16.8 billion for corn ethanol* and $12.2 billion for traditional renewables

Notes: * The subsidy figures for corn ethanol ignore the negative effects not only on world hunger but also on climate change that result from the massive conversion of forests for the production of ethanol as well as the amount of water needed to grow this water-intensive, fertilizer-intensive crop (Lester R. Brown, *Plan B 4.0: Mobilizing to Save Civilization* [New York: W. W. Norton, 2009], 131).

Source: Table based on David Roberts, "Fossil Fuel Subsidies Dwarf Clean Energy Subsidies: Obama Wants to Eliminate Them," *Grist*, September 23, 2009, http://www.grist.org/article/2009-09-22-fossil-fuel-subsidies-dwarf-clean-energy-subsidies-obama-wants.

The fossil fuel subsidy figures cited in this report are actually very conservative, since they do not include such indirect, but massive subsidies as military spending to protect our access to oil in the Middle East— military spending that is, itself, heavily petroleum-dependent. The subsidies for war do not, of course, go exclusively to fossil fuels. But if there were a way of including the share that does, the fossil fuel subsidy numbers would be greatly magnified.

In 2009 in the ARRA, or stimulus bill, incentives for developing clean energy had been expanded to include loan guarantees, cash grants, and contracts that require electrical customers to pay higher rates. At least temporarily, this had largely eliminated the risks to investors in wind and solar power, and created something of a gold rush mentality among them. Because these supports almost guaranteed profits for years to come, they came under considerable criticism. However, the federal loan guarantee program for wind and solar power expired in September 2011, and the US Treasury grant program for wind and solar expired at the end of that year.[39] By comparison, there are $4 billion of annual subsidies for oil and gas producers are *actually written into the US tax code*. Whereas aid for wind and solar power has simply expired, it would require congressional action to change the subsidies for oil and gas, according to Michael Gratz, professor of tax law at Columbia University.[40] These subsidies create market distortions that encourage wasteful consumption and undercut the position of clean energy, while effectively exacerbating climate change.

In congressional debates over energy bills, attempts to roll back some of the subsidies for fossil fuels are typically dubbed "raising taxes" and filibustered to death. Yet as Lester Brown of the Earth Policy Institute asserts, "... *it is tax shifting, not additional appropriations*, that is the key to restructuring the energy economy in order to stabilize the climate."[41] Brown notes that, worldwide, direct fossil fuel subsidies in 2010 amounted to roughly $500 billion, one-quarter of this amount supporting production and the remainder supporting consumption of fossil fuels, and that humanity is thereby spending nearly $1.4 billion per day to further destabilize the climate. In contrast to the $500 billion in fossil fuel supports, renewable energy received just $66 billion in subsidies in 2010, one-third of which went to biofuels.[42]

At least one conservative former US congressional representative, Bob Inglis of South Carolina, believes that a tax on carbon and the gradual phasing out of *all* energy subsidies would be the most effective approach. He declares that, if fossil fuels were made fully accountable for all of their health costs and other negative externalities, then wind and solar might in fact become more competitive *without* subsidies.[43] This is a battle that promises to continue to be fiercely fought, with one side of the political divide intent on phasing out fossil fuel subsidies entirely for the sake of addressing climate change, and the other side denying that climate change even exists as an issue.

Fuel for our cars versus food

Lester Brown has cautioned that global demands on the earth's natural systems are exceeding their sustainable regenerative capacity by an estimated 30 percent, warning that a more realistic view of the relationship between our economy and the natural environment is vital. The need is especially urgent, he adds, because the world is expected to add another three billion people by the middle of the twenty-first century.[44]

A stark example of this mismatch can be seen in the conflict between our expanding use of crops for automotive fuel and the needs of humanity for food. Edible crops such as corn, cassava, rapeseed, and sugarcane, are raised in the less developed countries explicitly for use as fuel in the US China, Europe, India, Indonesia, and Thailand, to meet strict biofuel targets that have been set in these countries.[45] Granted, this is only one of the reasons for the surge in the prices of food that has recently proven so devastating in impoverished nations. Other factors include the relentless growth of world population, extreme weather events such as floods and drought, a jump in meat and dairy consumption associated with rising affluence, and heavy market speculation in commodities, in particular grain and petroleum. But aggravating all of these factors is the production of crops for energy, which almost invariably competes with the production of food.

As remarked by Steven Rattner, former counselor to the US Secretary of the Treasury and lead economic advisor on the automobile industry, political support in the US for the conversion of corn into biofuels is linked to the Senate's heavy structural tilt toward the rural states, and to the fact that this support is nearly a prerequisite for candidates for the presidency—since Iowa, the nation's biggest corn-producing state, has held the lead position in the presidential sweepstakes for the past four decades. Rattner observes that, while conversion of corn into ethanol manages to drive up food prices, it simultaneously adds billions of dollars to the national deficit and harms the environment. Some studies, he notes, calculate that ethanol consumes more energy than it produces.[46] Its production also means that less land is available for growing food, so food prices go up.

For more than three decades, the US ethanol industry benefited from a "triple crown" of federal support: a law requiring that specific amounts of renewable fuels like ethanol be blended into gasoline; a tax credit that went to refiners for doing so; and a tariff on imported ethanol to protect the domestic industry. Both the tax credit and the tariff finally expired at the end of 2011. But the requirement that increasing amounts of ethanol be used in gasoline remains, and should be more than sufficient to ensure the profitability of a now-mature industry.[47]

The United States is by far the world's leading exporter of grain. And because the conversion of grain into ethanol has been mandated by the federal government in its Renewable Fuel Standard, an investment frenzy has developed around biofuels. In 2009, more than one-quarter of the US grain harvest was diverted into ethanol for fuel. By the following year this portion had increased to nearly 40 percent. This helped to boost grain prices well above historic levels—in a world that no longer has excess cropland capacity. As a result of this and the other factors noted above, between June and December 2010, the price of corn on the Chicago Mercantile Exchange rose 73 percent. While this may have meant a few cents difference in the typical box of cereal in a US supermarket, it has resulted in extreme hunger and hardship in the developing world.[48] People in low-income, grain-importing countries have been hit especially hard. Lester Brown has noted this irony:

The grain required to fill an SUV's 25-gallon tank with ethanol just once will feed one person for a whole year.... [There is] an emerging competition between the owners of the world's 910 million automobiles and the 2 billion poorest people.... The average income of the world's auto owners is roughly $30,000 a year. The poorest people earn on average less than $2,000 per year. The market says: "Let's fuel the cars."[49]

By July 2012, the hottest month in the United States since record keeping began in 1895, the devastating effects of severe heat waves and drought on the harvest had made it evident that it is neither sensible nor safe to build an energy sector that is even partially based on water- and weather-dependent crops. With the nation's worst drought in a half century, much of the corn crop had been lost, and the government had, by August 2012, reduced its estimate of the corn yield to the lowest level since 1995.[50]

(For years, the use of corn stover—the non-edible stalk portion of the plant—as a fuel for power in lieu of the corn itself—was thought to be unprofitable because of the high costs of harvesting, storing and transporting it.[51] But by early 2013, many years and millions of dollars of research on stover had been rewarded with the knowledge of how to break down this material so that it could be refined into ethanol. By March 2013, some seventy commercial-sized cellulosic plants were already under construction, and the Department of Agriculture had announced a model agreement with DuPont, one of the leading researchers, to help establish guidelines for how the company will collect stover for a new plant in central Iowa, while maintaining soil quality, since a certain amount of stover must be left in the ground to help replenish nutrients and control erosion.)[52]

The gas tax and a vehicle-miles traveled tax

The 2011 report, "Growing Wealthier," by the Center for Clean Air Policy, which was cited in chapter 1, found that cities that have invested in public transportation and downtown development are experiencing substantial economic benefits in the form of higher retail sales, increased property values, and growing tax revenues. The evidence of these benefits, when added to climate change and energy/national security considerations, should lead to a shift of policies away from support for building more highways and expanding suburbanization, and toward the strong support of city-reinforcing transit in general, and rail transit in particular.

On the contrary, we continue to see generous new subsidies for automobility. These have included the three billion dollar "cash for clunkers" program in 2009, as well as massive ongoing infusions of general funds into the Highway Trust Fund (HTF). The HTF was originally intended to be supported by the federal gasoline tax; however, this tax has not been increased since 1993, while inflation and the cost of building and maintaining transportation infrastructure have increased appreciably. In fact, between 1993 and the summer of 2011, the purchasing power of

HTF revenues had shrunken by 33 percent, while the needs of our increasingly dilapidated transportation infrastructure had only been growing.[53] So between 2008 and 2011, Congress was forced to top up the trust fund with repeated gifts, transferred from general funds, that totaled $30 billion.[54] There is no end in sight to these gifts, as the political will appears to be lacking for either increasing the gasoline tax or adjusting it for inflation. It has been reasonably argued by the National Association of Railroad Passengers that, to the extent that these subsidies are drawn from general funds, the states should at least have the option to spend them on rail projects instead of highways.[55]

Sir Nicholas Stern, the former chief economist for the World Bank from 2000 to 2003, in his 2006 study on the future costs of climate change, examined the huge gap that exists between the market prices for fossil fuels and an honest price that would incorporate their environmental costs to society.[56] Particularly in the US, where limitless driving appears to have taken on the status of a "right," the market ignores all of the indirect costs of gasoline. These include the impending costs of climate change, the military costs of protecting our access to petroleum in the Middle East, and the costs of health care for respiratory illnesses resulting from polluted air and for the obesity that results from sedentary lifestyles. When these amounts are counted, notes Lester Brown, gasoline in the US should actually cost nearly $15 per gallon (in 2009 dollars).[57] Typically, the argument is raised that increasing the gas tax to meet its true cost would be unfair to the poor.

The European countries generally tax gasoline and diesel fuel at the equivalent of around $5 or more per gallon. Not only do these taxes help to discourage private motoring, but the money collected is used to support higher-quality public transportation. Thomas Friedman, writing for the *New York Times*, has cited calculations by energy economist Phil Verleger that even a $1 increase in the tax on gasoline and diesel fuel in the United States would raise around $140 billion per year. Friedman points out that this money could be used to help cushion the burden of such a tax on the poor, while helping to pay down the national debt, affording better health care, and investing in higher-quality public transportation. Unfortunately, notes Friedman, in the current US Congress, "A gas tax is 'off the table.' But sending your neighbor's son or daughter to risk their lives in Afghanistan? No problem."[58]

There is, in any case, a fundamental drawback with relying on a gas tax to support our transportation needs. In addition to reductions in the purchasing power of gas tax revenues due to inflation, these revenues are shrinking even more as the fuel-efficiency of our cars increases. As a quasi-remedy, a number of states have adopted gas taxes that are tied to the price of fuel, but this has yielded too little revenue when fuel prices have declined. Other states have applied their regular sales tax rates to gas purchases, or have indexed their gas taxes to the rate of inflation.[59] Yet another solution has been recommended by several members of Congress and at least two former Secretaries of Transportation—replacement of the gas tax with a vehicle-miles-traveled (VMT) tax. The miles traveled could be tracked by electronic equipment installed on each car. Opponents of this idea have expressed concerns about privacy, while its proponents claim that any infringement on personal privacy need not exceed that already associated with other technological conveniences, such as credit cards and cell phones.[60] Thus, in July 2013, the legislature of the state of Oregon overcame these misgivings and passed a law to make that state the first in the US to adopt a VMT tax.[61]

By tradition in the United States, 20 percent of the revenues from the gasoline tax has been dedicated to public transportation. However, these funds were put under threat in February 2012 by an adverse congressional majority. And aside from the parsimony of the Congress in providing for the maintenance of the nation's highways and bridges, funding for intercity passenger rail—not to mention high-speed rail—was conspicuously absent in the budget that was signed into law in November 2011. Similarly, there was no funding for initiating a National Infrastructure Bank, which holds great potential for kick-starting HSR.[62] Such dreams will have to await the advent of a more progressive legislature.

Reducing the dominance of the automobile—four interrelated steps

A number of measures have been discussed in this book that could begin to redirect us away from the monoculture of automobile dependency, and toward the development of long-term urban infrastructure for a more energy- and land-conserving future. Some of these measures would be promising channels for the creation of good construction jobs that cannot be exported abroad. Some would demand heavy capital investments. Still, when one considers the billions of dollars our nation spends annually on wars fought for access to oil, it is not inconceivable that a sizable portion of these sums should be spent instead on *projects that would lessen our need for oil in the first place.*

These steps are summarized below in their approximate order from the least difficult to the most difficult to achieve:

1. Eliminating ubiquitous free car parking and changing minimum parking requirements to maximum

This is basic to discouraging ubiquitous private motoring, and to creating a "level playing field" for the use of transit. Charging for parking that was previously free, and lowering zoning requirements for parking will require a new mind-set on the part of both the public and public officials. As discussed in chapter 2, free parking, for starters, might be gradually eliminated, as a reflection of the true costs of providing that parking, and as a means of creating parity for public transportation. At the very least, employer-provided parking should be considered a taxable benefit that could be declined by the employee. As compensation for the loss of free parking, developers, building owners, and employers could offer free or deeply discounted transit passes and/or free car-share memberships, similar to those that are arranged through California's GreenTRIP program, also discussed in chapter 2. Certainly, unbundling the costs of providing parking from the costs of housing itself will be fundamental to clarifying peoples' perceptions of what they are buying.

2. Reversing road priorities currently given to cars—except on limited-access highways

These measures could be achieved in several ways:

• *a. Widespread establishment of 20 mph (32 km/h) zones in neighborhoods, shopping streets, and routes that lead to transit stations,* as described in chapter 5. This might in many cases serve as an alternative to creating separate bike paths, and could at the same time be establishing a safe network for the driving of mini-vehicles, while modifying speed limits in favor of pedestrians and cyclists.

• *b. Traffic calming in residential neighborhoods.* This has proven nearly universally popular worldwide, and has been highly successful in protecting people of all ages—children and the elderly, in particular—from speeding cars.

• *c. Developing safe and widespread networks of paths and lanes for walking and cycling, and safe bike parking facilities at transit stations and other destinations.* Many of these networks and facilities have already been initiated, and have proven extremely popular. As described in chapter 4, they are being promoted in the US through the "Complete Streets" movement, the Safe Routes to School program, and other organizations. The fine networks in the Netherlands, Denmark, and Germany are serving as highly successful models. Creating these networks often requires eliminating some traffic lanes for motorists, and this can be controversial. But the networks need to be extensive, and the walking and cycling they will encourage promise to have a very positive impact on our national crisis of obesity, while helping to restore a more substantial base of ridership for public transportation. They will be useful not only for more compact and flexible access to transit, but for all kinds of local trips—among places of residence, work, and school.

• *d. Pedestrian streets in downtowns.* For the pedestrianization of downtown streets, the most favorable cities are those that already possess rail public transport to their city centers, as this can help to ensure the presence of an abundance of pedestrians and retail shoppers, and with them, vibrant street life. Solutions need to be devised in pedestrian streets for the delivery of goods and services, either from side streets and/or at off-hours. With the right conditions, community agreement, mayoral backing, and favorable publicity, both traffic calming and pedestrianization can actually be achieved relatively quickly, and with highly positive results for both merchants and communities. The public space can be protected from vehicular traffic with speed humps and bollards, and enhanced with landscaping and amenities.

3. Developing comprehensive transit networks on all levels—local, regional and intercity

These should include local streetcars/trams, metros, regional rail, and ultimately, intercity high-speed rail, in addition to various types of express and local buses. Despite much current excitement about high-speed rail in the US, it is important to appreciate the indispensable role of intermediate- and low-speed systems of bus and rail—both for local travel and for access to longer-distance and high-speed lines. For if regional and high-speed rail is heavily reliant upon automobiles for passenger access to its stations, these stations will without a doubt, as previously noted, need to be surrounded by vast parking facilities instead of urban development. Ridership will then be constrained by the sizes of the parking facilities, bringing into question the relevance of the rail lines to our widely dispersed residences and workplaces. This is of course not an argument against regional and high-speed rail—quite the opposite.

Writing for the New America Foundation, authors Daniel Alpert of Westwood Capital, Cornell University law professor Robert Hockett, and New York University economics professor Nouriel Roubini have recommended a substantial five-to-seven-year public investment program that would repair the nation's crumbling infrastructure, and, in so doing, would not only put people back to work, but would "lay the foundation for a more efficient and cost-effective national economy."[63] These efforts will require multiple phases and many years, but would also, in the process, be generating thousands of jobs in the hard-hit construction industry. At the same time, we would be benefiting from one of the valuable lessons learned in the Great Depression of the 1930s, which is to build infrastructure during economic downtime, while interest rates are exceptionally low, and while the world economy is experiencing a glut of both labor and capital.

One possibility with the development of various levels of rail networks is to use trains and trams at off-peak hours for freight delivery, thereby ridding urban streets of a good deal of noxious trucking, and delivering goods via cleaner and much more energy-efficient rail.

There should also be opportunities to combine the construction of new rail networks together with new electric utility grids, thereby resolving in one fell swoop the issue of securing rights-of-way for both functions. For example, building HSR between Montréal and New York City, which had been called for in the 1970s by then-mayor of Montréal Jean Drapeau, was again cited in 2009 by Pierre Arcand, minister of international relations for the government of Quebec, as a golden opportunity to install new transmission lines to tap into Quebec's enormous hydroelectric power for New York City.[64]

4. Developing, in tandem with transit, increasing numbers of transit-oriented communities within existing urban areas

This is a long-term goal that would serve as a direct alternative to suburban sprawl, but faces hefty challenges. Certainly, the "Factor of Five" profits that can be achieved through land speculation, (cited in chapter 1) provide a powerful counter-incentive to induce developers toward outlying lands instead. And there exists in the US a practice of building new schools and other suburban facilities *after* greenfields have been developed. We need a clear policy of declining to do this.

There is also the relative ease of developing greenfields, compared with the complexities of redeveloping already-urban land. For example, brownfields require remediation, whose costs can be unpredictable. These barriers are added to the NIMBY ones, and to counterproductive zoning regulations that too often preclude compact and mixed-use development. As noted in chapter 2, *the fact that the mixed uses, relatively high densities, and reduced parking requirements that should characterize transit-oriented development are still illegal in many US municipalities is the first and most fundamental obstacle to be challenged.*

Densities of development should be determined by *transit* capacities, rather than by roadway capacities. And if a city has invested in transit, it should be a basic, underlying design principle that public transit investments will be recouped through coordination with major development, as occurs in the most successful systems in other highly developed nations. Planners Julia Parzen and Abby Jo Sigal have emphasized that enabling public investors to "capture the value" of public investments in TOD is key to obtaining the support of local governments and transit agencies for these projects. Especially in the medium and long term, successful TODs can produce substantial financial and social benefits, and the public sector should benefit when private land values increase as a result of these public investments.[65]

One of the persistent barriers to achieving comprehensive transit networks and TOD in the US is a common American resistance to central planning—no doubt enabled by, if not born of, our historic abundance of land. Yet central planning is essential for some purposes. Market indicators point to an increasing demand for transit-oriented communities in proximity to cities; and these will certainly call for central planning.

Cervero, Ferrell, and Murphy have noted the existence of numerous well-situated potential sites within existing urban areas for new rail rights-of-way and transit-oriented development:

Many transit lines across the United States are located along old railroad right-of-ways [sic] flanked by aging industrial properties and brownfield sites. While land tends to be plentiful in these corridors, developers face potentially costly bills for clean up and site remediation. Nonetheless, such parcels offer tremendous opportunities for forming new TODs and breathing life into once moribund industrial belts.[66]

The authors point to a number of supportive public policies that can help to balance the scales in favor of creating TOD in already-urban areas. These include government help in land assembly, such as land banking by a transit or redevelopment agency; assistance with the remediation of brownfield sites; the transfer of development rights; low-cost loans to lure developers to station areas; and tax abatements and other supportive finance and tax policies.[67]

In addition to mechanisms to encourage and support the construction of TODs, Cervero, Ferrell, and Murphy name a number of zoning types that can be used to promote their favorable design as pedestrian-friendly neighborhoods. These include incentive zoning (density bonuses); performance zoning (tying incentives to meeting minimum design criteria); inclusionary zoning (to encourage mixed uses); minimum-density (as-of-right) classifications; "floating" or overlay zoning (to encourage pedestrian-oriented planning in light-rail station areas, including the favorable location of small retail shops, restaurants, outdoor cafés and benches); and interim zoning (to prevent auto-oriented uses from precluding eventual TOD). Interim zoning has been used in the development of Portland's Westside light-rail corridor to set minimum densities, to control building placements in order to ensure direct pedestrian access to and from stations, to cap parking supplies, and to prevent auto-related uses within a half-mile of stations.[68]

Within the TOD, zoning changes should include an end to single-use zoning. Any land use might be permitted in a TOD, as long as it doesn't interfere with residential life. Thus, individuals and families who want to open a small retail business in their homes would have the presumed right to do so. In this way, goods and services could be brought back to within walking distance of places where people live and work, greatly reducing travel needs and saving time.

Vested interests and politics

Slowing the pace of change

By late June 2012, the US Congress had managed to pass a two-year, multi-billion-dollar transportation bill, but it had taken them three years to achieve this, and it was regrettably inadequate when it did pass. The bill failed to provide sufficient funding for the repair of the nation's many structurally deficient bridges, or for a significant increase in funding for public transportation, despite the clear needs for both. As remarked by Dr. Judith Rodin, president of the Rockefeller Foundation, these needs are especially relevant for today's public, since "transportation is the second highest cost in American households (and the highest if you are a low-wage worker)." Rodin points to the bill's lack of appropriate response to current demand:

American demographics are shifting significantly, and our transportation habits and needs are changing too. The new generation of Millennials—all those kids you see in your neighborhood biking and walking or staring at their smartphones on the bus—are driving less than the previous generation, and 25 percent less than people 10 years older than them. Within three years, over 15 million Americans above the age of 65—for whom transportation options are essential and even life-saving—will live in communities where public transportation is poor or woefully insufficient. As Baby Boomers age, this number will only get bigger. And racial minorities, who will be the country's majority in a few decades, are four times more likely to use public transportation to commute to work. These are the Americans we should be thinking about and building 21st century infrastructure for, yet we continue to fund and build the wrong things—highways—focusing on the needs of the loudest lobby rather than the needs of the next generation of Americans.[69]

The bill furthermore cut by 60 percent the already-modest funding for improvements designed to make walking and cycling safer.[70] Politics was unfortunately at play in this decision. As has been commented by former Bogotá mayor Enrique Peñalosa, "Politics is a dirty word. But politics is how societies make decisions.... There is something wrong if we assume that only automobile drivers deserve to have mobility without the risk of being killed."[71]

Nobel Prize–winning economist Paul Krugman, writing in the *New York Times*, has observed that changing our current patterns of behavior "would shuffle the economic deck, hurting some powerful vested interests even as it created new economic opportunities. And the industries of the past have armies of lobbyists in place right now; the industries of the future don't. Nor is it just a matter of vested interests. It's also a matter of vested ideas."[72]

Regardless of this resistance to change, the current conjunction of population increases and migratory trends toward the cities, and thus, increasing congestion in the cities, is making ever more obvious the need for a more rational use of urban space, and for more compact and sustainable forms of mobility—namely, walking, biking, and transit. While common wisdom has it that it is only progressives who favor the support of public transportation, there has been a movement on the part of prominent *conservatives* in support of passenger rail transport, in particular, for the many reasons that were cited in chapter 3. It was emphasized by co-authors and champions of both passenger rail and conservative causes, Paul Weyrich and William Lind, that conservatives sit in traffic just the same as progressives, and there are no special commuter lanes reserved for one party or the other.[73]

Privatization of public services and the implications for cities

One argument frequently heard against investing in public services and infrastructure is the theory that Europe is in economic trouble because it spends too much on its social safety net, and that we are watching the death throes of the welfare state—from which, we are told, the United States should learn a lesson. This line of thinking, however, has been soundly refuted by Krugman, who points out that Europe's problems have been mostly monetary, caused by the introduction of a single currency "without the institutions needed to make that currency work." If the economically troubled nations still had their own individual currencies, argues Krugman, they would be able to use devaluation to restore their competitiveness. He observes that Sweden, while retaining a very generous social safety net, currently has faster economic growth than that of any other wealthy nation, and that Germany, whose social safety net is greater than that of Italy, is a star performer economically.[74]

In contrast, we are witnessing in the US the gradual privatization/ conversion to for-profit status of our society's most essential public services—including schools, hospitals, libraries, postal services, fire and police protection, and urban transportation systems. Deprived of sufficient funds, many of these services and our vital infrastructure are becoming increasingly feeble and fragmented, no longer able to reliably serve the cities and the majority of the citizenry. As noted above, the nation's infrastructure in general is in dire need of heavy investments, not only in public transportation systems, but in the highway network (now rated as D-minus by the American Association of Civil Engineers and in water and sewer systems, power grids, roads and bridges.[75] While wealthy individuals and families may retreat to privately protected gated communities, the infrastructure and social services of the cities and their environs, which contain at least two-thirds of the US population, are particularly vulnerable to neglect. It should not be a question of choice between education and infrastructure. Both are needed, and both need to be of high quality.

The US is not alone in shortcutting quality for the bottom line. Despite the remarkable achievements of the European rail networks, a number of shocking, deadly rail crashes have occurred in recent years in Spain, France, Switzerland, and Belgium, as budget cuts have reduced the number of train employees and curtailed the ability to afford updated equipment, such as advanced automatic braking systems. In too many cases, high-speed vehicles are running on old rail, and leaving the systems vulnerable.[76]

The slashing of spending in the face of a depressed economy is a perfect recipe for increased unemployment and widespread suffering, as shown by today's extreme example of Greece. In contrast with the current scenario, during a much earlier economic crisis in the fifth century BC, the great Pericles did not respond by slashing budgets. Instead, he initiated a public works project and built the Parthenon.[77]

If we, on the other hand, choose to deprive our schools and infrastructure of sorely needed funds, we defeat our future. Difficult times call for vision and generosity, rather than austerity. Notes architect and Columbia University adjunct professor Thomas De Monchaux:

Economically, austerity—which the Germans, among others, are intent on forcing upon their southern brethren—can sound like a good idea, but might actually exacerbate the conditions it ostensibly ameliorates. One day, we might look back on cuts in public services and infrastructure during a downturn with the same disbelief with which today's doctors recall the medieval medicine of deliberately cutting and bleeding the sick.[78]

Box 7.1
Cities as the Leaders on Environmental Sustainability

Former Los Angeles mayor Villaraigosa governed his city with a strong environmental agenda, including major measures to revive and extend the city's public transportation system. He observed that at the 2009 climate negotiations in Copenhagen, it became crystal clear to the mayors of the great global cities—London, New York, Paris, and Mexico City—that, while the leaders of their nations were all outdoing each other to see who could do the *least* to mitigate climate change, the mayors were outdoing each other to see who could do the *most*. Villaraigosa has been looking to the global cities to take the lead in technology, innovation, and sustainability, "as they have in all else," rather than waiting for their national governments.[a]

Note

a. Greg Hanscom, "Mayor Awesome: Against All Odds, L.A.'s Mayor Stays Green," *Grist*, March 21, 2012, http://grist.org/cities/mayor-mas-awesome-against-all-odds-l -a-s-mayor-stays-green.

Some issues in conversion of the public from habitual driving to riding bikes and transit

A transition from ubiquitous automobility would not necessarily be smooth economically. For example, if a huge rail network with millions of daily passengers were ultimately developed in the US, a dynamic train industry could create hundreds of thousands of operating, maintenance, and administrative jobs. But the conversion of existing auto plants to the *manufacturing* of trains would be more of a challenge, because the factories would need to be largely modified, completely retooled, and the workers retrained. Furthermore, fewer people are needed in building trains than in building cars, since nowhere near as many trains will be needed by a train-riding society as cars are needed by a car-dependent society. This is basically because of mass transit's efficiency—its vehicles are shared by thousands of people rather than being possessed by one person or family.[79]

By the same token, the gradual conversion of large numbers of the public from habitual car-driving to habitual transit-riding would require far fewer vehicles would mean substantial savings in raw materials. For as a consumer of natural resources in its manufacture, the automobile has no equal. This fact was heralded in the 1930s as one of its great advantages for industrial prosperity, but can be viewed very differently from today's conservationist perspective. In the United States alone, the manufacture of automobiles consumes—in addition to enormous quantities of water—20 percent of the nation's steel, 95 percent of its nickel, 35 percent of its zinc, 10 percent of its copper, 6 percent of its rubber, and 5 percent of its lead—all of which are short-lived investments, since approximately 6 percent of our car population ends up on the scrap heap every year, where its material components leach into the groundwater.[80]

At present, the major rail manufacturers are in strong competition with each other for the relatively few rail projects currently on the drawing boards in the US. While much of the public is clamoring for new transit—light-rail, in particular—there is typically at least *some* community opposition to each new project, complicated by lengthy environmental reviews and the periodic turnover of local and state elected officials. All of these factors can slow or even halt the progress of a project. So the manufacturers typically cast low bids against each other, and often lose money in the process.[81] A resurgence of interest, enthusiasm, and particularly, funding for all types of rail might, nevertheless, alleviate these problems. And the experience of the amazingly speedy World War II conversion of America's peacetime factories into a mighty wartime industrial force is a dramatic example of how quickly the nation can mobilize once it is convinced of the necessity of doing so.

Current trends

Hyper-consumerism
Krugman has remarked that the recent rise in the prices of commodities is a sure indicator that we are living in a finite world, with finite quantities of resources. He notes that this will require that we gradually adapt our economy and lifestyles to the reality of more expensive resources.[82]

However, what has kept the economy going to date has been hyper-consumerism, which in turn implies the importance to the gross domestic product of promoting maximum acquisitions among the citizenry (conveniently referred to as "consumers"). Homes and cars are the main targets, as these are the major expenditures for most families. And toward the goal of maximum spending, the most effective tool is the deliberate promotion of aspirations to wealth and dominance. A prime example can be viewed in the car commercials, notably those that glamorize the speed of powerful vehicles on the open road—exactly the image to feed the fantasies of immature drivers, and a truly malign influence on their driving (with very negative repercussions for our neighborhoods and cities).

For years, the automobile industry has been a key spender when it comes to allotting dollars to advertising.[83] As noted by Robert Goodman, professor of environmental design at Hampshire College in Amherst, Massachusetts:

U.S. auto makers spend more by far for advertising—$20 billion a year—than any other industry in the world. Amtrak's $200 million budget shortfall in 2002, which threatened to shut down the nation's entire passenger rail system, could have been erased with less than the cost of four days of car ads.[84]

Certainly, spending beyond one's means has been unhealthy for the public in general, and has contributed heavily to the current rash of bankruptcies and home foreclosures. It is stunning that, between 1960 and 2007, the average ratio of personal debt to disposable income was exploding from around 55 to 133 percent.[85] By March 2009, the total outstanding personal debt in the US amounted to some $5.3 trillion. And the average rate of savings as a percentage of disposable income had fallen from 10 percent during the 1980s to approximately zero by the middle of the first decade of the twenty-first centurys.[86]

Writing in the *Wall Street Journal*, Daniel Gross points out that, for the past three decades in the United States, people have not so much bought their quality of life; rather they have borrowed it from banks and credit card companies. He notes that now, in our increasingly mobile economy, people are avoiding new financial encumbrances and getting over the idea that they need to *own* the American dream; rather, they are increasingly OK with *renting* it.[87] And the assumption that building and buying homes is synonymous with the "good life" and with a productive and prosperous economy has been losing relevance. On the contrary, higher rates of home ownership have become increasingly associated with *lower* wages in most parts of the country.[88]

Some cooling of the love affair between cars and young people

In fact, studies have shown that there is an increasing population of people in their twenties who are settling in locations where they are "transit-dependent by choice."[89] According to CNW Marketing Research, only 27 percent of the US purchases of new cars in 2010 were made by people ages 21 to 34, down from 38 percent in 1985. One likely reason is that this generation has been collectively hit by unemployment and unprecedented student debt.[90] Transportation planning expert Steven E. Polzin, in examining key trends between 2001 and 2008, just prior to the Great Recession, found substantial declines in vehicular travel by US youth compared with those of the same age eight years prior.[91] The percentage of potential drivers 19 years and younger with drivers' licenses had already been declining, from 64.4 percent in 1998 to 46.3 percent in 2008. Four years later, 46 percent of 18 to 24-year-olds indicated to the Gartner market research firm that they would choose Internet access over owning a car.[92]

In a 2009 study of auto-related online commentary among teens and young adults by the market research firm J.D. Power & Associates, hundreds of thousands of "conversations" were analyzed, which indicated a shift in perceptions regarding the necessity of and desire to own a car. The research firm suggested that, in light of the nation's ongoing recession, part of the reason could be economic, while part of it could be that—with the advent of social media and other forms of electronic communication—young people perceive less of a need to physically congregate, and thus less of a need for a car.[93] One young writer in 2012 expressed a very basic emotional reason to eschew driving:

> Another appeal of not driving is spending less time in isolation. We move to cities because we like to be close to each other; we like to know that there are other humans within easy reach. When I take the bus, I feel much more engaged in the life of my city than when I'm stuck in a car. On public transportation, even if I'm listening to music or texting my friends, I'm part of a micro-community populated by the bus driver and passengers, united by the fact that, even if just for a few minutes, we're all going in the same direction at the same time....
>
> Why do people take their laptops to cafés? Okay, sometimes for the free wireless. But also, I think, because while we're connecting virtually, we want to be assured that we belong to a tangible universe. We still get lonely when we're alone, even with the world at our fingertips.[94]

There is also the likelihood of another factor, at least as significant—that young people today are often more keenly aware than their parents, and care more deeply about the ecological damages to the planet caused by the omnipresence of automobiles. Many of them seem more ready to accept the fact that, if we want to solve our problems with oil, we have to use less of it.

Designing for smaller households—and downsizing for a lighter ecological footprint

Living modestly need not mean living poorly. Indeed, we might cheerfully envision a future of "frugal prosperity." If greater attention is being paid to the public urban realm, many of us could, in turn, find ourselves living happily in housing units that are far smaller and less costly than what we are used to. These might be a somewhat-larger variation on the "Nano" units that are being constructed in India. Tata, the Indian company that made headlines throughout the world in 2009 with its $2,000 Nano car, has embarked upon the design and construction of tiny apartments outside of Mumbai and other Indian cities, each unit of which will sell for the equivalent of only US$7,899 to US$13,400. The company's housing division is targeting a segment of the market that has hitherto been ignored—people who are unable to afford new condos in luxury buildings, but who comprise the bulk of the potential customers. The scale of these apartments is truly tiny, only 218 to 373 sf (20 to 35 m²), but the units will be coveted in a nation where the average call center employee with ten to twenty years of experience earns the equivalent of only US$6,400 a year.[95]

A similar phenomenon is occurring in our own country, where, with the ongoing recession, many young people are having a particularly difficult time establishing themselves financially—holding down two or even three part-time jobs, while paying off their student loans, and are e unable to afford market rents. Their housing needs are simple—basically a conveniently located and safe place to sleep, such as a loft, with a private bath and kitchenette tucked underneath—since they spend much of their non-work time at coffee shops, parks and plazas.

A Seattle developer has been answering these needs by erecting several buildings containing tiny apartments. In one of these buildings the units range from only 90 to 168 sf (8.36 to 15.61 m²), with rents of around $500 per month, which covers all utilities, including Wi-Fi. The developer files these buildings with the city as "rooming houses" so that parking requirements will be minimal. Renters are charged separately for the use of a parking stall, and most stalls go unused. The developer knows that good management is key to success with rental properties, so his staff makes sure that prospective tenants are carefully screened, and that public areas are scrupulously maintained. His success is indisputable: in 2011, he had waiting lists for his next three buildings.[96]

Similarly, a developer in Palo Alto has provided a building where the units range between 350 and 400 sf (32.52 and 37.16 m^2), and the rents range from less than $400 to $900 per month, in a city where market-rate studios rent for some $1,500 to $2,000. In this case, the developer provides free transit passes to the residents, so they will not need to own a car.[97]

And in 2012, New York City launched a pilot program, called adAPT NYC, to address its chronic housing shortage by developing "micro" rental apartments of between 275 and 300 sf (between 26 and 28 m^2), joining a trend that has prevailed for years in Paris, Tokyo, Barcelona, London, and other international urban centers.[98] In fact, in light of the limited land base of Japan, there has long been a tradition there of living well in small spaces, and out of necessity, "editing" non-essential possessions out of one's life.

In July 2013, an e-book by Alan Durning was released that advocates for an even less costly solution to affordable housing. In *Unlocking Home: Three Keys to Affordable Communities*, Durning points out that, since the mid-twentieth century, municipal laws in the United States have criminalized history's traditional answers to providing affordable dwellings—the rooming house, the roommate, the in-law apartment, and the backyard cottage. Banning what used to be the bottom end of the private housing market has made living quarters scarce and expensive, especially for low-income people, including seniors, students, artists, and others (who happen to add to the diversity of cities.)[99]

More typically, average households in the United States have an especially heavy ecological footprint—largely linked to the scale of our housing, our related acquisitions, and our predominantly automotive lifestyles. As noted earlier in this chapter, in the US, emissions of the greenhouse gases responsible for climate change amount to some 18 tons per person annually. In contrast, in Europe as a whole, annual emissions per person average less than half as much—mainly because of smaller houses, smaller cars, and fewer sprawling suburbs.[100] Additionally, a strong correlation has been found between affluent lifestyles and purchasing habits, and high volumes of greenhouse gases: emissions per person are sharply higher in the wealthier countries.[101] And with a US birthrate that is the very highest among the industrialized nations, our footprint is being accordingly multiplied.[102]

Compact, walkable, and transit-oriented development can be especially compatible for small-household living. Within such development, the ease of more incidental contact with neighbors than what normally occurs in spread-out suburbia creates possibilities for more sociable ways of life for small families and for people living alone (who now comprise a large percentage of the US population). Living in walkable, bikable, mixed-use communities, easily accessible to transit, can also allow more flexible lifestyles for young parents—having access to more educational and career opportunities, postponing having children until they are older, and having fewer children when they do. This can be of vital help in easing the environmental stresses that we are placing on the planet. Certainly, children living in these communities can also gain healthy independence at an earlier age, as they will not need to be chauffeured by their parents to every activity.

Indeed, there are many pleasures and rewards to be anticipated with the lightening of our ecological footprint. As commented by author William Greider:

Free of want and worry, we face a new challenge: to discover what it means to be truly human. That wondrous pursuit is what I recommend as the alternative to our old definition of progress. In the years ahead, Americans will suffer unavoidable losses of familiar pleasures and be compelled to alter some deeply ingrained habits of material consumption. These painful adjustments can be endured if the people are confident the country is progressing toward a more fulfilling transformation. The essential trade-off could be playfully expressed on a bumper sticker:

SMALLER CARS FOR LARGER LIVES.[103]

Abbreviations

ft	foot, feet
ha	hectare, hectares
kg	kilograms
km	kilometers
km²	square kilometers
km/h	kilometers per hour
lb	pound, pounds
mph	miles per hour
m	meters
m²	square meters
sf	square feet

Notes

Chapter 1

1. Worldwatch Institute, *State of the World 2012: Moving Toward Sustainable Prosperity* (Washington, DC: Island Press, 2012), 54–57.

2. Leon Kolankiewicz and Roy Beck, *Weighing Sprawl Factors in Large U.S. Cities: A Report on the Nearly Equal Roles Played by Population Growth and Land Use Choices in the Loss of Farmland and Natural Habitat to Urbanization* (analysis of US Bureau of the Census data on the hundred-largest urbanized areas of the United States, Arlington, VA, March 19, 2001), http://www.sprawlcity.org/studyUSA/index.html.

3. Aaron Betsky, "Smoke, Mirrors, and Oz," *Architecture*, October 9, 2012, http://www.architectmagazine.com/architecture/the-ideological-divide-between-cities-and-suburbs.aspx?utm_source=newsletter&utm_medium=email&utm_campaign=ABU_101612_content=full.

4. Tony Judt, *Ill Fares the Land* (New York: Penguin Press, 2010), 211, 215.

5. Robert Bruegmann, *Sprawl: A Compact History* (Chicago: University of Chicago Press), 2005.

6. Debra Kahn, "Transportation: Costs of U.S. Dependence on Petroleum Are Huge, Expert Says," *Climatewire*, September 5, 2012, http://www.eenews.net/climatewire/2012/09/05/5.

7. Robert Puentes, "Transportation and Climate Change: The Perfect Storm," Brookings Institution, Metropolitan Policy Program, September 8, 2009, http://www.brookings.edu/opinions/2009/0421_transportation_puentes.aspx.

8. Christopher B. Leinberger, remarks at the Forum for Urban Design symposium at the Century Association, New York, July 7, 2010.

9. Stacy C. Davis, Susan W. Diegal, and Robert G. Boundy, eds., *Transportation Energy Data Book: Edition 30* (prepared for the US Department of Energy, Oak Ridge National Laboratory, Oak Ridge, TN, June 2011), table 1.4, 1–5.

10. US Bureau of Transportation Statistics, *Transportation Statistics Annual Report* (Washington, DC: US Department of Transportation, 2008).

11. Lester R. Brown, *Plan B 4.0: Mobilizing to Save Civilization* (New York: W. W. Norton, 2009), 162.

12. US Department of Transportation, *The 2008 National Household Travel Survey*, sponsored by the Bureau of Transportation Statistics and Federal Highway Administration, http://www.bts.gov/programs/national_household_travel_survey.

13. Kaid Benfield, "National Geographic Surveys Countries' Transit Use: Guess Who Comes in Last?" *NRDC's Switchboard*, blog, posted May 18, 2009, http://switchboard.nrdc.org/blogs/kbenfield/natgeo_surveys_countries_trans.html.

14. Ralph Buehler and John Pucher, "Sustainable Transport That Works: Lessons from Germany," *World Transport Policy and Practice* 15, no. 1 (April 2009): 15, http://www.eco-logica.co.uk/pdf/wtpp15.1.pdf.

15. Boris S. Pushkarev and Jeffrey M. Zupan, *Public Transportation and Land Use Policy* (Bloomington: Indiana University Press, 1977), 121–171.

16. Sonia Hirt, "The Devil Is in the Definitions: Contrasting American and German Approaches to Zoning," *Journal of the American Planning Association* 73, no. 4 (fall 2007): 436–450.

17. Robert H. Nelson, *Zoning and Property Rights: An Analysis of the American System of Land Use Regulation* (Cambridge, MA: MIT Press, 1977).

18. US Department of Housing and Urban Development, *American Housing Survey* (Washington, DC: US Department of Housing and Urban Development, 2000).

19. Timothy Egan, "Urban Sprawl Strains Western States," *New York Times* (December 29, 1996), 1, 20.

20. American Farmland Trust, *Farming on the Edge: Sprawling Development Threatens America's Best Farmland* (Northampton, MA: American Farmland Trust, October 2002), https://wikis.uit.tufts.edu/confluence/download/attachments/29763335/Farming_on_the_Edge_2002.pdf?version=1&modificationDate=1257473715000.

21. A. Ann Sorensen, Richard P. Greene, and Karen Russ, *Farming on the Edge* (DeKalb, IL: American Farmland Trust for Agriculture in the Environment, March 1997), 2–23. It is calculated that if this rate continues, by the year 2050, we will have lost 13 percent of our best farmland, and by 2060 could well become a net importer rather than exporter of food.

22. US Environmental Protection Agency, Development, Community, and Environment Division, "Residential Construction Trends in America's Metropolitan Regions," January 2010, http://www.epa.gov/dced/pdf/metro_res_const_trends_09.pdf.

23. Kaid Benfield, "The 5 Most Important Sustainability Stories of 2013," *Atlantic Cities*, January 2, 2013, http://www.theatlanticcities.com/arts-and-lifestyle/2013/01/5-most-important-sustainability-stories-2013/4288.

24. Derek Mearns, "Multifamily Permits Jump 20 Percent, Highest Level in 4 Years," *Multifamily Executive*, October 18, 2012, http://www.multifamilyexecutive.com/permitting/multifamily-permits-are-up-more-than-20-percent

.aspx?utm_source=newsletter&utm_content=jump&utm_medium=email&utm _campaign=ANW_102212&day=2012-10-22.

25. US Department of Transportation, Federal Highway Administration, Bureau of Transportation Statistics, Federal Transit Administration, Census Transportation Planning Products, AASHTO Update, April 2009, 3.

26. Ibid., 5.

27. Todd Litman, "Why and How to Reduce the Amount of Land Paved for Roads and Parking Facilities," *Environmental Practice: Journal of the National Association of Environmental Professionals* 13, no. 1 (March 2011): 38–46.

28. Pushkarev and Zupan, *Public Transportation and Land Use Policy*, 4–7.

29. Donald C. Shoup, "Innovative Approaches to Parking and Land Use in Urban Areas" (remarks at a Rudin Center for Transportation Policy and Management seminar, NYU Wagner, New York. January 22, 2010.

30. Eric C. Brun and Preston L. Schiller. "How Cars Devour Urban Space and Time," *Urban Transport International* 5 (May–June 1996): 38, 39.

31. David Quammen, *The Song of the Dodo: Island Biography in an Age of Extinctions* (New York: Scribner, 1996), 602–625.

32. Stephen R. Kellert, "Values and Perceptions of Invertebrates," *Conservation Biology* 7, no. 4 (December 1993): 845–848.

33. F. Kaid Benfield, Matthew D. Raimi, and Donald D. T. Chen, *Once There Were Greenfields: How Urban Sprawl Is Undermining America's Environment, Economy, and Social Fabric* (Washington, DC: Natural Resources Defense Council, Surface Transportation Policy Project, 1999), 78–87.

34. Tom Schueler, *Site Planning for Urban Stream Protection* (Washington, DC: Center for Watershed Protection and Metropolitan Council of Governments, 1995), 38, 43, 75–76.

35. Haya El Nasser, "Suburban Growth Focused on Inner and Outer Communities," *USA Today*, April 26, 2011, http://www.usatoday.com/news/nation/2011 -04-26-suburbs-growth-census-demographics_n.htm.

36. Jonathan L. Freedman, "The Effects of Population Density on Humans," in *Psychological Perspectives on Population*, ed. James T. Fawcett (New York: Basic Books, 1973).

37. Israel Pressman and Arthur Carol, "Crime as a Diseconomy of Scale" (paper presented at the Operations Research Society of America convention, Denver, CO, June 1969); Jianling Li and Jack Rainwater, "The Real Picture of Land-Use Density and Crime: A GIS Application," study of Irving, TX, using GIS spatial analysis, based on 2000 and 1990 data, http://proceedings.esri.com/library/user-conf/proc00/professional/papers/PAP508/p508.htm; Brian Christens and Paul W. Speer, "Predicting Violent Crime Using Urban and Suburban Densities," study of Nashville, TN, Vanderbilt University, 2005, http://firstmonday.org/htbin/cgiwrap/ bin/ojs/index.php/bsi/article/viewFile/334/20.4.

38. Jonathan L. Freedman, Alan S. Levy, Roberta W. Buchanan, and Judy Price, "Crowding and Human Aggressiveness," *Journal of Experimental Social Psychology* 8, no. 6 (November 1972): 528–548.

39. Craig Karmin, "Housing Rebound Spurs Arizona Land Buy," *Wall Street Journal*, November 15, 2012, http://blogs.wsj.com/developments/2012/11/15/housing-rebound-spurs-arizona-land-buy; Real Estate Research Corporation, *The Costs of Sprawl: Environmental and Economic Costs of Alternative Residential Patterns at the Urban Fringe* (Washington, DC: Council on Environmental Quality, Office of Policy Development and Research, Department of Housing and Urban Development, and Office of Planning and Management, Environmental Protection Agency, 1974), chapter 6. There is a well-known "factor of five" by which the wholesale price of land beyond the urban fringe is commonly roughly quintupled as urban development approaches. When this land is furnished with services and infrastructural improvements (roads, sewer lines, water, and electricity), its value is further multiplied, again frequently by a factor of five. Speculators buy in anticipation of the extension of highways and utilities, or upon rezoning or subdivision, and willingly pay higher prices as soon as these measures are committed.

40. Smart Growth America, "Federal Involvement in Real Estate: A Call for Examination," January 2013, http://www.smartgrowthamerica.org/documents/federal-involvement-in-real-estate.pdf.

41. Michelle Ernst and Lilly Shoup, *Dangerous by Design: Solving the Epidemic of Preventable Pedestrian Deaths (and Making Great Neighborhoods)*, Transportation for America and Surface Transportation Policy Project, November 2009, http://t4america.org/docs/dangerousbydesign/dangerous_by_design.pdf.

42. Lewis Mumford, *The City in History: Its Origins, Its Transformations, and Its Prospects* (1989; repr., New York: Harcourt, Brace, 1961), 511.

43. Adie Tomer and Robert Puentes, "Transit Access and Zero-Vehicle Households," Brookings Institution, August 18, 2011, http://www.brookings.edu/papers/2011/0818_transportation_tomer_puentes.aspx.

44. Paul Krugman, "Stranded by Sprawl," *New York Times*, July 29, 2013.

45. Dan Bluemel, "Transit Panel Accuses MTA of Civil Rights Violations," *l.a.activist*, August 11, 2011, http://www.laactivist.com/2011/08/21/transit-panel-accuses-mta-of-civil-rights-violations; Jackie Orozco, "Memphis Bus Riders Union File Lawsuit against MATA," Local Memphis.com, March 18, 2012, http://www.localmemphis.com/news/local/story/Memphis-Bus-Riders-Union-File-Lawsuit-Against-MATA/PU09trMcLUC-Re5UFWdS5A.cspx.

46. Christopher Swope, "Faster Than a Speeding Turtle: New High-Tech Tools Can Make Buses a Lot More Efficient Than They Used to Be. Will That Be Enough to Satisfy Riders?" *Governing*, February 2006, http://www.governing.com/topics/transportation-infrastructure/Faster-Speeding-Turtle.html.

47. Jonathan Levine, "Is Bus versus Rail Investment a Zero-Sum Game? The Misuse of the Opportunity-Cost Concept," *Journal of the American Planning Association* 79, no. 1 (Winter 2013): 5–15.

48. Gregory R. Thompson and Tom Parkinson, "How the French Make Trams Succeed: State of the Art Light Rail" (presentation at the Ninety-Second Annual Meeting of the Transportation Research Board to the Light Rail Transit Committee AP075, Washington, DC, January 16, 2013).

49. Daniel Sperling, "Two Billion Cars and the Transformation of Transportation" (address at the University Transportation Research Center Region 2, City College of New York, June 12, 2010).

50. Amory B. Lovins and L. Hunter Lovins, "Reinventing the Wheels," *Atlantic Monthly* 275, no. 1 (January 1995): 75–85.

51. Carbonomics, "How to Fix the Climate and Charge It to OPEC," Zfacts.com, April 28, 2008, http://papers.ssrn.com/sol3/papers.cfm?abstract_id=1300126.

52. Eugene Mulero, "Transportation: Building EVs Could Create Twice the Emissions of Conventional Cars—Study," *E&E News*, October 10, 2012, http://www .eenews.net/eenewspm/2012/10/10/4.

53. Transportation for America, ITS America, Association for Commuter Transportation, and University of Michigan's SMART Initiative, "Smart Mobility for a 21st Century America: Strategies for Maximizing Technology to Minimize Congestion, Reduce Emissions, and Increase Efficiency," white paper, October 2010, http://t4america.org/wp-content/uploads/2010/10/ITS-White-Paper-100710 -FINAL.pdf.

54. Ben Klayman, "Who Needs a License? Self-Driving Cars Coming Our Way," *Finance*, Yahoo.com, August 15, 2012, http://www.reuters.com/article/2012/08/15/ us-autos-selfdriving-cars-idUSBRE87E04V20120815.

55. Tony Bizjak, "California's Taking the Lead on Self-Driving Cars," *Sacramento Bee*, June 3, 2012, http://www.modbee.com/2012/06/03/2226219_californias -taking-the-lead-on.html.

56. Associated Press, "Calif. Governor Signs Driverless Cars Bill: Nobody's Driving," *Finance*, Yahoo.com, September 25, 2012, http://finance.yahoo.com/news/ calif-governor-signs-driverless-cars-204943011.html.

57. John Markoff and Somini Sengupta, "Drivers with Hands Full Get a Backup: The Car," *New York Times*, January 13, 2013.

58. Scott Martelle, "Self-Driving Cars and the Liability Issues They Raise," Protect Consumer Justice.org, May 11, 2012, http://www.protectconsumerjustice .org/self-driving-cars-and-the-liability-issues-they-raise.html.

59. Transportation for America et al., "Smart Mobility for a 21st Century America."

60. Robert D. Yaro and Armando Carbonell, "Reinventing Megalopolis: The Northeast Megaregion, in *Smart Growth in a Changing World*, ed. Jonathan Barnett (Chicago: Planners Press, American Planning Association, 2007), 87.

61. Preservation Green Lab of the National Trust for Historic Preservation, "The Greenest Building: Quantifying the Environmental Value of Building Reuse," 2011, http://www.preservationnation.org/information-center/sustainable-commu nities/green-lab/lca/The_Greenest_Building_lowres.pdf.

62. Jane Jacobs, *The Death and Life of Great American Cities* (New York: Vantage Books, 1961), 150–151.

63. Benfield, Raimi, and Chen, *Once There Were Greenfields*, chapter 3.

64. American Public Transit Association, "Rising Gas Prices Allow Public Transit Riders to Ring in the New Year with an Average Savings of $805 This Month and

$9,656 Annually," *Transit News*, January 5, 2011, http://www.apta.com/media center/pressreleases/2011/Pages/110601_TransitSavingsReport.aspx.

65. Kaid Benfield, "'Growing Wealthier' Report Shows How Smart Growth Can Enhance Prosperity," Center for Clean Air Policy, Natural Resources Defense Council Switchboard, January 19, 2011. http://switchboard.nrdc.org/blogs/kben field/growing_wealthier_report_shows.html.

66. Joint Center for Housing Studies of Harvard University, Graduate School of Design, John F. Kennedy School of Government, "The State of the Nation's Housing 2011," http://www.jchs.harvard.edu/research/publications/state-nation %E2%80%99s-housing-2011.

67. Roger Vincent, "Apartments Are the Development Du Jour among Builders," *Los Angeles Times*, July 17, 2011, http://www.latimes.com/business/la-fi-commre -quarterly-apartments-20110717,0,6536545.story.

68. Richard Florida, *The Great Reset: How New Ways of Living and Working Drive Post-Crash Prosperity* (New York: HarperCollins, 2010), 173, 176–179.

69. Helen Chernikoff and Al Yoon, "Special Report: Smart Money in Real Estate Is on Smart Growth," Reuters.com, August 3, 2010, http://www.reuters.com/ article/2010/08/03/us-realestate-idUSTRE6722BG20100803.

70. Sabrina Tavernise, "Married Couples Are No Longer a Majority, Census Finds," *New York Times*, May 22, 2011.

71. Quoted in Blaine Weber, "Are You Ready for the New Urbanites?" *Seattle Daily Journal of Commerce*, July 28, 2011, http://www.djc.com/news/re/12031480 .html.

72. Christopher B. Leinberger, "The Next Slum?" *Atlantic*, March 2008, 72, 74.

73. Witold Rybczynski, *Makeshift Metropolis: Ideas about Cities* (New York: Scribner, 2010), 172, 173.

74. Sara Johnson, "Top 10 Small U.S. Cities Growing Faster Than Their Suburbs," *Atlantic Cities*, December 11, 2012.

75. Robert Steuteville, "Housing: An Irresistible Force Meets an Immovable Object," *New Urban Network*, April 29, 2011, http://newurbannetwork.com/news -opinion/blogs/robert-steuteville/14629/housing-irresistible-force-meets-immov able-object.

76. Robert Willis, "Multifamily Buildings to Lead U.S. Construction Gains: Economy," Bloomberg.com, February 13, 2012, http://www.bloomberg.com/ news/2012-02-13/multifamily-buildings-to-lead-u-s-construction-gains-this-year -economy.html.

77. Ellen Dunham-Jones and June Williamson, *Retrofitting Suburbia: Urban Design Solutions for Redesigning Suburbs* (Hoboken, NJ: John Wiley, 2009), 3, 27–29, 131.

78. Richard Florida, "Urban Home Values Are Rising Faster Than Suburban Ones," *Atlantic Cities*, June 25, 2013.

79. Christopher B. Leinberger, "Now Coveted: A Walkable, Convenient Place," *New York Times*, Sunday Review, May 27, 2012.

80. American Public Transportation Association, *Transit News*, March 9, 2009, http://www.apta.com/media/releases/090309_ridership.cfm.

81. New Urbanism Division, American Planning Association, *New Urbanism in Practice*, Fall 2010, http://www.planning.org/divisions/newurbanism/newsletter/2010/pdf/fall.pdf.

82. Greg Lindsay, "Texas Sprawl Goes Out with a Bang, Development Sprouts on Irving Transit Line," Fast Company.com, April 13, 2010, http://www.fastcompany.com/1615179/hasta-la-vista-cowboys-irving-texas-makes-room-for-transit-oriented-development.

83. Froma Harrop, "Is Houston Ready to Ditch Sprawl for More Urbanity?" *Cron*, April 29, 2010, http://www.chron.com/disp/story.mpl/editorial/outlook/6982670.html.

84. Steuteville, "Housing."

85. Amy Cortese, "New Rail Lines Spur Urban Revival," *New York Times*, June 14, 2010.

86. Kaid Benfield, "How California Legislated Its Way to Smarter Growth," *Atlantic Cities*, September 25, 2012.

87. Ibid.

88. Mark L. Hinshaw, *True Urbanism: Living In and Near the Center* (Chicago: American Planning Association, 2007), 106–107.

89. Tony Dutzick and Benjamin Davis, "Do Roads Pay for Themselves? Setting the Record Straight on Transportation Funding," Phineas Baxandall, US PIRG Education Fund, NJPIRG Law and Policy Center, January 2011, http://njpirg.org/sites/pirg/files/reports/Do-Roads-Pay-for-Themselves_-wNJ.pdf.

90. Eric Jaffe, "We Shouldn't Be Surprised That Most Transit Referendums Won," *Atlantic Cities*, November 13, 2012.

91. Cortese, "New Rail Lines."

92. Reuters, "Nightmare Roads Identified in Congestion Study," *Today Travel*, November 15, 2011, http://today.msnbc.msn.com/id/45304661/ns/today-travel/t/nightmare-roads-identified-congestion-study/#.TsLbLfGMaZw.

93. Adam Nagourney, "In Los Angeles, Big Step Ahead for Mass Transit," *New York Times*, November 25, 2010.

94. Allison Brooks and Darnell Chadwick Grisby, "LA Vision; US Promise: Implications of the America Fast Forward Proposal," *Reconnecting America: People—Places—Possibility* (Fall 2011): 4; "Senate Panel Gives Los Angeles Mayor's Transit Plan Bipartisan Boost," *Los Angeles Times*, November 9, 2011, http://latimesblogs.latimes.com/lanow/2011/11/senate-committee-gives-bipartisan-boost-to-mayors-transit-plan.html.

95. Emily Badger, "Why Mayors Should Run the Department of Transportation," *Atlantic Cities*, November 21, 2012.

96. Henry Grabar, "A Guide to America's Most Ambitious Transit Projects," *Atlantic Cities*, January 23, 2013.

97. Ashley Halsey III, "Reports Foresee Trillion-Dollar Spending Gap for U.S. Infrastructure," *Washington Post*, January 15, 2013, http://www.washington post.com/local/trafficandcommuting/trillion-dollar-gap-seen-in-infrastructure -spending/2013/01/15/0a511c30-5f01-11e2-b05a-605528f6b712_story.html.

98. Banking on the Future conference, organized by Manhattan borough president Scott M. Stringer, Steven L. Newman Real Estate Institute, New York, March 14, 2011, http://www.libertycontrol.net/uploads/mbpo/infrastructureprogramfin .pdf.

99. Remarks by Bernard L. Schwartz, chair and CEO, BLS Investments, LLP, at the Banking on the Future conference, New York, March 14, 2011.

100. Michael Cooper, "Bank Sought by Senators to Finance Infrastructure," *New York Times*, March 16, 2011, http://www.nytimes.com/2011/03/16/us/ politics/16infrastructure.html?_r=1.

101. Sphere Consulting, LLC, "The Benefits of Private Investment in Infrastructure," updated July 2011, http://www.politico.com/static/PPM170_110816 _investmentinfrastructure.html.

102. Tony Dutzik and Jordan Schneider, "High-Speed Rail: Public, Private, or Both? Assessing the Prospects, Promise, and Pitfalls of Public-Private Partnerships," Phineas Baxandall, US PIRG Education Fund, Summer 2011, http://cdn .publicinterestnetwork.org/assets/85a40b6572e20834e07b0da3e66e98bf/HSR -PPP-USPIRG-July-19-2011.pdf.

103. Deirdre Shesgreen, "With Federal Funds Threatened, States Look for New Ways to Pay for Transit," *CT Mirror*, September 20, 2011, http://ctmirror.com/ story/13953/stateinfrabank; Keith Laing, "Infrastructure Bank to Get a House Hearing," *Hill*, October 6, 2011, http://thehill.com/blogs/transportation-report/ highways-bridges-and-roads/186109-infrastructure-bank-to-get-a-house-hearing.

104. Joe McDonald, "Minister: China Wants to Invest in US Roads, Rails," Associated Press, December 2, 2011, http://seattletimes.com/html/businesstechnology/ 2016912000_apaschinausinvestment.html.

105. Bill Bradley, Tom Ridge, and David Walker, *Road to Recovery: Transforming America's Transportation*, Carnegie Endowment for International Peace, Leadership Initiative on Transportation Solvency, 2011, http://carnegieendowment.org/ files/road_to_recovery.pdf.

106. Enrique Peñalosa, Remarks from a response at the Our Cities, Ourselves: Visions for 2030 symposium at the American Institute of Architects, New York chapter, New York, July 1, 2010.

Chapter 2

1. Boris S. Pushkarev and Jeffrey M. Zupan, *Public Transportation and Land Use Policy* (Bloomington: Indiana University Press, 1977).

2. Center for Transit-Oriented Development, Transportation Research Board, "CDFIs (Community Development Finance Institutions) and Transit-Oriented

Development," October 2010, http://www.trb.org/Main/Blurbs/CDFIs_and_
TransitOriented_Development_164350.aspx?utm_medium=etmail&utm_source
=Transportation%20Research%20Board&utm_campaign=TRB+E-Newsletter+-
+11-09-2010&utm_content=Web&utm_term=; Stephanie Pollack, "Maintaining Diversity in America's Transit-Rich Neighborhoods," Dukakis Center for
Urban and Regional Policy, Northeastern University, October 2010, http://www
.dukakiscenter.org/storage/TRNEquityFull.pdf.

3. Reconnecting America, *Planning for TOD at the Regional Scale: The Big Pic-
ture*, TOD 204: One in a series of best practices from the Center for Transit-
Oriented Development, August 2011, 9, http://reconnectingamerica.org/assets/
Uploads/RA204REGIONS.pdf.

4. Pollack, "Maintaining Diversity," 40–49.

5. Ibid., 50–54.

6. Gerrit Knaap, Stuart Meck, Terry Moore, and Robert Parker, *Zoning as a Barrier to Multifamily Housing Development*, Planning Advisory Service Report no.
548 (Chicago: American Planning Association, 2007), 44, 68, http://www.huduser
.org/Publications/pdf/zoning_MultifamilyDev.pdf.

7. Reconnecting America and Center for Transit-Oriented Development, "Mixed-
Income Housing: Increasing Affordability with Transit" (Washington, DC: Federal Transit Administration, September 2009).

8. Donald C. Shoup, *The High Cost of Free Parking* (Chicago: American Planning
Association, 2005), 185, 190, 258.

9. Shelley L. Smith, "The Stuff of Parking," *Urban Land* 49, no.2 (February
1990): 38.

10. Donald C. Shoup and Richard W. Willson, "Employer-Paid Parking: The In-
fluence of Parking Prices on Travel Demand," in *Proceedings of the Commuter
Parking Symposium* (Seattle, WA: Association for Commuter Transportation and
Municipality of Metropolitan Seattle, December 6–7, 1990), 10.

11. Shoup, *The High Cost of Free Parking*, 590, 591.

12. Institute of Transportation Engineers, *Parking Generation*, 3rd ed. (Washington, DC: Institute of Transportation Engineers, 2004).

13. Shoup, *The High Cost of Free Parking*, 102–103, 121.

14. Todd Litman, *Parking Management Best Practices* (Chicago: American Planning Association, 2006), 96, 97.

15. Urban Land Institute and Ernst & Young, *Infrastructure 2009: Pivot Point*
(Washington, DC: Urban Land Institute, 2009), 38–39.

16. Tom Vanderbilt, "There's No Such Thing as Free Parking: How Eliminating
Parking Spaces Could Make Cities More Nimble and Efficient," Slate.com, June
22, 2010, http://www.slate.com/id/2257814.

17. Nate Berg, "The Future of Intelligent Parking," *Atlantic Cities*, March
23, 2012, http://www.theatlanticcities.com/commute/2012/03/future-intelligent
-parking/1573.

18. Noah Kazis, "D.C. Planning Chief Urges New York City to Scrap Parking Minimums," *Streetsblog*, November 16, 2011, http://www.streetsblog.org/2011/11/16/d-c-planning-chief-urges-new-york-city-to-scrap-parking-minimums.

19. Michael Bernick and Robert Cervero, *Transit Villages in the 21st Century* (New York: McGraw-Hill, 1997), 45.

20. Shoup, *The High Cost of Free Parking*, 131, 132.

21. Jeremy Kutner, "Downtown Need a Makeover? More Cities Are Razing Urban Highways," *Christian Science Monitor*, March 2, 2011, http://www.csmonitor.com/USA/2011/0302/Downtown-need-a-makeover-More-cities-are-razing-urban-highways.

22. Jeffrey Spivak, "Top 10 Highway Removal Projects," *Urban Land*, September 13, 2011, http://urbanland.uli.org/Articles/2011/September/SpivakTopTenHighway.

23. David Flick, "Dallas 'Downtown 360' Plan Envisions a Dense Urban Center Connected by Streetcars," *Architectural Record*, April 10, 2010, cited in *Dallas Morning News*.

24. Katherine Fung, "Feature > Go Down Moses," *Architect's Newspaper*, June 23, 2011. http://archpaper.com/news/articles.asp?id=5476.

25. Richard Peiser and Anne Frej, *Professional Real Estate Development: The ULI Guide to Business*, 2nd ed. (Washington, DC: Urban Land Institute, 2003), 173.

26. Eduardo C. Serafin, "SJSU/VTA Collaborative Research Project: A Parking Utilization Survey of Transit-Oriented Development Residential Properties in Santa Clara County," San Jose State University, Department of Urban and Regional Planning, November 2010, http://www.sjsu.edu/urbanplanning/docs/VTA-TODParkingSurveyReport-VolI.pdf.

27. Shoup, *The High Cost of Free Parking*, 133.

28. Wenyu Jia and Martin Wachs, "Parking and Affordable Housing," *Access* 13 (Fall 1998): 22–25.

29. Bay Area Rapid Transit, *TOD Guidelines*, June 2003, 38, http://www.bart.gov/docs/planning/TOD_Guidlines.pdf.

30. Shoup, *The High Cost of Free Parking*, 150, 151.

31. Ibid., 166.

32. Ibid., 153–165.

33. Adam Millard-Bell, "Putting on Their Parking Caps," *Planning* 68, no.4 (April 2002): 19.

34. Shoup, *The High Cost of Free Parking*, 153.

35. Ibid., 98–101.

36. Donald C. Shoup, "Yes, Parking Reform Is Possible," *Planning* 77, no.10 (October 2011): 31–35.

37. Shoup, *The High Cost of Free Parking*, 134.

38. Inga Saffron, "Renovated Independence Mall Fails to Win Hearts of Philly Residents," *Philadelphia Inquirer*, December 26, 2010, http://archrecord.con struction.com/yb/ar/article.aspx?story_id=153885585.

39. Peter Calthorpe, *The Next American Metropolis: Ecology, Community, and the American Dream* (Princeton, NJ: Princeton Architectural Press, 1993), 62.

40. Peter Calthorpe, *Think Tank*, Reconnecting America, posted July 26, 2007, http://www.reconnectingamerica.org/public/thinktank/176.

41. Calthorpe, *The Next American Metropolis*, 57.

42. Reconnecting America, *2010 Inventory of TOD Programs: A National Review of State, Regional, and Local Programs That Fund Transit-Oriented Development Plans and Projects.* January 2011.

43. Steve McLinden, "It Takes a Transit Village," *National Real Estate Investor*, November 1, 2006, http://nreionline.com/property/mixed_use/real_estate_takes _transit_village.

44. Robert Cervero, Steven Murphy, Christopher Ferrell, Natasha Goguts, Yu-Hsin Tsai, G. B. Arrington, John Boroski, Janet Smith-Heimer, Robert Dunphy, and others, *Transit-Oriented Development in the United States: Experiences, Challenges, and Prospects.* Transit Cooperative Research Report 102. Washington, DC: Transportation Research Board, January 1, 2004, http://www.reconnect ingamerica.org/resource-center/browse-research/2004/tcrp-102-transit-oriented -development-in-the-united-states-experiences-challenges-and-prospects.

45. Tom Fairchild, "Arlington Focuses on Moving People, Not Cars, in the Nation's Worst Traffic Metro Area," *Mobility Lab*, February 5, 2013, http://mobilitylab .org/2013/02/05/arlington-focuses-on-moving-people-not-cars-in-the-nations -worst-traffic-metro-area.

46. Steven Higashide, "Connecticut Officials, TOD Advocates Tour New Jersey's Transit Villages," *Tri-State Transportation Campaign, Mobilizing the Region*, December 13, 2012, http://blog.tstc.org/2012/12/13/connecticut-officials-tod -advocates-tour-new-jerseys-transit-villages.

47. Ibid.

48. Robert Cervero, "Infrastructure and Development: Planning Matters," in *Transportation Infrastructure: The Challenges of Rebuilding America*, ed. Marlon G. Boarnet, report no. 557 (Chicago: American Planning Association, July 2009), 44, 45.

49. Cervero et al., *Transit-Oriented Development in the United States*.

50. Ron Nyren, "Transit-Oriented Development Outlook," *Urban Land*, August 27, 2012, http://www.urbanland.uli.org/Articles/2012/Aug/ul/NyrenTransit.

51. Allison Brooks and Darnell Chadwick Grisby, "LA Vision; US Promise: Implications of the America Fast Forward Proposal," *Reconnecting America: People— Places—Possibility* (Fall 2011): 4, 5.

52. McLinden, "It Takes a Transit Village."

53. Ibid.

54. Bay Area Rapid Transit, *TOD Guidelines*, 9, 37.

55. Robert Cervero, Christopher Ferrell, and Steven Murphy, *Transit-Oriented Development and Joint Development in the United States: A Literature Review*, Transportation Cooperative Research Program, no. 52 (Washington, DC: Transportation Research Board, October 2002), 78.

56. Bernick and Cervero, *Transit Villages*, 121.

57. Steve Nadis and James J. MacKenzie, *Car Trouble* (Washington, DC: World Resources Institute, 1993), iv.

58. Cervero, Ferrell, and Murphy, *Transit-Oriented Development*, 2, 7, 8, 20.

59. Calthorpe, *The Next American Metropolis*.

60. Cervero, Ferrell, and Murphy, *Transit-Oriented Development*.

61. Ibid., 72.

62. Ibid., 4.

63. Ibid., 78–79.

64. Chris Sikich, "Welcome Trend or Unfulfilled Vision? 'New Urbanism' Communities Have Struggled to Lure Businesses," Indystar.com, June 12, 2011, http://www.indystar.com/article/20110612/LOCAL/106120360/New-Urbanism-communities-struggled-lure-business?odyssey=tab%7Ctopnews%7Ctext%7CIndyStar.com.

65. Mark L. Hinshaw, *True Urbanism: Living In and Near the Center* (Chicago: American Planning Association, 2007), x, xi.

66. Bernick and Cervero, *Transit Villages*, 121, 122.

67. Dylan Rivera, "Residents of Transit-Oriented Orenco Station Still Driving Cars to Work," *Oregonian*, October 17, 2009, http://www.oregonlive.com/news/index.ssf/2009/10despite_urban_design_most_oren.html.

68. Lee Fehrenbacher, "REACH Eyes Passive House Design for Multifamily Project," *Daily Journal of Commerce*, February 24, 2012, http://reachcdc.org/main/docs/housing_development/DJC_Article_2012-02-24.pdf.

69. Casey Parks, "Affordable Housing Coming to Orenco Station in $13.5 Million Project," *Oregonian*, March 1, 2012, http://www.oregonlive.com/hillsboro/index.ssf/2012/03/affordable_housing_coming_to_o.html.

70. Bay Area Rapid Transit, *TOD Guidelines*, 38.

71. Hollie Lund, Robert Cervero, and Richard W. Willson, "Travel Characteristics of Transit-Oriented Development in California," 2004, www.csupomona.edu/~rwwillson/tod/Pictures/TOD2.pdf.

72. Bay Area Rapid Transit, *TOD Guidelines*, 38.

73. Shoup, *The High Cost of Free Parking*, 258.

74. "Fruitvale: Challenged TOD," Boho Center Source, from *New Urban News*, April 4, 2007, http://bohosource.blogspot.com/2007/04/fruitvale-model-for-livable-communities.html.

75. "Retail Seen as 'The Achilles' Heel' of Some TODs," *New Urban Network*, December 1, 2006, http://newurbannetwork.com/article/retail-seen-%E2%80%98 -achilles%E2%80%99-heel%E2%80%99-some-tods.

76. G. B. Arrington and Robert Cervero, *Effects of TOD on Housing, Parking, and Travel*, Transit Cooperative Research Program, report 128 (Washington, DC: Transportation Research Board, 2008), 4, 5, 54, 55.

77. Ibid., 4.

78. Erick Guerra and Robert Cervero, "Cost of a Ride: The Effects of Densities on Fixed-Guideway Transit Ridership and Costs," *Journal of the American Planning Association* 77, no. 3 (Summer 2011): 267–290.

79. Arrington and Cervero, *Effects of TOD, on Housing, Parking, and Travel*, 3, 5.

80. Joanna Lin, "California Commute Times Rank 10th Longest in U.S.," *California Watch*, November 1, 2012, http://californiawatch.org/dailyreport/calif -commute-times-rank-10th-longest-us-18614.

81. Bay Area Rapid Transit, *TOD Guidelines*, 38.

82. Matthew Kaufman, Matthew Formanack, and Jodie Gray, and Rachel Weinberger, "Contemporary Approaches to Parking Pricing: A Primer" (Washington, DC: Federal Highway Administration, US Department of Transportation, June 2012). http://www.ops.fhwa.dot.gov/publications/fhwahop12026/fhwahop 12026.pdf.

83. Matt Flengenheimer, "Data Show a City's Car Sharing May Be Working, but Doubts Persist," *New York Times*, September 3, 2012, http://www.nytimes .com/2012/09/03/nyregion/car-sharing-gamble-in-hoboken-has-mixed-reactions .html.

84. Robert Cervero and Cathleen Sullivan, "TODs for Tots," *Planning* 77, no. 2 (February 2011): 26–31.

85. G. B. Arrington, "TOD and Transit: Making It Great" (presentation at Rail~Volution conference, Washington, DC, October 18, 2011).

86. Ann Cheng, "Reducing Driving and Vehicle Ownership in New Developments" (presentation at Rail~Volution conference, Washington, DC, October 18, 2011), http://www.transformca.org/GreenTRIP.

87. Ann Cheng, GreenTRIP program director, email update, February 3, 2014.

88. Shishir Mathur and Christopher Ferrell, "Effect of Suburban Transit-Oriented Developments on Residential Property Values," San Jose, CA: Mineta Transportation Institute, College of Business, San Jose State University, August 2007), http:// www.transweb.sjsu.edu/MTIportal/research/publications/documents/Effects%20 of%20Sub-Urban%20Transit%20(with%20Cover).pdf.

89. Claire Easley, "The Cost of NIMBYism: Towns with Few Housing Options Are Forced to Bear the Economic Consequences," *Builder Online*, June 7, 2011, http://www.builderonline.com/affordable-housing/the-cost-of-nimby.aspx.

90. Cervero, Ferrell, and Murphy, *Transit-Oriented Development*, 72, 73.

91. Ibid., 19, 26, 61.

92. Bernick and Cervero, *Transit Villages*, 175–177.

93. Ibid., 156.

94. Cervero, Ferrell, and Murphy, *Transit-Oriented Development*, 81, 82.

95. Ibid., 19, 26.

96. James M. Daisa, "Traffic, Parking, and Transit-Oriented Development," in *The New Transit Town: Best Practices in Transit-Oriented Development*, ed. Hank Dittmar and Gloria Ohland (Washington, DC: Island Press, 2004), 121–123.

97. Ibid.

98. Arrington, "TOD and Transit."

Chapter 3

1. Vukan R. Vuchic, *Urban Transit Systems and Technology* (Hoboken, NJ: John Wiley, 2007), 7, 8.

2. Ibid., 10–15.

3. Quoted in Sam Bass Warner, *Streetcar Suburbs: The Process of Growth in Boston, 1870–1900* (New York: Atheneum, 1973), 23.

4. Vuchic, *Urban Transit Systems and Technology*, 37–39.

5. William D. Middleton, *The Interurban Era* (Milwaukee, WI: Kalmbach Publications, 1961).

6. Vuchic, *Urban Transit Systems and Technology*, 33–37.

7. Ibid., 436.

8. Jonathan Bennet, "Who Wrecked America's Trains?" *Utne Reader*, June–July 1986, 106–108.

9. Steve Nadis and James J. MacKenzie, *Car Trouble* (Washington, DC: World Resources Institute, 1993), 6.

10. James Flink, *The Automobile Age* (Cambridge, MA: MIT Press, 1988).

11. Vuchic, *Urban Transit Systems and Technology*, 431.

12. Ibid., 47–50.

13. Ibid.

14. Diego Diaz, "Perspectives on French Light Rail Success" (paper presented at the 91st Annual Meeting of the Transportation Research Board, Washington, DC, January 23, 2012), no. 12-5809; Margarita Novales, "Light Rail Systems in Spain" (presentation to the Railroads and Transportation Group at the 91st Annual Meeting of the Transportation Research Board, Washington, DC, January 24, 2012).

15. Gregory R. Thompson, "How the French Make Trams Succeed: State of the Art Light Rail" (presentation at the 92nd Annual Meeting of the Transportation Research Board to the Light Rail Transit Committee AP075, Washington, DC, January 16, 2013).

16. Ibid.

17. American Public Transportation Association, *2009 Public Transportation Fact Book*, 60th ed., April 2009. http://www.apta.com/resources/statistics/Documents/FactBook/APTA_2009_Fact_Book.pdf.

18. Lester Brown, *Plan B 4.0: Mobilizing to Save Civilization* (New York: W. W. Norton, 2009), 147, 148.

19. Walter Hook, "Stimulating a Car-Free Recovery," *Sustainable Transport* 20 (Winter 2008): 3–4.

20. Institute for Transportation and Development Policy, "Recapturing Global Leadership in Bus Rapid Transit: A Survey of Select U.S. Cities," in *BRT in the U.S. Today*, May 2011, http://www.itdp.org/documents/20110526ITDP_USBRT _Report-HR.pdf.

21. Nathanial Gronewold, "NYC Tries 'Rapid' Buses in Bid to Cut Transit Costs," *New York Times Greenwire*, January 3, 2011. http://www.nytimes .com/gwire/2011/01/03/03greenwire-nyc-tries-rapid-buses-in-bid-to-cut-transit -co-71909.html?pagewanted=all

22. Discussion with Eric Beaton, director of Bus Rapid Transit Planning and Implementation group for NYC Department of Transportation, March 21, 2012.

23. Michael Kanellos, "The Greening of the City Bus," *CNET News*, June 1, 2006, http://news.cnet.com/The-greening-of-the-city-bus/2100-11389_3-6079090 .html.

24. Lester R. Brown, *Plan B 3.0: Mobilizing to Save Civilization* (New York: W. W. Norton, 2008), 194.

25. Vukan R. Vuchic, *Transportation for Livable Cities* (New Brunswick, NJ: Center for Urban Policy Research, Rutgers University, 1999), 41.

26. Vuchic, *Urban Transit Systems and Technology*, 297–298.

27. Ibid., 49.

28. Ibid., 297–298.

29. Ron Nyren, "Transit-Oriented Development Outlook," *Urban Land*, August 27, 2012, http://urbanland.uli.org/Articles/2012/Aug/ul/NyrenTransit.

30. Jonathan Boyer, "Potential Light Rail Replacements for NYC's Busiest Bus Routes" (presentation to vision42 Working Group, New York, December 16, 2008).

31. Jonathan Yazer, "Express Bus Corridors Increasingly Popular Transit Option, *Globe and Mail*, May 22, 2011, http://www.theglobeandmail.com/news/national/toronto/express-bus-corridors-increasingly-popular-transit-option/article2031689.

32. Vivian Sequera and Frank Bajak, "Bogotá's Vaunted Transit System in Distress," Associated Press, Boston.com, March 14, 2012, http://www.boston.com/business/articles/2012/03/14/bogotas_vaunted_transit_system_in_distress.

33. John Phythyon, "The Future Is Here: Catenary-Less Power for Light Rail," *Mass Transit Magazine*, June 3, 2011, http://www.masstransitmag.com/article/10262406/the-future-is-here-catenary-less-power-for-light rail?page=3.

34. Mattias Gripsrud and Randi Hjorthol, "Working on the Train: From 'Dead Time' to Productive and Vital Time," *Transportation* 39, no. 5 (2012): 941–956, DOI: 10.1007/s11116-012-9396-7, http://www.springerlink.com/content/y582k 7t821t74005.

35. Boris S. Pushkarev and Jeffrey M. Zupan, *Public Transportation and Land Use Policy* (Bloomington: Indiana University Press, 1977), 98.

36. Edward L. Tennyson, "Issues in Public Transportation," in *Proceedings of a Conference Held by the Highway Research Board at Henniker, NH, July 9–14, 1972*, special report no. 144 (Washington, DC: Transportation Research Board, 1974), 38–42.

37. "Modern American Passenger Rail: The Amtrak Era," American Rail blog, October 20, 2009, http://americanrail.blogspot.com/2009/10/modern-american -passenger-rail-amtrak.html.

38. Angela Greiling Keane, "Amtrak Chief Says Railroad's Subsidy Dwarfed by Highway Bailout," *Bloomberg News*, September 20, 2012, http://www.bloomberg .com/news/2012-09-20/amtrak-chief-says-railroad-s-subsidy-dwarfed-by-high way-bailout.html.

39. Joan Lowy, "Amtrak's Annual Losses at Lowest Level since 1975," *Business News*, Boston.com, January 10, 2013, http://www.boston.com/business/ news/2013/01/10/amtrak-annual-losses-lowest-level-since/let28tQX6RrSajGo 9r7ApK/story.html.

40. Richard L. Lobron, "The Future of the Northeast Corridor," *Eno Brief Newsletter*, June 2013, http://www.enotrans.org/eno-brief/the-future-of-the-northeast -corridor.

41. "Long-distance Buses Piling Up in Midtown," *Crain's Insider*, November 17, 2009, http://www.crainsnewyork.com/apps/pbcs.dll/article?AID=/20091117/ INS/911169982/1006.

42. Christine Berthet, "ARC Funding Needs to Be Allocated to Building a Bus Garage," *Chekpeds News*, posted November 4, 2010, http://chekpeds.com/?p=1363.

43. Stephen Smith, "NYC Officials Take Notice of Astronomical Subway Construction Costs," *Forbes*, November 29, 2011; Michael M. Grynbaum, "Stringer Tries to Give Transportation Projects a Push," *New York Times*, November 21, 2011, http://cityroom.blogs.nytimes.com/2011/11/21/stringer-tries-to-give-trans portation-projects-a-push.

44. James S. Russell, "As U.S. Dithers, China, UK Pursue Major Rail Projects," Bloomberg.com, December 27, 2010, http://www.bloomberg.com/news/2010-12 -27/as-u-s-dithers-china-u-k-push-ahead-on-major-rail-projects.html.

45. Subramaniam Sharma, "India Plans 960 Billion Rupees of Urban Rail Investment in Next 7 Years," October 26, 2010, http://www.bloomberg.com/ news/2010-10-26/india-plans-960-billion-rupees-of-urban-rail-investment-in -next-7-years.html.

46. Andrew Salzberg, "Urban Rail in China: Challenges Ahead" (paper presented at the ninety-first annual meeting of the Transportation Research Board, January 25, 2012), no. 12-3574.

47. "Beijing Opens Five New Metro Lines amid Increasing Traffic Pressures," Xinhuanet.com, December 30, 2010, http://news.xinhuanet.com/english2010/china/2010-12/30/c_13670970.htm.

48. Yonah Freemark, "China Expands Its Investment in Rapid Transit, Paving Way for Future Urban Growth," *Transport Politic,* May 13, 2010, http://www.thetransportpolitic.com/2010/05/13/china-expands-its-investment-in-rapid-transit-paving-way-for-future-urban-growth.

49. "Chinese Increase Rail Spending Plan for Second Time," *Bloomberg Business Week*, July 30, 2012, http://www.businessweek.com/news/2012-07-30/china-increases-railway-spending-plan-for-second-time.

50. Aaron Back, "Beijing Plans Infrastructure Binge," *Wall Street Journal*, September 8, 2012, http://online.wsj.com/article/SB10000872396390443686004577637002372028464.html.

51. "Concentration on Infrastructure in China in Light of Increasingly Extensive Transport Networks," editorial, *World Architecture News*, August 21 2012, http://backstage.worldarchitecturenews.com/index.php?fuseaction=wanappln.projectview&upload_id=20444.

52. Todd Litman, "Rail Transit in America: A Comprehensive Evaluation of Benefits" (Victoria, BC: Victoria Transport Institute, March 10, 2009).

53. American Public Transportation Association, *Transit News*, March 9, 2009, http://www.apta.com/media/releases/090309_ridership.cfm.

54. Herbert A. Sample, "It's Costly, but Los Angeles Is Getting Its Rail Mojo Back," *Sacramento Bee*, May 30, 2012, http://www.modbee.com/2012/05/27/2217130_its-costly-but-los-angeles-is.html http://www.sacbee.com/2012/05/27/4519118/its-costly-but-los-angeles-is.html.

55. Terry Pristin, "In Westside Los Angeles, a Rail Line Stirs a Revival," *New York Times*, July 7, 2010. http://www.nytimes.com/2010/07/07/realestate/commercial/07angeles.html?pagewanted=all.

56. Dana Rubinstein, "What New York City Can Learn from Los Angeles about the Transit Biz," *Capital New York*, July 16, 2012, http://www.capitalnewyork.com/article/politics/2012/07/6192057/what-new-york-city-can-learn-los-angeles-about-transit-biz.

57. Yonah Freemark, "The Future of American Streetcars: Are They Coming to Your City?" *Infrastructurist*, December 7, 2009, http://www.infrastructurist.com/2009/12/07/the-future-of-american-streetcars-are-they-coming-to-your-city/#more-6215.

58. William J. Angelo, "Minnesota Light Rail Delivers People, Pride, and Progress," *Design-Build*, McGraw-Hill Construction, November–December 2005, cover story, http://designbuild.construction.com/features/archive/2005/0511_cover.asp.

59. Associated Press, "Feds Approve $140M Woodward Light Rail Project," CBS Detroit, April 22, 2013, http://detroit.cbslocal.com/2013/04/22/feds-approve-woodward-light-rail-project.

60. Mary Newsom, "Charlotte Does Light Rail Right," *Grist*, June 25, 2010, http://www.grist.org/article/2010-06-25-charlotte-does-light rail-right.

61. Shaun Courtney, "All Eyes on DC Streetcar Plan: International Experts Weigh in on Proposed 22-Mile 'Priority Network' of Streetcar Lines, Including Route from Union Station to Georgetown," *Georgetown Patch*, September 5, 2012, http://georgetown.patch.com/articles/all-eyes-on-dc-streetcar-plan.

62. Gerald Fox, "LRT v. Buses: Why Portland Chose Light Rail," *Tramways and Urban Transit: The International Light Rail Magazine* 72, no. 862 (October 2009): 390–392.

63. Brown, *Plan B 3.0*, 196.

64. Shelley Poticha, "Transportation in the Multi-City Regions," in *Smart Growth in a Changing World*, ed. Jonathan Barnett (Chicago: American Planning Association, 2007), 51.

65. Craig Canine, "On the Fast Track," *On Earth* (Spring 2009): 41–43.

66. Rod Diridon Sr., Executive Director of Mineta Transportation Institute (presentation on California high-speed rail to the executive meeting of the Advanced Transit Association at the ninety-second annual meeting of the Transportation Research Board, Washington, DC, January 13, 2013.)

67. Brown, *Plan B 3.0*, 226–228.

68. Canine, "On the Fast Track."

69. Elisabeth Fischer, "How Japan's Rail Network Survived the Earthquake," Railway Technology.com, June 28, 2011, http://www.railway-technology.com/features/feature122751.

70. Charlie M. Hetland, "Tokyo's High Speed Rail Network Gains Momentum on the Global Stage," *Atlantic Cities*, December 3, 2012. http://www.theatlanticcities.com/sponsored/inspiring-global-cities/2012/12/tokyos-high-speed-rail-network-gains-momentum-global-stage/49.

71. Alex Davies, "Japan Is Testing Its New 300 MPH Floating Train," *Business Insider*, June 11, 2013, http://www.businessinsider.com/japan-tests-300-mph-maglev-train-2013-6.

72. European Commission, Directorate-General for Mobility and Transport, "High-Speed Europe: A Sustainable Link between Citizens," 2010, http://bookshop.europa.eu/is-bin/INTERSHOP.enfinity/WFS/EU-Bookshop-Site/en_GB/-/EUR/ViewPublication-Start?PublicationKey=KO3109174.

73. Brown, *Plan B 3.0*.

74. Tony Dutzik and Erin Steva, "Next Stop: California: The Benefits of High-Speed Rail around the World and What's in Store for California," report for Calpirg Education Fund, June 2010, http://cdn.publicinterestnetwork.org/assets/ff178505134e5feffbd9dc8faf2ece7d/Next-Stop-California.pdf.

75. Agence France Presse, "French Companies Eye Australian High-Speed Rail," August 15, 2011, http://www.google.com/hostednews/afp/article/ALeqM5iKLIOT9lYfk3TWIMtLONURlJfnYA?docId=CNG.f4027ad3fcc2408e8d-cbb1b13ccc42a4.871.

76. Bruce Selcraig, "Taking High-Speed Trains into the Future," *Miller-McCune*, August 16, 2010, http://www.miller-mccune.com/politics/taking-high-speed-trains-into-the-future-20305/?utm_source=Newsletter122&utm_medium=email&utm_content=0817&utm_campaign=newsletters.

77. Chris Nelder, "California's High-Speed Rail as an Energy Lifeline," *Smart Planet*, July 11, 2012, http://www.smartplanet.com/blog/energy-futurist/californias-high-speed-rail-as-an-energy-lifeline/523.

78. Keith Bradsher, "A High-Speed Economy: As China Builds a Vast Network of Fast Trains, the U.S. Falls Further Behind," *New York Times*, February 13, 2010, B1, B6.

79. Guo, "Bullet Train Slashes Travel Time between Beijing and SW China," CRIENGLISH.com, January 4, 2011, http://english.cri.cn/6909/2011/01/04/2743s613311.htm.

80. Keith Bradsher, "On the Longest Bullet Train Line, Chinese Ride 1200 Miles in 8 Hours," *New York Times*, December 27, 2012, B1.

81. Associated Press, "Crash Raises Doubts about China's High-Speed Rail Plans," July 25, 2011, http://www.foxnews.com/world/2011/07/25/crash-raises-doubts-about-chinas-high-speed-rail-plans.

82. Sharon LaFraniere, "Study Cites Blunders in China Train Crash," *New York Times*, December 29, 2011. http://www.nytimes.com/2011/12/29/world/asia/design-flaws-cited-in-china-train-crash.html

83. Keith Bradsher, "High-Speed Rail Poised to Alter China," *New York Times*, June 23, 2011, B1, B2.

84. "Haramain High Speed Rail Project," Railway Technology.com, November 7, 2011, http://www.railway-technology.com/projects/haramain-high-speed.

85. Sian Disson, 14-Strong Saudi and Spanish Consortium Handed Phase II of SR 30,815 m HHR Scheme, News Review, *World Architecture News*, November 8, 2011, http://www.worldarchitecturenews.com/index.php?fuseaction=wanappln.projectview&upload_id=17984.

86. Siraj Wahab, "Trains Will Be Up and Running in Three Years, Says Saudi Railways Chief," Railway Technology.com, February 19, 2012, http://www.railway-technology.com/projects/haramain-high-speed.

87. "Mexico to Have High-Speed Rail System," *Caribbean News*, January 30, 2013, http://www.caribbeannews.net/index.php/sid/212226075/scat/80f72651582f2c13/ht/Mexico-to-have-high-speed-rail-system.

88. Jack May, Vice President of NJ Association of Railway Passengers (presentation to vision42 Working Group on rail development in Turkey, New York, February 19, 2013.)

89. Diridon, presentation on California high-speed rail.

90. Robert D. Yaro, "Houston Embraces Its Region," *Spotlight on the Region* (New York: Regional Plan Association, October 6, 2009).

91. Ron Nixon, "Frustrations of Air Travel Push Passengers to Amtrak," *New York Times*, August 15, 2012. http://www.nytimes.com/2012/08/16/business/hassles-of-air-travel-push-passengers-to-amtrak.html?pagewanted=all.

92. Daniel B. Wood, "A Lot Riding on California Dream of High-Speed Rail," *Christian Science Monitor*, August 21, 2012, http://www.csmonitor.com/USA/2012/0821/A-lot-riding-on-California-dream-of-high-speed-rail.

93. Poticha, "Transportation in the Multi-City Regions," 45–48.

94. Ruan Holeywell, "Texas and Calif.'s Contrasting High-Speed Rail Attempts," *Governing*, September 6, 2012, http://www.governing.com/blogs/fedwatch/gov -texas-pursuing-dallas-houston-high-speed-rail-bullet-train.html.

95. Jeffrey Spivak, "The Next Big Thing," *Planning* 75, no. 9 (October 2009): 10–15.

96. Ibid.

97. Bradsher, "A High-Speed Economy."

98. Yuwei Zhang, "Chinese Funds Could Help Strengthen US Infrastructure," *China Daily*, February 14, 2012, http://www.chinadaily.com.cn/usa/epaper/2012-02/14/content_14606475.htm.

99. Mike Rosenberg, "GOP House Aims to Take $2 Billion Back from California High-Speed Rail," *Mercury News*, November 22, 2010, http://www.mercury news.com/san-mateo-county/ci_16687559?nclick_check=1.

100. Senanu Ashiabor and Wenbin Wei, "Advancing High-Speed Rail Policy in the United States" (San Jose: Mineta Transportation Institute, San JoseState University, June 2012), http://transweb.sjsu.edu/PDFs/research/2905-US-hsr-high -speed-rail-policy.pdf.

101. Robert Cervero, "Infrastructure and Development: Planning Matters," in *Transportation Infrastructure: The Challenges of Rebuilding America*, ed. Marlon G. Boarnet, report no. 557 (Chicago: American Planning Association, July 2009), 43.

102. G. B. Arrington and Robert Cervero, *Effects of TOD on Housing, Parking, and Travel*, Transit Cooperative Research Program, report 128 (Washington, DC: Transportation Research Board, 2008), 2.

103. Vukan R. Vuchic, "Rapid Transit Automation and the Last Crew Member," in *Railway Gazette* (London: IPC Transport Press, Ltd., October 1973).

104. Rongfang (Rachel) Liu, "The Spectrum of Automated Guideway Transit (AGT) and Its Applications," in vol. 2, *Handbook of Transportation Engineering*, ed. Myer Kutz, 2nd ed. (New York: McGraw-Hill, 2010).

105. Vuchic, *Urban Transit Systems and Technology*, 72, 431.

106. Liu, "The Spectrum of Automated Guideway Transit."

107. Vuchic, *Urban Transit Systems and Technology*, 456–458.

108. ULTra, London Heathrow Airport, http://www.ultraglobalprt.com/wheres-it-used/heathrow-t5.

109. Ingmar Andréasson, "Personal Rapid Transit as Feeder and Distributor to Rail" (paper presented at the 91st annual meeting of the Transportation Research Board, January 23, 2012), no. 12-1080.

110. Ingmar Andréasson, update, KTH Royal Institute of Technology, Sweden, January 15, 2013.

111. Advanced Transit Association, "Asian PRT Progress," *TransitPulse Newsletter*, July–August 2013.

112. "Govt May Turn to Pod Cars to Boost Public Transport," *Indian Express*, April 27, 2011, http://www.indianexpress.com/news/govt-may-turn-to-pod-cars -to-boost-public-transport/781954; Timothy B. Hurst, "Catching a Ride in a Driverless Vehicle: Masdar City's PRT," *Matter Network*, December 20, 2011. http://theenergycollective.com/tbhurst/50376/masdar-city-s-prt-catching-ride -driverless-electric-vehicle.

113. Vuchic, *Urban Transit Systems and Technology*, 472–474.

114. The Office of Technology Assessment was established by Congress in the early 1970s for the purpose of developing descriptions and assessments (and of setting these forth in lay terms comprehensible to the lawmakers) of the ongoing variety of technologies that are frequently proposed to Congress for funding. The bylaws of the OTA were carefully constructed so that political and business interests could not influence the office's deliberations and conclusions. Highly respected scientists and experts in the fields relevant to these investigations were invited to serve on OTA panels, and over a period of more than two decades, the OTA functioned as a valuable and cost-effective screening organization in the setting of congressional priorities. The OTA was nevertheless dismantled by Congress in September 1995 as a "cost-cutting" measure.

115. Office of Technology Assessment, *Automated Guideway Transit: An Assessment of PRT and Other New Systems* (Washington, DC: US Government Printing Office, June 1975), 377–379.

116. Ibid., 378.

117. Vuchic, *Transportation for Livable Cities*, 220.

Chapter 4

1. Rick Leisner and David T. Retzsh, "Resurgent Urbanism," reprinted in *New Urbanism in Practice* 3 (2008), with permission from *Jacobs Quarterly* 6, no. 4 .

2. Donald C. Shoup and Richard W. Willson, "Employer-Paid Parking: The Influence of Parking Prices on Travel Demand," in *Proceedings of the Commuter Parking Symposium* (Seattle, WA: Association for Commuter Transportation, December 6–7, 1990), 10.

3. Robert Cervero, Christopher Ferrell, and Steven Murphy, *Transit-Oriented Development and Joint Development in the United States: A Literature Review*, Transportation Cooperative Research Program, no. 52 (Washington, DC: Transportation Research Board, October 2002), 29, http://onlinepubs.trb.org/online pubs/tcrp/tcrp_rrd_52.pdf.

4. Joseph Berger, "Slump Opens Space at the Station," *New York Times*, June 28, 2009, 1, 8.

5. Shelly Banjo, "Where Spots Are Hot," *Wall Street Journal*, October 24, 2011, http://online.wsj.com/article/SB10001424052970204485304576643411720265 644.html?mod=googlenews_wsj.

6. Gary Gardner, "Power to the Pedals," *World Watch* (July–August 2010): 6–11.

7. John Pucher and Lewis Dijkstra, "Promoting Safe Walking and Cycling to Improve Public Health: Lessons from the Netherlands and Germany," *American Journal of Public Health* 93, no. 9 (September 2003): 7, 9, 10, http://policy .rutgers.edu/faculty/pucher/AJPHfromJacobsen.pdf.

8. League of American Bicyclists, "Ride for the Environment," Washington, DC, 2011, http://www.csus.edu/org/eso/bicycle.htm.

9. Lester R. Brown, *Plan B 4.0: Mobilizing to Save Civilization* (New York: W. W. Norton, 2009), 151, 152.

10. Pucher and Dijkstra, "Promoting Safe Walking and Cycling," 21, 11.

11. Ibid., 3.

12. Neal Peirce, "Biking and Walking: Our Secret Weapon?" Citiwire.net, July 16, 2009, http://citiwire.net/columns/biking-and-walking-our-secret-weapon.

13. Peter L. Jacobsen, "Safety in Numbers: More Walkers and Bicyclists, Safer Walking and Bicycling," *Injury Prevention* 9 (2003): 205–209, http:// ip.bmjjournals.com/cgi/content/full/9/3/205.

14. Elly Blye, "There's Safety in Numbers for Cyclists," *Grist*, October 11, 2011, http://www.grist.org/article/2010-10-11-theres-safety-in-numbers-for-cyclists.

15. John Pucher and Ralph Buehler, "Analysis of Bicycling Trends and Policies in Large North American Cities: Lessons for New York," Research and Innovative Technology Administration, US Department of Transportation, March 2011, http://policy.rutgers.edu/faculty/pucher/UTRC_29Mar2011.pdf.

16. Ibid.

17. Ibid.

18. Victoria Bekiempis, "Department of Transportation Hits Back at John Liu's Bike Share Criticism (UPDATE)," *Village Voice*, June 26, 2012, http://blogs .villagevoice.com/runninscared/2012/06/department_of_t.php.

19. Pucher and Buehler, "Analysis of Bicycling Trends and Policies," 33, 34.

20. Ibid.

21. Ibid., 42, 43.

22. Quoted in Jay Walljasper, "Unjamming the Future," *Ode*, October 2005, 40, www.bikepartners.nl.

23. Alex Marshall, "Better Ways to Promote Bike Transit," *New York Times*, opinion pages, update December 22, 2010; Alex Marshall, "To Make Cycling and Walking Safer, Put the Burden on Drivers," *Spotlight on the Region*, August 9, 2012.

24. Ross Hirsch, "First-of-Its-Kind Cyclist Anti-Harassment Becomes Law in Los Angeles. LA Streetsblog, September 27, 2011, http://la.streetsblog.org/2011/09/27/ first-of-its-kind-cyclist-anti-harassment-becomes-law-in-los-angeles.

25. Patrick Madden, "D.C. Considers Allowing Cyclists to Sue Drivers," WAMU 88.5, November 3, 2011, http://wamu.org/news/morning_edition/11/11/03/dc _considers_allowing_cyclists_to_sue_drivers.

26. Ralph Buehler and John Pucher, "Sustainable Transport That Works: Lessons from Germany," *World Transport Policy & Practice* 15, no. 1 (April 2009): 18, 23, http://www.eco-logica.co.uk/pdf/wtpp15.1.pdf.

27. Faith Cable, "Design First, Codify Second: Germany Offers Lessons for U.S. Planners," *Planning* (July 2009): 24–27.

28. Buehler and Pucher, "Sustainable Transport That Works," 18–22.

29. Pucher and Dijkstra, "Promoting Safe Walking and Cycling."

30. Buehler and Pucher, "Sustainable Transport That Works," 19, 20.

31. John Pucher, "Germany's Bicycle Boom," *Transportation Quarterly*, April 1998, http://www.tstc.org/bulletin/19980410/mtr16906.htm.

32. Timothy Beatley, *Green Urbanism: Learning from European Cities* (Washington, DC: Island Press. 2000), 169.

33. Brown, *Plan B 4.0*, 153.

34. Leah Shahum, "Lessons from Copenhagen for Bicycling in the Bay Area," Streetsblog.org, June 23, 2010, http://sf.streetsblog.org/2010/06/23/lessons-from -copenhagen-for-bicycling-in-the-bay-area.

35. Alice Rawsthorn, "Bicycle Lanes for Multitudes," *New York Times*, June 24, 2013, http://www.nytimes.com/2013/06/24/arts/design/bicycle-lanes-for-multi tudes.html.

36. Beatley, *Green Urbanism*, 173.

37. Buehler and Pucher, "Sustainable Transport That Works," 37.

38. Brown, *Plan B 4.0*, 154.

39. John Pucher and Ralph Buehler, "Integrating Bicycling and Public Transport in North America," *Journal of Public Transportation* 12, no. 3 (2009), http://policy .rutgers.edu/faculty/pucher/PUCHER_BUEHLER.pdf.

40. Ibid.

41. David Alpert, "Metro Proposes Quintupling Bicycle Access Mode Share," GreaterGreater Washington.org. December 6, 2010, http://greatergreaterwashing ton.org/post/8398/metro-proposes-quintupling-bicycle-access-mode-share.

42. Michelle Ernst and Lilly Shoup, *Dangerous by Design: Solving the Epidemic of Preventable Pedestrian Deaths (and Making Great Neighborhoods)*, Transportation for America and the Surface Transportation Policy Project, November 2009, http://www.transact.org/PDFs/2009-11-09-Dangerous%20by%20Design .pdf.

43. Eoin O'Carroll, "Can Bikes and Cars Share the Road?" *Christian Science Monitor*, August 25, 2009, http://features.csmonitor.com/environment/2009/08/25/ can-bikes-and-cars-share-the-road.

44. LA County, "Model Design Manual for Living Streets," 2011, chapter 1, http://modelstreetdesignmanual.com/model_street_design_manual.pdf; Linda Baker, "Cities for Cycling Embrace European Street Designs," *Governing*, January 2010, http://www.governing.com/article/cities-cycling-embrace-european-street -designs.

45. Karen Rouse, "New Jersey Highways to be Made Safer," New Jersey.com, December 25, 2009, http://www.northjersey.com/news/transportation/122509 _Aid_for_walkers_bikers.html.

46. Alex Goldmark, "NY Governor Will Sign Complete Streets Law," *Transportation Nation*, August 15, 2011, http://transportationnation.org/2011/08/15/ny-gov -will-sign-complete-streets-law.

47. Paul Winters, "Complete Streets: Changing the Rules for the Better," *Spotlight on the Region*, Regional Plan Association, October 13, 2011.

48. National Complete Streets Coalition, "On the Hill," 2011, http://www .completestreets.org/federal-policy/on-the-hill.

49. Jay Walljasper, "How Portland Is Planning to Become the First World-Class Bike City in America," Alternet.org, December 1, 2010, http://www.alternet.org/ environment/149042/how_portland_is_planning_to_become_the_first_world -class_bike_city_in_america_.

50. Pucher and Buehler, "Analysis of Bicycling Trends and Policies."

51. Frank Bruni, "Bicycle Visionary *New York Times*, Sunday Review, September 10, 2011, http://www.nytimes.com/2011/09/11/opinion/sunday/bruni-janette -sadik-khan-bicycle-visionary.html?pagewanted=all.

52. Rachel Gordon and Jill Tucker, "Ruling Paves Way for San Francisco Bike Lanes," *San Francisco Chronicle*, August 7, 2010, http://articles.sfgate.com/2010 -08-07/bay-area/22210318_1_bike-lanes-bike-plan-san-francisco-bicycle-plan.

53. Justin Gerdes, "A Two-Wheeled Future?" *Chinadialogue,* June 9, 2011, http:// www.chinadialogue.net/article/show/single/en/4344.

54. Tim De Chant, "Minneapolis? More Like Bike-opolis," *Grist*, August 25, 2011, http://www.grist.org/biking/2011-08-25-minneapolis-a-rising-bike-metro polis.

55. Adam Nagourney, "Los Angeles Lives by Car, but Learns to Embrace Bikes," *New York Times*, May 20, 2012. http://www.nytimes.com/2012/05/20/us/in-los -angeles-drivers-and-bicyclists-learn-to-co-exist.html.

56. City of Philadelphia, "The Bicycle Network," http://www.phila.gov/streets/ Bike_Network.html; telephone interview with Charles R. Carmalt, pedestrian and bicycle coordinator, Mayor's Office of Transportation and Utilities, Philadelphia, September 12, 2011.

57. Jon Hurdle, "U.S. Cities Spur Bike Use for Climate, Health," *Reuters*, December 14, 2009, http://www.reuters.com/article/idUSTRE5BD4WF20091214; Ami Cholia, "The Top 10 US Cities for Biking," *Huffington Post*, August 5, 2009, http://www.huffingtonpost.com/2009/08/05/the-top-10-us-cities-for_n_252092 .html; Nate Berg, "Creating 'The Most Bicycle Friendly City in America' … in Southern California," *Atlantic Cities*, January 26, 2012.

58. Pucher and Buehler, "Analysis of Bicycling Trends and Policies," 42.

59. Bruni, "Bicycle Visionary."

60. Shaun Courtney, "D.C. Is Tops for Investing in Bicycling and Walking," Georgetown Patch.com, January 26, 2012, http://georgetown.patch.com/articles/ d-c-is-tops-for-investing-in-bicycling-and-walking.

61. Alpert, "Metro Proposes Quintupling Bicycle Access Mode Share."

62. Yamiche Alcindor, "Bike Center Aims to Be Haven for Riders," *Washington Post*, August 13, 2009, http://www.washingtonpost.com/wp-dyn/content/article/2009/08/12/AR2009081202508.html; J. David Goodman, "City Prepares for Law Allowing Bikes in Buildings," *New York Times*, November 10, 2009; http://cityroom.blogs.nytimes.com/2009/11/10/city-prepares-for-law-allowing-bikes-in-buildings; "Free Wheelin': DC Gets First Stand-Alone Bike Hub on East Coast," *Architect's Newspaper*, November 4, 2009, 10.

63. Jon Orcutt, "Bicycles as Transport—From Alternative to Mainstream" (address at the American Institute of Architects symposium, New York, August 12, 2010).

64. Pucher and Buehler, "Analysis of Bicycling Trends and Policies," March 2011. 36. http://policy.rutgers.edu/faculty/pucher/UTRC_29Mar2011.pdf.

65. Tom Vanderbilt, "What Would Get Americans Biking to Work? Decent Parking," *Slate*, August 19, 2009, http://www.slate.com/id/2225511.

66. Andrea Bernstein, "NYC Biking Is Up 14 Percent from 2010; Overall Support Rises," *Transportation Nation*, July 28, 2011, http://transportationnation.org/2011/07/28/breaking-new-york-city-biking-is-up-14-percent-from-2010.

67. Quoted in "Biking Fastest Way to Get around NYC," WCBSTV online, February 2010, http://wcbstv.com/topstories/biking.around.nyc.2.1130374.html.

68. Pucher and Buehler, "Analysis of Bicycling Trends and Policies," 40.

69. NYC Department of City Planning, "Zoning for Bicycle Parking—Approved!" April 22, 2009, http://www.nyc.gov/html/dcp/html/bicycle_parking/index.shtml.

70. Gardner, "Power to the Pedals."

71. Tanja Rieckmann, "European Cities Get the Bike Bug," *Der Spiegel*, December 1, 2010, http://www.spiegel.de/international/europe/0,1518,725229,00.html.

72. Brown, *Plan B 4.0*, 149.

73. Steven Erlanger, "French Ideal of Bicycle-Sharing Meets Reality," *New York Times*, October 30, 2009, http://www.nytimes.com/2009/10/31/world/europe/31bikes.html?pagewanted=all.

74. Transportation Alternatives, "Keep Calm and Carry On with Bikeshare," *Reclaim*, Summer 2011, 19.

75. J. David Goodman, "Spokes/Cities Engage in Vast Biking Conspiracy," *New York Times*, August 5, 2010. http://cityroom.blogs.nytimes.com/2010/08/05/spokes-cities-engage-in-vast-biking-conspiracy-shh/?_php=true&_type=blogs&_r=0.

76. Didi Tang, "Bike-Sharing Programs Spin across U.S. Campuses," *USA Today*, September 22, 2010, http://www.usatoday.com/news/education/2010-09-21-college-bike-sharing_N.htm.

77. Bike Rentals: Coming of Age and Linking to Transit" (Rail~Volution Conference session, Boston, October 31, 2009).

78. Matt Friedman, "The Morning Dig: D.C. Bikeshare System Is a Model for U.S. Cities," *Infrastructurist*, June 22, 2011, http://www.planetizen.com/node/50017.

79. Rachel Tepper, "Capital Bikeshare Moves Forward toward Corporate Sponsorship," *Huffington Post*, January 4, 2012, http://www.huffingtonpost.com/2012/01/04/capital-bikeshare-sponsorship_n_1181741.html.

80. Martin Di Caro, "From A to B: Bike Shop Owners See Big Returns from Capital Bikeshare," *Metro Connection*, WAMU 88.5, June 29, 2012, http://wamu.org/programs/metro_connection/12/06/29/from_a_to_b_bike_shop_owners_see_big_returns_from_capital_bikeshare.

81. Edward D. Reiskin, "Mobility Initiatives in San Francisco" (paper presented at the ninety-first annual meeting of the Transportation Research Board, January 23, 2012), P12-5754.

82. "Chicago Welcomes Divvy Bike Sharing System," City of Chicago.com, July 1, 2013, http://www.cityofchicago.org/city/en/depts/cdot/provdrs/bike/news/2013/jul/chicago_welcomesdivvybikesharingsystem.html.

83. "Bike-Share Program Is Off to a Fast Start," *Fort Worth City News*, June 12, 2013, http://fortworthtexas.gov/citynews/default.aspx?id=112190.

84. Andrea Bernstein, "New York City Chooses Alta for Wide-Ranging Bike Share," *Transportation Nation*, September 14, 2011, http://transportationnation.org/2011/09/14/new-york-city-chooses-alta-for-wide-ranging-bike-share.

85. Rail~Volution Conference, Westin Boston Waterfront Hotel. Session: "Bike Rentals: Coming of Age and Linking to Transit," October 31, 2009.

86. Friedman, "The Morning Dig."

87. J. David Goodman, "Expansion of Bike Lanes in City Brings Backlash," *New York Times*, November 22, 2010. http://www.nytimes.com/2010/11/23/nyregion/23bicycle.html.

88. Thomas Tracy, "Bikelash! Cops to Crack Down on Two-Wheelers," *Brooklyn Paper*, January 5, 2011, http://www.brooklynpaper.com/stories/34/1/34_1_crackdown.html.

89. Alex Marshall, "Two Wheels Are Becoming as Chic as Four," *Spotlight on the Region*, October 20, 2010, http://www.rpa.org/node/6352.

90. J. David Goodman, "An Electric Boost for Cyclists," *New York Times*, February 1, 2010, B1, B8.

91. Ibid.

92. Nicole Foletta and Simon Field, *Europe's Vibrant New Low Car(bon) Communities*, Institute for Transportation and Development Policy, Summer 2011, 48, http://www.itdp.org/documents/092611_ITDP_NED_Desktop_Print.pdf.

93. William J. Mitchell, "Mobility on Demand" 2008. http://smartcities.media.mit.edu/pdf/Mobility_on_Demand_Introduction.pdf.

94. Steven Ashley, "Shrink-to-Fit Car for City Parking," *New York Times*, Automobiles, July 15, 2012, http://www.nytimes.com/2012/07/15/automobiles/shrink-to-fit-car-for-city-parking.html; Antony Ingram, "Hiriko Folding Electric Car Now Set for Production," *Green Car Reports*, December 19, 2012, http://www.greencarreports.com/news/1081235_hiriko-folding-electric-car-now-set-for-production.

95. K. M. Hunter-Zaworski, *Impacts of Low-Speed Vehicles on Transportation Infrastructure and Safety*. Oregon Transportation Research and Education Consortium, final report, OTREC-RR-10–19, December 2010.

96. Pucher and Buehler, "Analysis of Bicycling Trends and Policies," 39.

97. Seth Fletcher, "GM Unveils the P.U.M.A., and Possibly the Future of Urban Transportation," *Popular Science*, April 7, 2009, http://www.popsci.com/cars/article/2009-04/gm-unveils-puma-and-perhaps-future-urban-transportation; "Segway Advanced Development: Applying Cutting Edge Technology to the Future of Small Electrical Transportation," 2010, http://www.segway.com/puma.

98. Conversation with NYC Transportation commissioner Janette Sadik-Khan and Alta Bicycle Share president Alison Cohen, Center for Architecture, New York, January 11, 2012.

Chapter 5

1. Shawn Cohen and Cathey O'Donnell, "Cops: Extreme Speeders Are Easy Targets," *Journal News*, Lohud.com, July 15, 2009, http://www.lohud.com/article/20090715/NEWS01/907150341/1019/RSS0102.

2. National Highway Traffic Safety Administration, US Department of Transportation, "Traffic Safety Facts: Early Estimate of Motor Vehicle Traffic Fatalities in 2010," April 2011, http://www-nrd.nhtsa.dot.gov/Pubs/811451.pdf. A statistical projection of traffic fatalities in the United States in 2010 indicates that an estimated 32,788 people died in motor vehicle crashes, as compared with the 33,808 fatalities that occurred in 2009.

3. Rajesh Subramanian, "Motor Vehicle Traffic Crashes as a Leading Cause of Death in the United States, 2008 and 2009," National Highway Traffic Safety Administration, US Department of Transportation, May 2012, http://www-nrd.nhtsa.dot.gov/Pubs/811620.pdf.

4. Michelle Ernst, *Dangerous by Design: Solving the Epidemic of Preventable Pedestrian Deaths*, Transportation for America, 2011, http://t4america.org/docs/dbd2011/Dangerous-by-Design-2011.pdf.

5. Ibid.; Lizette Alvarez, "On Wide Florida Roads, Running for Dear Life," *New York Times*, August 16, 2011, A1, A3.

6. Peter D. Norton, *Fighting Traffic: The Dawn of the Motor Age in the American City* (Cambridge, MA: MIT Press, 2008), 29–46.

7. Ibid., 96–101.

8. Karen Sprattler, "Speeding and Aggressive Driving: Survey of the States," Governors' Highway Safety Association, March 1, 2012, http://www.ghsa.org/html/publications/pdf/survey/2012_speed.pdf.

9. Charles Marohn, "Confessions of a Recovering Engineer," *Grist*, November 22, 2010, http://www.grist.org/article/2010-11-22-confessions-of-a-recovering-engineer.

10. Tom Vanderbilt, "The Traffic Guru," *Wilson Quarterly*, Summer 2008, http://www.wilsonquarterly.com/article.cfm?AID=1234.

11. James G. Hanley and Norman Garrick, "How Shared Space Challenges Conventional Thinking about Transportation Design," December 16, 2010, http://www.planetizen.com/node/47317.

12. US Census Bureau, "World's Older Population to Triple by 2050," *infoZine*, June 24, 2009, http://www.infozine.com/news/stories/op/storiesView/sid/36418.

13. Transportation Alternatives, "Testimony: Public Safety Committee of the New York City Council on Res. No. 338 on Deadly Drivers," January 10, 2005, http://transalt.org/newsroom/testimony/1862.

14. Ibid.

15. Ibid.

16. Donald Appleyard with M. Sue Gerson, and Mark Lintell, *Livable Streets* (Berkeley: University of California Press, 1981).

17. Transportation Alternatives, "Traffic's Human Toll: A Study of the Impacts of Vehicular Traffic on New York City Residents," October 2006.

18. Noah Kazis, "How London Is Saving Lives with 20 mph Zones," Streetsblog, March 22, 2010, http://www.streetsblog.org/2010/03/22/how-london-is-saving-lives-with-20-mph-zones.

19. Matthew Beard, "London Could See 20mph Speed Limit on Nearly All Residential Streets by 2020," *London Evening Standard*, June 7, 2013, http://www.standard.co.uk/news/transport/london-could-see-20mph-speed-limit-on-nearly-all-residential-streets-by-2020-8648655.html.

20. Kazis, "How London Is Saving Lives."

21. Irma Venter, "European Parliament Adopts 30 km/h Urban Speed Limit Resolution," *Engineering News*, September 28, 2011, http://www.engineeringnews.co.za/article/european-parliament-adopts-30-kmh-urban-speed-limit-resolution-2011-09-28.

22. Kazis, "How London Is Saving Lives."

23. Beard, "London Could See 20mph Speed Limit."

24. Sheena Craig, "Mayor Must Review 20mph Limit on London Roads, Says Assembly," London.gov.uk, January 16, 2013, http://www.london.gov.uk/media/press_releases_london_assembly/mayor-must-review-20mph-limit-london-roads-says-assembly.

25. Michelle Ernst, "Groundbreaking NYCDOT Pedestrian Study Recommends Testing 20 mph Limit for Neighborhoods," *Mobilizing the Region: News and Opinion from the Tri-State Transportation Campaign*, August 18, 2010, http://blog.tstc.org/2010/08/18/groundbreaking-nycdot-pedestrian-study-recommends-testing-20-mph-limit-for-neighborhoods.

26. Drew Grant, "Department of Transportation Introduces First 20 Miles-Per-Hour 'Slow Zone' in the Bronx … Is Manhattan Next?" *New York Observer*, November 21, 2011, http://www.observer.com/2011/11/department-of-transportation-introduces-first-20-miles-per-hour-slow-zone-in-the-bronx.

27. Josh Robin, "Slow Zones Come to 13 Additional Neighborhoods," NY1.com, July 10, 2012, http://www.ny1.com/content/news_beats/political_news/164538/-slow-zones--come-to-13-additional-city-neighborhoods.

28. New York City DOT: About DOT: Neighborhood Slow Zones, 2012, http://www.nyc.gov/html/dot/html/about/slowzones.shtml.

29. Ibid.

30. Jim O'Grady, "Manhattan on Track to Get Its First Slow Zone," *Transportation Nation*, June 11, 2012, http://transportationnation.org/2012/06/11/manhattan -on-track-to-get-its-first-slow-zone.

31. Matt Flegenheimer, "City Expands 20 mph Zones across More Neighborhoods," *New York Times*, July 11, 2012. A19. http://www.nytimes.com/2012/07/11/nyregion/new-york-expanding-20-mph-slow-zones-in-neighborhoods.html?_r=0.

32. Andrew Grossman, "New Push to Snap Speeders' Photos," *Wall Street Journal*, December 6, 2010, http://online.wsj.com/article/SB10001424052748704584804575644814140025890.html?mod=djemAmsterdam_t.

33. Ibid.

34. Matt Flegenheimer, "Police Officer Not Needed: Bill Would Let Cameras Catch City's Speeders," *New York Times*, June 20, 2012, A23, http://www.nytimes.com/2012/06/20/nyregion/in-new-york-cameras-to-catch-speeders-may-arrive -soon.html?_r=2.

35. Paul Melia, "Drivers Facing Car Ban in Major Towns under New Transport Plan," independent.ie, *National News*, March 1, 2011, http://www.independent .ie/national-news/drivers-facing-car-ban-in-major-towns-under-new-transport -plan-2560153.html.

36. Lester R. Brown, *Plan B 3.0: Mobilizing to Save Civilization* (New York: W. W. Norton, 2008), 193, 194.

37. Enrique Peñalosa, keynote address, Manhattan Borough President's Manhattan on the Move: A Transportation Agenda for a Growing City conference, Lerner Hall, Columbia University, New York, October 12, 2006; subsequent author conversations with Peñalosa.

Chapter 6

1. "Laurie Olin: Noted Landscape Architect Discusses the Profession and the State of Public Space Today," *Architect's Newspaper*, June 15, 2012, http://archpaper .com/news/articles.asp?id=6117.

2. Tom Vanderbilt, "The Traffic Guru," *Wilson Quarterly*, Summer 2008, http://www.wilsonquarterly.com/article.cfm?AID=1234.

3. Carmen Hass-Klau, *The Pedestrian and City Traffic* (London: Belhaven Press, 1990), 211–247.

4. TEST, *Quality Streets: How Traditional Urban Centers Benefit from Traffic Calming* (London: TEST, May 1988), 8, 89.

5. Ralph Buehler and John Pucher, "Four Decades of Planning for Livable Communities: Insights from Freiburg, Germany," in *Transportation Systems for Livable Communities: Summary of a Conference, October 18-19, 2010* (Washington,

DC: Transportation Research Board, 2010), 70–72, http://onlinepubs.trb.org/onlinepubs/conf/cpw6.pdf.

6. Ralph Buehler and John Pucher, "Sustainable Transport That Works: Lessons from Germany," *World Transport Policy and Practice* 1 (April 2009): 22–23, http://www.eco-logica.co.uk/pdf/wtpp15.1.pdf.

7. Ibid., 36.

8. Ibid., 23.

9. Andrea Broaddus, "A Tale of Two Eco-Suburbs in Freiburg, Germany: Parking Provision and Car Use,' in *Proceedings of the 89th Annual Meeting of the Transportation Research Board* (Washington, DC: Transportation Research Board, January 13, 2010).

10. Elisabeth Rosenthal, "In German Suburb, Life Goes On without Cars," *New York Times*, May 12, 2009, A-1, A-6.

11. Broaddus, "A Tale of Two Eco-Suburbs in Freiburg."

12. Ibid.

13. Nicole Foletta and Simon Field, *Europe's Vibrant New Low Car(bon) Communities*, Institute for Transportation and Development Policy, Summer 2011, 97, 102, 104, http://www.itdp.org/documents/092611_ITDP_NED_Desktop_Print.pdf.

14. Ibid.

15. Ibid.

16. Ibid., 32, 33, 34, 43.

17. Ibid., 32, 35, 42.

18. "Carfree Projects, Carfree Vacation Destinations, and Large Pedestrian Areas in Germany and Worldwide," Autofrei Wohnen, Office of Architecture Heller, http://www.autofrei-wohnen.de/projects.html#prelim-proj-ini.

19. Institute for Community Design Analysis, "Improving the Viability of Two Dayton Communities: Five Oaks and Dunbar Manor," Great Neck, NY, 1994, https://www.ncjrs.gov/pdffiles1/Digitization/153096NCJRS.pdfhttps://www.ncjrs.gov/pdffiles1/Digitization/153096NCJRS.pdf.

20. Communications with Sherman Lewis, president of the Hayward Planning Association, January and February 2012, http://www.bayviewvillage.us.

21. Reid Ewing and Steven J. Brown, "Traffic Calming Progress Report," *Planning* 75, no. 10 (November 2009): 32–35.

22. "Maryland County Draws a 'Car-Free Blueprint for Growth,'" *Climate Progress*, Center for American Progress Action Fund, November 22, 2009, http://climateprogress.org/2009/11/11/smart-growth-maryland-montgomery-county-car-free.

23. Office of Governor Martin O'Malley, "Governor Martin O'Malley Kicks Off Transit-Oriented Development Project in Montgomery County," July 16, 2012, http://www.governor.maryland.gov/blog/?p=6207.

24. Organization for Economic Cooperation and Development, ed., *Streets for People* (Paris: Organization for Economic Cooperation and Development, 1974) (chapter authors include Victor Gruen, Brian Richards, N. M. Thompson, C. Kenneth Orski, J. Kuehnemann and R. Witherspoon, Wilheim Niehusener, Curt M. Elmberg, Kai Lemburg, A. A. Wood, A. Gasperini, H. M. Goodappel, and P. B. Van Gurp); TEST, *Quality Streets*.

25. A.E.J. Morris, *History of Urban Form: Before the Industrial Revolutions* (New York: John Wiley and Sons, 1979), 136.

26. Hass-Klau, *The Pedestrian and City Traffic*, 9, 23, 97.

27. Palisades Consulting Group, Inc., ITE Technical Committee 6A-47, *Final Draft Report: Update of Transit and Pedestrian Malls in 13 U.S. Cities:* (Tenefly, NJ: Palisades Consulting Group, Inc., September 1996), table 6; Jonathan Barnett, "What's New in Downtown Planning," *Urban Design* (Spring 1977): 18–23.

28. Hannelore Cobet, "Retail Development in Germany," *Urban Land* 50, no. 10 (October 26, 1991): 25, 26.

29. TEST, *Quality Streets*, 8, 89.

30. Ibid., 10.

31. Timothy Beatley, *Green Urbanism: Learning from European Cities* (Washington, DC: Island Press, 2000), 94.

32. Jan Gehl, *Cities for People* (Washington, DC: Island Press. 2010).

33. Ing Manfred Droste, *Ausländische Erfahrungen mit Möglichkeiten der räumlichen und sektoralen Umverteilung des städtischen Verkehrs*, Urbanistic Research Papers series, no. No. 03.063, Bundesministers für Raumordnung, Bauwesen and Städtebau, Auswertung von OECD—Fallstudien, Forschungsprojekt BMBau RS II 6–704102–234, Bonn, 1978.

34. TEST, *Quality Streets*.

35. Werner Heinz, Herbert Hübner, Berd Meinecke, and Erhart Pfotenhauer, *Siedlungsstrukturelle Folgen der Einrichtung verkehrsberuhigter Zonen in Kernbereichen*, Urbanistic Research Papers series, no. 03.065, Bundesministers für Raumordnung, Bauwesen and Städtebau, Forschungsprojekt BMBau RS II 6–704102–74.08, Bonn, 1978; Ronald Wiedenhoeft, "Downtown Pedestrian Zones: Experiments in Germany," *Urban Land* 34, no. 4 (April 1975): 3–11.

36. Cobet, "Retail Development in Germany," 25, 26.

37. Trans21, *TransitPulse* (Boston: Advanced Transit Association, January–February 1997), 2.

38. Lester R. Brown, *Plan B 4.0: Mobilizing to Save Civilization* (New York: W. W. Norton, 2009), 163–164.

39. Victor Gruen, "Vienna, Austria," in *Streets for People*, edited by Organization for Economic Cooperation and Development (Paris: Organization for Economic Cooperation and Development, 1974), 49–55.

40. Norman Klein and Walter Arensberg, "Auto-Free Zones: Giving Cities Back to People," *City* (March–April 1972).

41. TEST, *Quality Streets*, 10.

42. Cobet, "Retail Development in Germany," 25, 26.

43. Wiedenhoeft, "Downtown Pedestrian Zones."

44. Lawrence Houstoun, "Give Pedestrian Malls a Second Look," *Planning* 76, no. 5 (May–June 2010): 25–26.

45. Linda Baker, "Walking Wins Out: Pedestrian Streets Are in Style Again," *Planning* 76, no. 5. (May–June 2010): 24–27.

46. Maureen McAvey, "Urban Opportunities," in *Developing around Transit: Strategies and Solutions That Work*, ed. Robert T. Dunphy (Washington, DC: Urban Land Institute, 2004), 107–108.

47. Janet Moore, "Aging Nicollet Mall Gets a Team to Make It Young Once More," *Star Tribune Minneapolis*, September 19, 2013, http://www.startribune.com/local/minneapolis/224480761.html.

48. Baker, "Walking Wins Out."

49. Mike Lydon, "Talking Tactical Urbanism," *Architect's Newspaper*, June 18, 2012, http://archpaper.com/news/articles.asp?id=6120.

50. Sarah Goodyear, "Taming the Mean Streets of New York: A Talk with NYC Transportation Chief Janette Sadik-Khan," *Grist*, December 21, 2010, http://www.grist.org/article/2010-12-21-Taming-the-mean-streets-of-new-york-a-talk-with-nyc-dot.

51. Michael Barbaro, "Recalling, Vividly, a Visit to a Much Grittier Times Square," *New York Times*, April 14, 2011.

52. Eric Jaffe, "That's Right, Los Angeles Is Giving Up Car Lanes for Pedestrians," *Atlantic Cities*, July 5, 2013. http://www.theatlanticcities.com/jobs-and-economy/2013/07/s-right-los-angeles-giving-car-lanes-pedestrians/6116.

53. Janette I. Sadik-Khan, "New Mobility Initiatives in New York: Select Bus Service, Bike Share, Wayfinding, and Midtown in Motion" (paper presented at the ninety-first annual meeting of the Transportation Research Board, January 23, 2012).

54. Emily Badger, "The Street Hacker, Officially Embraced," *Atlantic Cities*, May 7, 2012. http://www.theatlanticcities.com/neighborhoods/2012/05/street-hacker-officially-embraced/1921.

55. Kaid Benfield, "In San Francisco, a One-Stop Shop for Building Better Streets," *Atlantic Cities*, June 26, 2012. http://www.theatlanticcities.com/politics/2012/06/san-francisco-one-stop-shop-better-streets/2378.

56. Nate Seltenrich, "San Francisco Parklets Swap Parking Spots for Community Space," *San Francisco Examiner*, October 23, 2011, http://www.sfexaminer.com/local/2011/10/san-francisco-parklets-swap-parking-spots-community-space; William Bostwick, "Life in the Slow Lane," *Architectural Record*, October 28, 2011.

57. Nate Berg, "Los Angeles Seeks Pedestrians," *Atlantic Cities*, March 5, 2012.

58. Linh Thoi, "Sidewalk Sipping with Sadik-Khan at NYC Pop-Up Café," *Architect's Newspaper*, August 19, 2010, http://blog.archpaper.com/wordpress/archives/8545.

59. "Talking Tactical Urbanism," *Architect's Newspaper*, June 18, 2012, http://archpaper.com/news/articles.asp?id=6120.

60. Buehler and Pucher, "Sustainable Transport That Works," 20–21.

61. Ibid., 15–22.

62. Ibid., 18–22.

63. Ibid., 17.

64. Bonnie Kavoussi, "Gas Prices in U.S. Are among Lowest in World, Report Finds," *Huffington Post*, May 16, 2012, http://www.huffingtonpost.com/2012/05/15/united-states-low-gas-prices_n_1518169.html.

65. G. B. Arrington, "Beyond the Field of Dreams: Light Rail and Growth Management in Portland," in vol. 2, *Seventh National Conference on Light Rail Transit* (Washington, DC: Transportation Research Board, September 1996), 9.

66. Interview with Director of Traffic Management Ruedi Ott, Leiter, Verkersplanning, Zürich, July 12, 2000.

67. Pete Donohue, "M42 Wins Slowest Bus of the Year Award, with Average Speed of 3.6 mph," *New York Daily News*, December 7, 2010, http://www.nydailynews.com/ny_local/2010/12/07/2010-12-07_m42_wins_slowest_bus_of_the_year_award_with_average_speed_of_36_mph.html.

68. John Phythyon, "The Future Is Here: Catenary-Less Power for Light Rail," *Mass Transit Magazine*, June 3, 2011, http://www.masstransitmag.com/article/10262406/the-future-is-here-catenary-less-power-for-light-rail?page=3.

69. Schaller Consulting, "Necessity or Choice? Why People Drive in Manhattan," February 2006, http://www.transalt.org/files/newsroom/reports/schaller_Feb2006.pdf.70. Times Square Alliance, report released to Mayor's Midtown Citizens' Committee, February 23, 2010.

71. "Closing the Crossroads," *Architect's Newspaper*, February 11, 2010, http://archpaper.com/e-board_rev.asp?News_ID=4236.

72. Philip Habib & Associates and Allee King Rosen and Fleming, Inc., *42nd Street Light Rail Transit Line: Final Environmental Impact Statement, CEQR No. 92DOT008M*, report prepared for NYC Department of Transportation, March 23, 1994; Jonathan Boyer, "New York Council Votes to Plan to Build 42nd Street Trolley Line," *LRT News* 9, no. 1 (December 1994): 2, 3.

73. Halcrow, Inc., *vision42 Complete Construction Cost Study*, March 31, 2005, http://www.vision42.org/_pdf/cost_study.pdf; Halcrow, Inc., *Vision42 2007 Construction Cost Update*, http://www.vision42.org/about/documents/08.02.01Cost EstimateUpdated.pdf.

74. Urbanomics, Inc., *vision42 Economic Study, Phase 2*, November 15, 2006, http://www.vision42.org/about/documents/vision42retail_061115.pdf.

75. Urbanomics, Inc., *vision42 Financing Report, Phase 3*, February 2008, http://www.vision42.org/about/documents/Financing_Report_080318.pdf.

76. Urbanomics, Inc., *vision42 Phase V Technical Studies: A Comparison of Relative Benefits of a Proposed River-to-River Auto-Free Light Rail Boulevard on*

42nd Street with a New 10th Avenue #7 Subway Station, May 23, 2012, http://www.vision42.org/about/documents/vision42_5FinalReport.pdf.

77. Halcrow, Inc., *vision42 Construction Phasing Study*, October 23, 2006, http://www.vision42.org/about/documents/vision42constr.phasing_061023.pdf.

78. Urbanomics, *vision42 Economic Study, Phase 2*.

79. Sam Schwartz Engineering, *vision42 Traffic Study, Phase 1*, March 31, 2005, http://www.vision42.org/_pdf/traffic_study.pdf.

80. Sam Schwartz Engineering, *vision42 Phase II Traffic Study: Traffic Analysis and Truck Loading*, October 23, 2006, http://www.vision42.org/about/documents/vision42traffic_061023.pdf.

81. Jonathan Barnett, "What's New in Downtown Planning," *Urban Design* (Spring 1977): 18–23.

82. Philip L. Walker, "Myths of Downtown Planning," *Planning* 75, no. 6 (June 2009): 38–40.

83. US Environmental Protection Agency, Development, Community, and Environment Division, "Residential Construction Trends in America's Metropolitan Regions," January 2010, http://www.epa.gov/dced/construction_trends.htm

84. Marc G. Berman, John Jonides, and Stephen Kaplan, "The Cognitive Benefits of Interacting with Nature," *Psychological Science* (December 2008), http://pss.sagepub.com/content/19/12/1207.short.

85. Interview with NYC transportation commissioner Janet Sadik-Kahn, "A Fresh Look," *Forbes*, September 17, 2009, http://www.forbes.com/2009/09/17/sadik-khan-cities-thought-leaders-transportation.html.

86. Adrian Benepe, "Landscape by Bloomberg" (presentation at a meeting of the Forum for Urban Design, Century Association, November 2, 2011).

87. Amanda Kolson Hurley, "Feature: A New Morning in Washington," *Architect's Newspaper*, June 20, 2012, http://archpaper.com/news/articles.asp?id=6124.

88. John Vidal, "Away with the Grey," *Guardian*, March 25, 2009, http://www.guardian.co.uk/environment/2009/mar/25/green-infrastructure.

89. Mark L. Hinshaw, *True Urbanism: Living In or Near the Center* (Chicago: American Planning Association, 2007), 72.

Chapter 7

1. "EMISSIONS: C2ES President Eileen Claussen Says Natural Gas Development Can Be Leveraged to Reduce Emissions," *E&E TV: OnPoint*, June 4, 2013, transcript, http://www.eenews.net/tv/videos/1693/transcript.

2. International Energy Agency, "Global Carbon-Dioxide Emissions Increase by 1.0 Gt in 2011 to Record High," May 24, 2012, http://www.iea.org/newsroomandevents/news/2012/may/name,27216,en.html.

3. Ibid.

4. "World Carbon Dioxide Emissions Data by Country: China Speeds Ahead of the Rest," *Guardian*, January 31, 2011, http://www.guardian.co.uk/news/data blog/2011/jan/31/world-carbon-dioxide-emissions-country-data-co2.

5. International Energy Agency, "Global Carbon-Dioxide Emissions Increase"; Jenny Mandel and Gayathri Vaidyanathan, "Energy Markets: Natural Gas Goals in India Seem Ever-Distant after Unprecedented Blackout," *Energywire*, August 2, 2012, http://www.eenews.net/energywire/2012/08/02/1.

6. John M. Broder, "Climate Change Will Cause More Energy Breakdowns, U.S. Warns," *New York Times*, July 11, 2013, A12.

7. Michael T. Klare, "The New Fossil Fuel Fever," *Nation*, March 19, 2012, 15–22.

8. Ibid.

9. Ian Urbina, "Hunt for Gas Hits Fragile Soil, and South Africans Fear Risks," *New York Times*, December 31, 2011,http://www.nytimes.com/2011/12/31/world/south-african-farmers-see-threat-from-fracking.html?_r=0.

10. Klare, "The New Fossil Fuel Fever."

11. Christopher Helman, "Billionaire Father of Fracking Says Government Must Step Up Regulation," *Forbes*, July 19, 2012, http://www.forbes.com/sites/christo pherhelman/2012/07/19/billionaire-father-of-fracking-says-government-must -step-up-regulation.

12. Gayathri Vaidyanathan and Ellen M. Gilmer, "Oil and Gas: Water Flows to Money in Drought-Stricken Drilling Regions," *Energywire*, July 30, 2012, http:// www.eenews.net/energywire/2012/07/30/1.

13. Mike Soraghan, "Earthquakes: Man-Made, Drilling-Related Quakes Getting Harder to Ignore," *Energywire*, August 7, 2012, http://www.eenews.net/energy wire/2012/08/07/1.

14. Anthony R. Ingraffea, "Gangplank to a Warm Future," op-ed, *New York Times*, July 29, 2013, A17.

15. Gayathri Vaidyanathan, "Energy Policy: Natural Gas Can Help, for a While, with Climate Change—IEA," *E&E News*, July 18, 2012, http://www.eenews.net/ energywire/2012/07/18/6.

16. Steve LeVine, "Amid Frenzy of Discoveries, a New Energy Player Stokes Political Unrest," *Energywire*, July 18, 2012, http://www.eenews.net/energy wire/2012/07/18/2.

17. National Renewable Energy Laboratory, *Renewable Electricity Futures Study*, June 2012, http://www.nrel.gov/analysis/re_futures.

18. Center for Climate and Energy Solutions, "Renewable and Alternative Energy Standards," August 2, 2012, http://www.c2es.org/us-states-regions/policy -maps/renewable-energy-standards.

19. Ibid.

20. Union of Concerned Scientists, "Production Tax Credit for Renewable Energy," September 13, 2011, http://www.ucsusa.org/clean_energy/smart-energy -solutions/increase-renewables/production-tax-credit-for.html.

21. Rainer Baake, "German Energy Transition Architect Baake Discusses U.S. Clean Energy policy," *E&E News: On Point*, May 14, 2013, http://www.eenews.net/tv/videos/1685/transcript.

22. Michael Grunwald, *The New New Deal: The Hidden Story of Change in the Obama Era* (New York: Simon and Schuster, 2012).

23. Jeff Himmelman, "Here Comes the Sun," *New York Times Magazine*, August 12, 2012, 24–27, http://www.nytimes.com/2012/08/12/magazine/the-secret-to-solar-power.html?_r=1.

24. Solar Energy Market Growth, Solarbuzz.com, 2010, http://www.solarbuzz.com/facts-and-figures/markets-growth/market-growth.

25. Himmelman, "Here Comes the Sun."

26. "Experts Expect Big Boom in U.S. Solar Installation Due to Bond Financing," Getsolar.com, July 12, 2012, http://www.getsolar.com/News/Solar-Energy-Facts/General/Experts-Expect-Big-Boom-in-US-Solar-Installation-Due-to-Bond-Financing-800817433.

27. Blaine Brownell, "Solar Cells for Windows Harvest Infrared Light," *Architect Magazine*, August 7, 2012, http://www.architectmagazine.com/photovoltaics/solar-cells-for-windows-harvest-infrared-light.aspx.

28. Robert S. Eschelman, "Technology: Solar Heating Has Vast, Overlooked Potential—Report," *Climatewire*, August 21, 2012, http://www.eenews.net/climatewire/2012/08/21/3.

29. Himmelman, "Here Comes the Sun."

30. Ibid.

31. "Interior Unveils First-Ever National Solar Energy Plan for Public Lands," *Power Engineering*, July 26, 2012, http://www.power-eng.com/news/2012/07/25/interior-unveils-first-ever-national-solar-energy-plan-for-public-lands.html; John Timmer, "US to Make Solar Energy Development on Public Land Easier," Arstechnic.com, July 27, 2012, http://arstechnica.com/science/2012/07/us-to-make-solar-energy-development-on-public-land-easier.

32. Nick Juliano, "Renewable Energy: In California Desert, the Future Is Now for Solar Plant," *E&E News*, August 20, 2012, http://www.eenews.net/Greenwire/2012/08/20/2.

33. J. Matthew Roney, "Offshore Wind Development Picking Up Pace," *Earth Policy Institute, Plan B Updates*, August 16, 2012, http://www.earth-policy.org/plan_b_updates/2012/update106.

34. Nick Juliano, "Offshore Wind: Cape Wind Purchases Massachusetts Marina to Use as Operations Hub," *E&E News*, August 23, 2012, http://www.eenews.net/eenewspm/2012/08/23/10.

35. Mike Lock, "Annual Report: Wind Power Bringing Innovation, Manufacturing Back to American Industry," American Wind Energy Association, April 12, 2012, http://todayeco.com/pages/3641280-annual-report-wind-power-bringing-innovation-manufacturing.

36. Ehren Goossens and Justin Doom, "U.S. Wind Energy Capacity Growth Up 31 Percent in 2011," *Business Week*, April 12, 2012, http://www.bloomberg.com/news/2012-04-12/kansas-texas-led-31-gain-in-u-s-wind-energy-capacity-in-2011.html; Eileen O'Grady, "Texas Sets Wind Power Record as Coastal Wind Grows," Reuters, October 18, 2011, http://www.reuters.com/article/2011/10/18/us-utilities-texas-wind-idUSTRE79H5ZL20111018.

37. Dan Voorhis, "Tax Break's End Is a Blow to Wind Power in Kansas," *Wichita Eagle*, March 19, 2012, http://www.kansas.com/2012/03/11/2261041/tax-breaks-end-a-blow-to-wind.html.

38. "U.S.: 200,000 GW of Solar Power Could Be Installed," Evwind.es, July 27, 2012, http://www.evwind.es/2012/07/27/u-s-200000-gw-of-solar-power-could-be-installed.

39. Eric Lipton and Clifford Krauss, "Rich Subsidies Powering Solar and Wind Projects," *New York Times*, November 12, 2011, http://www.wind-watch.org/news/2011/11/12/rich-subsidies-powering-solar-and-wind-projects.

40. Ben Sills, "Fossil Fuel Subsidies Six Times More Than Renewable Energy," *Bloomberg News*, November 9, 2011, http://www.bloomberg.com/news/2011-11-09/fossil-fuels-got-more-aid-than-clean-energy-iea.html.

41. Lester R. Brown, *Plan B 4.0: Mobilizing to Save Civilization* (New York: W. W. Norton, 2009), 265.

42. Lester R. Brown, "Governments Spend $1.4 Billion per Day to Destabilize Climate," Earth Policy Institute data release, January 19, 2012, http://www.earth-policy.org/data_highlights/2011/highlights24.

43. "Energy Policy: Former Representative Inglis Says Subsidy Phaseout, Carbon Tax the Future of Conservative Energy Narrative," *E&E News*, July 25, 2012, http://www.eenews.net/tv/transcript/1561.

44. Brown, *Plan B 4.0*, chapters 1–2.

45. Elisabeth Rosenthal, "Rush to Use Crops as Fuel Raises Food Prices and Hunger Fears," *New York Times*, April 7, 2011, 1, 3.

46. Steven Rattner, "The Great Corn Con," *New York Times*, Opinion Pages, June 24, 2011, http://www.nytimes.com/2011/06/25/opinion/25Rattner.html.

47. Robert Pear, "After three Decades, Tax Credit for Ethanol Expires," *New York Times*, January 2, 2012, http://www.nytimes.com/2012/01/02/business/energy-environment/after-three-decades-federal-tax-credit-for-ethanol-expires.html.

48. Rosenthal, "Rush to Use Crops as Fuel Raises Food Prices."

49. Brown, *Plan B 4.0*, 50.

50. Ron Nixon and Annie Lowrey, "Drought Forces Reductions in U.S. Crop Forecasts," *New York Times*, August 11, 2012, http://www.nytimes.com/2012/08/11/business/projections-for-corn-yield-falls-to-17-year-low.html?pagewanted=all.

51. Jena Thompson and Wallace E. Tyner, "Corn Stover for Bioenergy Production: Cost Estimates and Farmer Supply Response," Purdue University Agriculture

Extension, September 2011, http://www.extension.purdue.edu/extmedia/EC/RE
-3-W.pdf.

52. Ibid.

53. Samuel I. Schwartz, "An Indecent Proposal for Our Country's Infrastructure,"
Need to Know, PBS.org, July 27, 2011, http://www.pbs.org/wnet/need-to-know/
voices/an-indecent-proposal-for-our-countrys-infrastructure-future/10707.

54. "Life in the Slow Lane," *Economist*, April 30, 2011, 29–31.

55. "National Association of Railroad Passengers," *NARP News* 44, no. 9 (October–November 2009): 3, 4.

56. Nicholas Stern, *The Stern Review on the Economics of Climate Change* (London: HM Treasury, 2006), http://webarchive.nationalarchives.gov.uk/+/http:/
www.hm-treasury.gov.uk/sternreview_index.htm.

57. Brown, *Plan B 4.0*, 16, 17.

58. Thomas L. Friedman, "Real Men Tax Gas," *New York Times*, Week in Review, September 20, 2009, 8.

59. Josh Goodman, "Marilyn Governor O'Malley Takes a Risk on Gas Tax,"
Stateline, February 10, 2012, http://www.stateline.org/live/details/story?cont
entId=631108.

60. Saquib Rahim, "Tax on Vehicle Miles Traveled Gains Support, but Raises
Orwellian Questions," *New York Times*, October 7, 2010, http://www.nytimes
.com/cwire/2010/10/07/07climatewire-tax-on-vehicle-miles-traveled-gains
-support-22995.html?pagewanted=all.

61. Eric Jaffe, "The Era of Pay-per-Mile Has Begun," *Atlantic Cities*, July 10,
2013, http://www.theatlanticcities.com/commute/2013/07/era-pay-mile-driving
-has-begun/6150.

62. Ken Orski, "The Precarious State of the Highway Trust Fund," *Cascadia
Prospectus*, November 28, 2011, http://www.cascadiaprospectus.org/2011/11/
the_precarious_state_of_the_hi.php.

63. Daniel Alpert, Robert Hockett, and Nouriel Roubini, "The Way Forward:
Moving from the Post-Bubble, Post-Bust Economy to Renewed Growth and Competitiveness," *New America Foundation*, October 10, 2011, http://newamerica
.net/publications/policy/the_way_forward.

64. Dan Heath, "Montréal–New York City High-Speed Rail a Priority for Quebec," PressRepublican.com, October 19, 2009, http://www.pressrepublican.com/
homepage/local_story_292220028.html.

65. Julia Parzen and Abby Jo Sigal, "Financing Transit-Oriented Development,"
in *The New Transit Town: Best Practices in Transit-Oriented Development*, ed.
Hank Dittmar and Gloria Ohland (Washington, DC: Island Press, 2004), 84–112.

66. Robert Cervero, Christopher Ferrell, and Steven Murphy, *Transit-Oriented
Development and Joint Development in the United States: A Literature Review*,
Transit Cooperative Research Report 52 (Washington, DC: Transportation Re-
search Board, October 2002), 62–63.

67. Ibid., 46–64.

68. Ibid., 53–61.

69. Judith Rodin, "How the Transportation Bill Failed America," *Atlantic Cities*, June 30, 2012.

70. Mary Lauren Hall, "New Transportation Bill Cuts Biking and Walking Funding by More Than 60 Percent," *America Bikes*, June 28, 2012, http://www.america bikes.org/new_transportation_bill_cuts_biking_walking_funding_by_more _than_60_percent.

71. Enrique Peñalosa, "Our Cities, Ourselves: Visions for 2030" (remarks at the American Institute of Architects symposium, New York, July 1, 2010).

72. Paul Krugman, "Cassandra of Climate," op-ed, *New York Times*, September 28, 2009, A23.

73. Paul Weyrich and William S. Lind, *Moving Minds: Conservatives and Public Transportation* (Washington, DC: Free Congress Foundation, 2009).

74. Paul Krugman, "What Ails Europe?" *New York Times*, February 27, 2012, http://www.nytimes.com/2012/02/27/opinion/krugman-what-ails-europe.html.

75. Schwartz, "An Indecent Proposal for Our Country's Infrastructure."

76. Doreen Carvalja, "European Rail Crashes Show Gaps in an Increasingly Precarious System," *New York Times*, September 10, 2013, A4, A6.

77. Nicholas D. Kristof, "In Athens, Austerity's Ugliness," *New York Times*, March 8, 2012, http://www.nytimes.com/2012/03/08/opinion/kristof-in-athens -austeritys-ugliness.html.

78. Thomas De Monchaux, "Why Less Isn't Always More," *New York Times*, Sunday Review, February 26, 2012, http://www.nytimes.com/2012/02/26/ opinion/sunday/why-less-isnt-always-more.html?pagewanted=all.

79. Yonah Freeman, "Can High-Speed Rail Save American Manufacturing?" *Transport Politic*, June 6, 2009, http://www.thetransportpolitic.com/2009/06/06/ can-high-speed-rail-save-american-manufacturing.

80. Steve Nadis and James J. MacKenzie, *Car Trouble* (Washington, DC: World Resources Institute, 1993), 11.

81. Bill Conis, director of business development for Siemens Transportation, presentation to the vision42 Working Group, Transportation Alternatives, New York, March 17, 2009.

82. Paul Krugman, "The Finite World," op-ed, *New York Times*, December 27, 2010, A19.

83. Beverly Crandon, "Auto Industry Growth Good News for Marketers," *Adition*, March 2, 2011, http://www.ad-ition.com/2011/03/02/auto-industry -growth-good-news-for-marketers.

84. Robert Goodman, "The Truth about Sustainability," *Planning*74, no. 5 (May 2008): 13.

85. David Brooks, "The Next Culture War," op-ed, *New York Times*, September 29, 2009, A39.

86. Richard Florida, "Unraveling," in *The Great Reset: How New Ways of Living and Working Drive Post-Crash Prosperity* (New York: HarperCollins, 2010), 43, 44.

87. Daniel Gross, "Renting Prosperity," *Wall Street Journal*, May 4, 2012, http://online.wsj.com/news/articles/SB10001424052702304746604577382321021920372.

88. Richard Florida, "Homeownership Means Little to Economic Growth," *Atlantic Cities*, June 20, 2012.

89. Reconnecting America, "Planning for TOD at the Regional Scale," *TOD 204:* One in a series of best practices from the Center for Transit-Oriented Development, August 2011, http://www.reconnectingamerica.org/resource-center/browse-research/2011/tod-204-planning-for-tod-at-the-regional-scale.

90. Jordan Weissmann, "Young People Aren't Buying Cars Because They're Buying Smart Phones Instead," *Atlantic Cities*, August 8, 2012. http://www.theatlanticcities.com/technology/2012/08/young-people-arent-buying-cars-because-theyre-buying-smart-phones-instead/2873.

91. Steven E. Polzin, "Exploring Changing Travel Trends" (presentation at the National Household Travel Survey conference, Transportation Research Board, June 6–7, 2011), Washington, DC, http://onlinepubs.trb.org/onlinepubs/conferences/2011/NHTS1/Polzin2.pdf.

92. Amy Chozick, "As Young Lose interest in Cars, GM Turns to MTV for Help," *New York Times*, March 23, 2012, http://www.nytimes.com/2012/03/23/business/media/to-draw-reluctant-young-buyers-gm-turns-to-mtv.html?pagewanted=all.

93. Martin Zimmerman, "Rebel without a Car?" *Los Angeles Times*, October 8, 2009, http://latimesblogs.latimes.com/uptospeed/2009/10/james-dean-.html.

94. Claire Thompson, "Slow Ride: Buses Are the New Vehicles of Youth Rebellion," *Grist*, March 26, 2012, http://grist.org/transportation/slow-ride-buses-are-the-new-vehicles-of-youth-rebellion.

95. Prashant Gopal, "Tata's Nano Home: Company behind World's Cheapest Car to Sell $7,800 Apartments," *Bloomberg Business Week*, May 7, 2009, http://www.businessweek.com/stories/2009-05-06/tatas-nano-home-company-behind-worlds-cheapest-car-to-sell-7-800-apartments.

96. Mark L. Hinshaw and Brianna Holan, "Rooming House Redux," *Planning* (November 2011): 16–19.

97. Ibid.

98. John Caulfield, "The Big Apple Aims Smaller in Its Housing Plans," *Builder*, July 18, 2012, http://www.builderonline.com/multifamily/the-big-apple-aims-smaller-in-its-housing-plans.aspx?cid=ANW:072012:FULL.

99. Alan Durning, *Unlocking Home: Three Keys to Affordable Communities* (Seattle: Sightline Institute, July 15, 2013).

100. James Fallows, "Dirty Coal, Clean Future," *Atlantic*, December 2010, http://www.theatlantic.com/magazine/archive/2010/12/dirty-coal-clean-future/308307.

101. Daniel Hoornweg, Lorraine Sugar, and Claudia Lorena Trejos Gómez, "Cities and Greenhouse Gas Emissions: Moving Forward," *Environment and Urbanization* (2011), http://eau.sagepub.com/content/23/1/207; Tim De Chant, "Dirty 'Hoods: Is Your Neighborhood Bad for the Climate?" *Grist*, September 5, 2011, http://www.grist.org/cities/2011-09-04-bad-neighborhood-is-yours-bad-for-the -climate.

102. Associated Press, "Baby Boomlet Pushes U.S. Birth Rates to 45-Year High," January 15, 2008, http://www.foxnews.com/story/0,2933,323028,00.html.

103. William Greider, *Come Home, America* (New York: Rodale, 2009), 263.

Selected Bibliography

Appleyard, Donald, with M. Sue Gerson and Mark Lintell. *Livable Streets*. Berkeley: University of California Press, 1981.

Arrington, G. B. "Beyond the Field of Dreams: Light Rail and Growth Management in Portland." In vol. 2, *Seventh National Conference on Light Rail Transit*. Washington, DC: Transportation Research Board, September 1996.

Arrington, G. B., and Robert Cervero. *Effects of TOD on Housing, Parking, and Travel*. Transit Cooperative Research Program, report 128. Washington, DC: Transportation Research Board, 2008.

Badger, Emily. "The Street Hacker, Officially Embraced." *Atlantic Cities*, May 7, 2012.

Badger, Emily. "Why Mayors Should Run the Department of Transportation." *Atlantic Cities*, November 21, 2012.

Baker, Linda. "Walking Wins Out: Pedestrian Streets Are in Style Again." *Planning* 76, no. 5 (May–June 2010): 24–26.

Beatley, Timothy. *Green Urbanism: Learning from European Cities*. Washington, DC: Island Press, 2000.

Benfield, F. Kaid. "'Growing Wealthier' Report Shows How Smart Growth Can Enhance Prosperity." Center for Clean Air Policy, Natural Resources Defense Council Switchboard. January 19, 2011.

Benfield, F. Kaid. "In San Francisco, a One-Stop Shop for Building Better Streets." *Atlantic Cities*, June 26, 2012.

Benfield, F. Kaid. "How California Legislated Its Way to Smarter Growth." *Atlantic Cities*, September 25, 2012.

Benfield, F. Kaid, Matthew D. Raimi, and Donald D. T. Chen. *Once There Were Greenfields: How Urban Sprawl Is Undermining America's Environment, Economy, and Social Fabric*. Washington, DC: Natural Resources Defense Council, Surface Transportation Policy Project, 1999.

Bennet, Jonathan. "Who Wrecked America's Trains?" *Utne Reader*, June–July 1986, 106–108.

Berg, Nate. "The Future of Intelligent Parking." *Atlantic Cities*, March 23, 2012.

Bergen, Mark. "India's Cities Risk Repeating America's Congestion Mistakes." *Atlantic Cities*, September 7, 2012.

Bernick, Michael, and Robert Cervero. *Transit Villages in the 21st Century*. New York: McGraw-Hill, 1997.

Brooks, Allison, and Darnell Chadwick Grisby. "LA Vision; US Promise: Implications of the America Fast Forward Proposal." *Reconnecting America: People—Places—Possibility* (Fall 2011): 4, 5.

Brown, Lester R. *Plan B 3.0: Mobilizing to Save Civilization*. New York: W. W. Norton, 2008.

Brown, Lester R. *Plan B 4.0: Mobilizing to Save Civilization*. New York: W. W. Norton, 2009.

Bruegmann, Robert. *Sprawl: A Compact History*. Chicago: University of Chicago Press, 2005.

Brun, Eric C., and Preston L. Schiller. "How Cars Devour Urban Space and Time." *Urban Transport International 5* (May–June 1996): 38, 39.

Bureau of Transportation Statistics. *Transportation Statistics Annual Report*. Washington, DC: US Department of Transportation, 2008.

Buehler, Ralph, and John Pucher. "Sustainable Transport That Works: Lessons from Germany." *World Transport Policy and Practice* 1 (April 2009): 22–23. http://www.eco-logica.co.uk/pdf/wtpp15.1.pdf.

Cable, Faith. "Design First, Codify Second: Germany Offers Lessons for U.S. Planners." *Planning* 75, no. 7 (July 2009): 24–27.

Cairns, Sally, Carmen Hass-Klau, and Phil Goodwin. *Traffic Impact of Highway Capacity Reductions: Assessment of the Evidence*. London: Landor Publishing and London Transport, March 1998.

Calthorpe, Peter. *The Next American Metropolis: Ecology, Community, and the American Dream*. Princeton, NJ: Princeton Architectural Press, 1993.

Cervero, Robert. "Infrastructure and Development: Planning Matters." In *Transportation Infrastructure: The Challenges of Rebuilding America*, edited by Marlon G. Boarnet. Report no. 557. Chicago: American Planning Association, July 2009.

Cervero, Robert, Christopher Ferrell, and Steven Murphy. *Transit-Oriented Development and Joint Development in the United States: A Literature Review*. Transportation Cooperative Research Program, no. 52 Washington, DC: Transportation Research Board, October 2002.

Cervero, Robert, Steven Murphy, Christopher Ferrell, Natasha Goguts, Yu-Hsin Tsai, G. B. Arrington, John Boroski, Janet Smith-Heimer, Robert Dunphy, and others. *Transit-Oriented Development in the United States: Experiences, Challenges, and Prospects*. Transit Cooperative Research Report 102. Washington, DC: Transportation Research Board, January 1, 2004.

Cervero, Robert, and Cathleen Sullivan. "TODs for Tots." *Planning* 77, no. 2 (February 2011).

Cobet, Hannelore. "Retail Development in Germany." *Urban Land* 50, no. 10 (October 26, 1991): 25, 26.

Daisa, James M. "Traffic, Parking, and Transit-Oriented Development." In *The New Transit Town: Best Practices in Transit-Oriented Development*, edited by Hank Dittmar and Gloria Ohland. Washington, DC: Island Press, 2004.

Davis, Stacy C., Susan W. Diegal, and Robert G. Boundy, eds. *Transportation Energy Data Book: Edition 30*. Prepared for the US Department of Energy, Oak Ridge National Laboratory, Oak Ridge, TN, June 2011.

Dunham-Jones, Ellen, and June Williamson. *Retrofitting Suburbia: Urban Design Solutions for Redesigning Suburbs*. Hoboken, NJ: John Wiley, 2009.

Durning, Alan. *Unlocking Home: Three Keys to Affordable Communities*. Seattle: Sightline Institute, 2013.

Ewing, Reid, and Steven J. Brown. "Traffic Calming Progress Report." *Planning* 75, no. 10 (November 2009): 32–35.

Fallows, James. "Dirty Coal, Clean Future." *Atlantic*, December 2010, 68.

Flink, James. *The Automobile Age*. Cambridge, MA: MIT Press, 1988.

Florida, Richard. *The Great Reset: How New Ways of Living and Working Drive Post-Crash Prosperity*. New York: HarperCollins, 2010.

Florida, Richard. "Homeownership Means Little to Economic Growth." *Atlantic Cities*, June 20, 2012.

Florida, Richard. "Urban Home Values Are Rising Faster Than Suburban Ones." *Atlantic Cities*, June 25, 2013.

Fox, Gerald. "LRT v. Buses: Why Portland Chose Light Rail." *Tramways and Urban Transit: The International Light Rail Magazine* 72, no. 862 (October 2009): 390–392.

Freedman, Jonathan L. "The Effects of Population Density on Humans." In *Psychological Perspectives on Population*, edited by James T. Fawcett. New York: Basic Books, 1973.

Freedman, Jonathan L., Alan S. Levy, Roberta W. Buchanan, and Judy Price. "Crowding and Human Aggressiveness." *Journal of Experimental Social Psychology* 8, no. 6 (November 1972): 528–548.

Gannet, Henry. "Settled Areas and the Density of Our Population." *International Review* 12, no. 1 (1882): 70–77.

Gardner, Gary. "Power to the Pedals." *World Watch* (July–August 2010): 6–11.

Gehl, Jan. *Cities for People*. Washington, DC: Island Press, 2010.

Goodman, Robert. "The Truth about Sustainability." *Planning* 74, no. 5 (May 2008): 12–15.

Grabar, Henry. "A Guide to America's Most Ambitious Transit Projects." *Atlantic Cities*, January 23, 2013.

Greider, William. *Come Home, America*. New York: Rodale, 2009.

Gripsrud, Mattias, and Randi Hjorthol. "Working on the Train: From 'Dead Time' to Productive and Vital Time." *Transportation* 39, no. 5 (2012): 941–956. doi:10.1007/s11116-012-9396-7.

Grunwald, Michael. *The New New Deal: The Hidden Story of Change in the Obama Era*. New York: Simon and Schuster, 2012.

Guerra, Erick, and Robert Cervero. "Cost of a Ride: The Effects of Densities on Fixed-Guideway Transit Ridership and Costs." *Journal of the American Planning Association* 77, no. 3 (Summer 2011): 267–290.

Hass-Klau, Carmen. *The Pedestrian and City Traffic*. London: Belhaven Press, 1990.

Heinz, Werner, Herbert Hübner, Berd Meinecke, and Erhart Pfotenhauer. *Siedlungsstrukturelle Folgen der Einrichtung verkehrsberuhigter Zonen in Kernbereichen*, Urbanistic Research Papers series, no. 03.065, Bundesministers für Raumordnung, Bauwesen and Städtebau, Forschungsprojekt BMBau RS II 6–704102–74.08, Bonn, 1978.

Hetland, Charlie M. "Tokyo's High Speed Rail Network Gains Momentum on the Global Stage." *Atlantic Cities*, December 3, 2012.

Hinshaw, Mark L. *True Urbanism: Living In and Near the Center*. Chicago: American Planning Association, 2007.

Hinshaw, Mark L., and Brianna Holan. "Rooming House Redux." *Planning* 77, no. 11 (November 2011).

Hirt, Sonia. "The Devil Is in the Definitions: Contrasting American and German Approaches to Zoning." *Journal of the American Planning Association* 73, no. 4 (Fall 2007): 436–450.

Hook, Walter. "Stimulating a Car-Free Recovery." *Sustainable Transport* 20 (Winter 2008): 3–4.

Houstoun, Lawrence. "Give Pedestrian Malls a Second Look." *Planning* 76, no. 5 (May–June 2010): 25–26.

Hunter-Zaworski, K. M. *Impacts of Low-Speed Vehicles on Transportation Infrastructure and Safety*. Oregon Transportation Research and Education Consortium, final report, OTREC-RR-10–19, December 2010.

Institute of Transportation Engineers. *Parking Generation*. 3rd ed. Washington, DC: Institute of Transportation Engineers, 2004.

Jacobs, Jane. *The Death and Life of Great American Cities*. New York: Vantage Books, 1961.

Jaffe, Eric. "We Shouldn't Be Surprised That Most Transit Referendums Won." *Atlantic Cities*, November 13, 2012.Jaffe, Eric. "That's Right, Los Angeles Is Giving Up Car Lanes for Pedestrians." *Atlantic Cities*, July 5, 2013.

Jaffe, Eric. "The Era of Pay-per-Mile Has Begun." *Atlantic Cities*, July 10, 2013.

Johnson, Sara. "Top 10 Small U.S. Cities Growing Faster Than Their Suburbs." *Atlantic Cities*, December 11, 2012.

Judt, Tony. *Ill Fares the Land*. New York: Penguin Press, 2010.

Kellert, Stephen R. "Values and Perceptions of Invertebrates." *Conservation Biology* 7, no. 4 (December 1993): 845–848.

Klare, Michael T. "The New Fossil Fuel Fever." *Nation*, March 19, 2012, 15–22.

Klein, Norman, and Walter Arensberg. "Auto-Free Zones: Giving Cities Back to People." *City* (March–April 1972).

Kolankiewicz, Leon, and Roy Beck, *Weighing Sprawl Factors in Large U.S. Cities: A Report on the Nearly Equal Roles Played by Population Growth and Land Use Choices in the Loss of Farmland and Natural Habitat to Urbanization*. Analysis of US Bureau of the Census data on the hundred-largest urbanized areas of the United States, Arlington, VA, March 19, 2001.

Leinberger, Christopher B. "The Next Slum?" *Atlantic*, March 2008, 72, 74.

Leisner, Rick, and David T. Retzsh. "Resurgent Urbanism." Reprinted in *New Urbanism in Practice* 3 (2008), with permission from *Jacobs Quarterly* 6, no. 4.

Levine, Jonathan. "Is Bus versus Rail Investment a Zero-Sum Game? The Misuse of the Opportunity-Cost Concept." *Journal of the American Planning Association* 79, no. 1 (Winter 2013): 5–15.

Litman, Todd. *Parking Management Best Practices*. Chicago: American Planning Association, 2006.

Litman, Todd. "Why and How to Reduce the Amount of Land Paved for Roads and Parking Facilities." *Environmental Practice: Journal of the National Association of Environmental Professionals* 13, no. 1 (March 2011): 38–46.

Liu, Rongfang (Rachel). "The Spectrum of Automated Guideway Transit (AGT) and Its Applications." In vol. 2, *Handbook of Transportation Engineering*, edited by Myer Kutz. 2nd ed. New York: McGraw-Hill, 2010.

Lovins, Amory B., and L. Hunter Lovins. "Reinventing the Wheels." *Atlantic Monthly* 275, no. 1 (January 1995): 75–85.

Marshall, Alex. "Two Wheels Are Becoming as Chic as Four." *Spotlight on the Region*, Regional Plan Association, New York (October 20, 2010).

Marshall, Alex. "To Make Cycling and Walking Safer, Put the Burden on Drivers." *Spotlight on the Region*, Regional Plan Association, New York (August 9, 2012).

McAvey, Maureen. "Urban Opportunities." In *Developing around Transit: Strategies and Solutions That Work*, edited by Robert T. Dunphy. Washington, DC: Urban Land Institute, 2004.

Middleton, William D. *The Interurban Era*. Milwaukee, WI: Kalmbach Publications, 1961.

Morris, A.E.J. *History of Urban Form: Before the Industrial Revolutions*. New York: John Wiley, 1979.

Mumford, Lewis. *The City in History: Its Origins, Its Transformations, and Its Prospects*. 1989. Reprint, New York: Harcourt, Brace, 1961.

Nadis, Steve, and James J. MacKenzie. *Car Trouble*. Washington, DC: World Resources Institute, 1993.

Nelson, Robert H. *Zoning and Property Rights: An Analysis of the American System of Land Use Regulation*. Cambridge, MA: MIT Press, 1977.

New Jersey Public Interest Research Group. "Do Roads Pay for Themselves?" January 4, 2011.

Norton, Peter D. *Fighting Traffic: The Dawn of the Motor Age in the American City.* Cambridge, MA: MIT Press, 2008.

Office of Technology Assessment. *Automated Guideway Transit: An Assessment of PRT and Other New Systems.* Washington, DC: US Government Printing Office, June 1975.

Organisation for Economic Co-operation and Development. *Streets for People.* Paris: Organisation for Economic Co-operation and Development, 1974.

Parzen, Julia, and Abby Jo Sigal. "Financing Transit-Oriented Development." In *The New Transit Town: Best Practices in Transit-Oriented Development,* edited by Hank Dittmar and Gloria Ohland. Washington, DC: Island Press, 2004.

Peiser, Richard, and Anne Frej. *Professional Real Estate Development: The ULI Guide to Business.* 2nd ed. Washington, DC: Urban Land Institute, 2003.

Philip Habib and Associates and Allee King Rosen and Fleming, Inc. *42nd Street Light Rail Transit Line: Final Environmental Impact Statement, CEQR No. 92DOT008M.* Report prepared for NYC Department of Transportation, March 23, 1994.

Pollack, Stephanie. "Maintaining Diversity in America's Transit-Rich Neighborhoods." Dukakis Center for Urban and Regional Policy, Northeastern University, October 2010. http://nuweb9.neu.edu/dukakiscenter/wp-content/uploads/TRN_Equity_final.pdf.

Poticha, Shelley. "Transportation in the Multi-City Regions." In *Smart Growth in a Changing World,* edited by Jonathan Barnett. Chicago: American Planning Association, 2007.

Pushkarev, Boris S., and Jeffrey M. Zupan. *Public Transportation and Land Use Policy.* Bloomington: Indiana University Press, 1977.

Quammen, David. *The Song of the Dodo: Island Biography in an Age of Extinctions.* New York: Scribner, 1996.

Real Estate Research Corporation. *The Costs of Sprawl: Environmental and Economic Costs of Alternative Residential Patterns at the Urban Fringe.* Washington, DC: Council on Environmental Quality, Office of Policy Development and Research, Department of Housing and Urban Development, and Office of Planning and Management, Environmental Protection Agency, 1974.

Reconnecting America. 2010 *Inventory of TOD Programs: A National Review of State, Regional, and Local Programs That Fund Transit-Oriented Development Plans and Projects.* January 2011.

Reconnecting America and Center for Transit-Oriented Development. "Mixed-Income Housing: Increasing Affordability with Transit." Washington, DC: Federal Transit Administration, September 2009.

Rodin, Judith. "How the Transportation Bill Failed America." *Atlantic Cities,* June 30, 2012.

Rybczynski, Witold. *Makeshift Metropolis: Ideas about Cities.* New York: Scribner, 2010.

Schueler, Tom. *Site Planning for Urban Stream Protection.* Washington, DC: Center for Watershed Protection and Metropolitan Council of Governments, 1995.

Shoup, Donald C. *The High Cost of Free Parking*. Chicago: American Planning Association, 2005.

Shoup, Donald C. "Yes, Parking Reform Is Possible." *Planning* 77, no. 10 (October 2011): 31–35.

Smith, Shelley L. "The Stuff of Parking." *Urban Land* 49, no. 2 (February 1990): 36–39.

Sorensen, A. Ann, Richard P. Greene, and Karen Russ. *Farming on the Edge*. DeKalb, IL: American Farmland Trust for Agriculture in the Environment, March 1997.

Spivak, Jeffrey. "The Next Big Thing." *Planning* (October 2009): 10–15.

TEST. *Quality Streets: How Traditional Urban Centers Benefit from Traffic Calming*. London: TEST, May 1988.

Transportation Alternatives. "Traffic's Human Toll: A Study of the Impacts of Vehicular Traffic on New York City Residents." October 2006.

Urban Land Institute and Ernst & Young. *Infrastructure 2009: Pivot Point*. Washington, DC: Urban Land Institute, 2009.

Vuchic, Vukan R. "Rapid Transit Automation and the Last Crew Member." In *Railway Gazette*. London: IPC Transport Press, Ltd., October 1973.

Vuchic, Vukan R. *Transportation for Livable Cities*. New Brunswick, NJ: Center for Urban Policy Research, Rutgers University, 1999.

Vuchic, Vukan R. *Urban Transit Systems and Technology*. Hoboken, NJ: John Wiley, 2007.

Walker, Philip L. "Myths of Downtown Planning." *Planning* 75, no. 6 (June 2009): 38–40.

Walljasper, Jay. "Unjamming the Future." *Ode*. October 2005. 36–41. Note 16. Interface for cycling Expertise (I-ce). "Bicycle Partnership Program."

Warner, Sam B., Jr. *Streetcar Suburbs: The Process of Growth in Boston, 1870–1900*. New York: Atheneum, 1973.

Weissmann, Jordan. "Young People Aren't Buying Cars Because They're Buying Smart Phones Instead." *Atlantic Cities*, August 8, 2012.

Weyrich, Paul, and William S. Lind. *Moving Minds: Conservatives and Public Transportation*. Washington, DC: Free Congress Foundation, 2009.

Wiedenhoeft, Ronald. "Downtown Pedestrian Zones: Experiments in Germany." *Urban Land* 34, no. 4 (April 1975): 3–11.

Worldwatch Institute. *State of the World 2012: Moving Toward Sustainable Prosperity*. Washington, DC: Island Press, 2012.

Yaro, Robert D., and Armando Carbonell. "Reinventing Megalopolis: The Northeast Megaregion." In *Smart Growth in a Changing World*, edited by Jonathan Barnett. Chicago: Planners Press, American Planning Association, 2007.

Index

Urban and Industrial Environments

Series editor: Robert Gottlieb, Henry R. Luce Professor of Urban and Environmental Policy, Occidental College

Eran Ben-Joseph, *The Code of the City: Standards and the Hidden Language of Place Making*

Nancy J. Myers and Carolyn Raffensperger, eds., *Precautionary Tools for Reshaping Environmental Policy*

Kelly Sims Gallagher, *China Shifts Gears: Automakers, Oil, Pollution, and Development*

Kerry H. Whiteside, *Precautionary Politics: Principle and Practice in Confronting Environmental Risk*

Ronald Sandler and Phaedra C. Pezzullo, eds., *Environmental Justice and Environmentalism: The Social Justice Challenge to the Environmental Movement*

Julie Sze, *Noxious New York: The Racial Politics of Urban Health and Environmental Justice*

Robert D. Bullard, ed., *Growing Smarter: Achieving Livable Communities, Environmental Justice, and Regional Equity*

Ann Rappaport and Sarah Hammond Creighton, *Degrees That Matter: Climate Change and the University*

Michael Egan, *Barry Commoner and the Science of Survival: The Remaking of American Environmentalism*

David J. Hess, *Alternative Pathways in Science and Industry: Activism, Innovation, and the Environment in an Era of Globalization*

Peter F. Cannavò, *The Working Landscape: Founding, Preservation, and the Politics of Place*

Paul Stanton Kibel, ed., *Rivertown: Rethinking Urban Rivers*

Kevin P. Gallagher and Lyuba Zarsky, *The Enclave Economy: Foreign Investment and Sustainable Development in Mexico's Silicon Valley*

David N. Pellow, *Resisting Global Toxics: Transnational Movements for Environmental Justice*

Robert Gottlieb, *Reinventing Los Angeles: Nature and Community in the Global City*

David V. Carruthers, ed., *Environmental Justice in Latin America: Problems, Promise, and Practice*

Tom Angotti, *New York for Sale: Community Planning Confronts Global Real Estate*

Paloma Pavel, ed., *Breakthrough Communities: Sustainability and Justice in the Next American Metropolis*

Anastasia Loukaitou-Sideris and Renia Ehrenfeucht, *Sidewalks: Conflict and Negotiation over Public Space*

David J. Hess, *Localist Movements in a Global Economy: Sustainability, Justice, and Urban Development in the United States*

Julian Agyeman and Yelena Ogneva-Himmelberger, eds., *Environmental Justice and Sustainability in the Former Soviet Union*